Scene of t

Scene of the Crime

The Importance of Place in Crime and Mystery Fiction

DAVID GEHERIN

McFarland & Company, Inc., Publishers
Jefferson, North Carolina, and London

LIBRARY OF CONGRESS CATALOGUING-IN-PUBLICATION DATA

Geherin, David, 1943–
    Scene of the crime : the importance of place
in crime and mystery fiction / David Geherin.
        p.   cm.
    Includes bibliographical references and index.

    ISBN 978-0-7864-3298-1
    softcover : 50# alkaline paper ∞

    1. Detective and mystery stories, American — History and criticism.
2. Place (Philosophy) in literature.   3. American fiction — 20th
century — History and criticism.   4. Detective and mystery stories,
English — History and criticism.   5. English fiction — 20th
century — History and criticism.   6. Popular literature — History
and criticism.   I. Title.
PS374.D4G395   2008
809.3'87209358 — dc22   2007052694

British Library cataloguing data are available

Cover photograph ©2008 Shutterstock

Manufactured in the United States of America

*McFarland & Company, Inc., Publishers
    Box 611, Jefferson, North Carolina 28640
    www.mcfarlandpub.com*

Table of Contents

For Anna, Gino, Sofia,
Maxine, Giada, and Katherine

Preface

I first became interested in how novelists use setting in their fiction when I wrote a doctoral dissertation on British novelist Christopher Isherwood and his portrayal of Berlin during the years of Hitler's rise to power in *The Berlin Stories*. My first publication on crime fiction in 1975 was a study of Ross Macdonald's use of Hollywood in his Lew Archer books. Over the years, I continued to explore the subject and devoted significant portions of books I wrote on John D. MacDonald and Elmore Leonard to their use of place in their fiction. *Scene of the Crime* is the culmination of my thinking about the subject over several decades.

A few basic books on setting in fiction already exist. Two essential studies are Leonard Lutwack's *The Role of Place in Literature* (1984) and Gillian Tindall's *Countries of the Mind: The Meaning of Place to Writers* (1991). However, given the important role setting often plays in crime and mystery fiction, it is surprising that this subject hasn't received more critical attention than it has. Gary Hausladen's *Places for Dead Bodies* is a useful beginning, but the book is restricted to police procedurals, and because it covers almost three dozen examples it takes more of a survey approach. Gillian Mary Hanson's *City and Shore: The Function of Setting in the British Mystery* is also helpful, though it is limited to a consideration of only two settings.

The focus of this book is different: through in-depth analyses of fifteen authors, including some of the most acclaimed writers of contemporary crime fiction, I aim to illustrate some of the various ways setting functions in a literary work. I am primarily concerned with two basic issues: how setting informs a writer's fiction, and how these writers employ language to make the settings they choose come alive to the reader. After an introduction offering a general consideration of the use of place in fiction, the remaining chapters are devoted to writers for whom setting is

1

an integral part of their overall design. Settings in their novels range from the familiar to the exotic, from large cities to wide open spaces, and from the U.S. to France, Italy, Scotland, Sweden, Mexico, Africa, and even to ancient Rome. For some of these writers, place is geographical; for others, it is social, political, or even cultural in nature. In every case, however, setting plays such an indispensable role in their fiction that it is impossible to imagine their works set in any other location.

Introduction

The Importance of Place in Fiction

Setting — the physical space where the action of a story or novel takes place — is an important yet often undervalued component of fiction. In her essay "Place in Fiction," writer Eudora Welty conceded that place is often regarded as one of the "lesser angels" that gaze "benignly enough from off to one side" while other elements like plot, character and symbol do all the heavy lifting (39). On the other hand, Leonard Lutwack, author of the first comprehensive study of the subject, *The Role of Place in Literature,* argued that "the most elemental orientation of a reader to a narrative text is through its evocation of places" (37).

While all stories and novels must take place somewhere, it is certainly true that in many cases the setting is either minimally described or essentially generic (a farmhouse, a cabin in the woods, a room in a hotel, etc.). In such instances place serves mainly an ornamental purpose, a decorative background to the action. Lengthy description of setting can actually be an impediment in literary works where plot is the dominant feature. Novels that employ a specific or unusual setting are sometimes categorized as regional literature, a dismissive term implying that a reader might expect to get a dash of local color as a reward for reading the story.

But when a writer uses location as more than backdrop by weaving it into the very fabric of the novel, affecting every other element of the work, the reader gets far more than local color. As Thomas Hardy in his Wessex novels and William Faulkner in his Yoknapatawpha books demonstrate (to cite but two of the most obvious examples), setting in the hands of certain writers assumes extraordinary importance. It becomes so essential to their overall artistic vision that one could not imagine these novels taking place anywhere else.

Faulkner, for example, set most of his novels and short stories in and around Oxford, Mississippi. This area, which he likes to call his "own little postage stamp of native soil" (Stein 24), he transformed into fictional Yoknapatawpha County. Faulkner made the local setting so much his own that he was able to draw a detailed map of the territory, on which he inscribed "William Faulkner, sole owner and proprietor." Countless other writers have followed Faulkner's example and staked out claims on promising territory of their own.

While there are many notable differences between the two, the function of setting can be compared to that of a movie soundtrack. Music, like any geographical location, has its own separate existence, but when it is integrated into a film the connection between the two produces special effects. In some cases, of course, the background music is barely heard, adding little to the overall effect of the film. Or it may exist largely to market the film or to sell more CDs by cashing in on the film's popularity. But used effectively by a film director, music can evoke or even intensify the emotion of a scene. Think of the opening scene of *Jaws,* where John Williams's pulsating music anticipates the imminent shark attack. Music can serve as a commentary on the action (Simon and Garfunkel's music for *The Graduate*) or be an ironic counterpoint to what is being depicted on the screen (Rossini's "Thieving Magpie" played against the brutal rape in *A Clockwork Orange*). A film may also employ familiar music (e.g., popular songs of the '50s and '60s in *American Graffiti*) to evoke a specific time period by playing off of the viewer's memories. Music is oftentimes so well integrated into a film that one cannot think of that film without hearing the music (e.g., Nino Rota's score for *The Godfather* or Ennio Morricone's distinctive music for Sergio Leone's spaghetti Westerns).

As Leonard Lutwack points out, "The novelist enjoys a wide range of choice in the amount of emphasis he puts upon place in his work, from the barest suggestion of the scene of his action to the most detailed description, from geographical verisimilitude to symbolical reference" (17–18). Some authors avoid virtually any description of place. Some, like Daniel Defoe in *Robinson Crusoe* or Franz Kafka in *The Castle,* provide a vivid sense of place, but without establishing an exact geographical location. Some, like Joseph Conrad in *Nostromo* and Gabriel García Márquez in *One*

Hundred Years of Solitude, provide detailed descriptions of wholly imaginary countries. Others, like James Joyce in his description of Dublin in *Ulysses*, are so detailed and specific about streets and places that one can actually retrace the steps the characters take in the novel.

Lutwack defines place as "the reconstitution in words of those aspects of the actual environment that a writer puts together to make up the 'world' in which his characters, events, and themes have their show of existence" (37). In an author's use of setting, there are two separate but closely related issues to consider. The first is how writers actually create setting, i.e., how they artistically transform geographical space into literary space. The important point here is not how accurate the description is but how effective the writer is in using language to capture the way the setting feels, sounds, smells — all that goes into conveying a palpable sense of place. Writers often do more than simply map out street names and familiar landmarks. They evoke such a vivid sense of location that they capture the spirit or soul of that place. Employing words the way an artist might draw upon an entire palette of colors, writers can make setting resonate in the reader's imagination every bit as powerfully as the fictional characters they create.

What reader hasn't had the experience of reading a novel and immediately wishing to hop on the first plane to experience firsthand the place described so picturesquely by the author? Indeed, the power of literary description is so great that *representation* of place often contributes to the overall *perception* of that place. Many famous cities — London, Paris, Venice, to name but a few — have been described so often and so effectively that they have in a very real sense been created by literary texts. Writers can be said to have contributed as much to the construction of such places (at least in readers' minds) as those who designed the buildings or laid out the streets.

A second issue worth examining is how writers use place in the service of other fictional ends, i.e., how they transform topography into metaphor. In Ernest Hemingway's famous short story "Hills Like White Elephants," an American couple is awaiting the next train at a station in the remote Spanish countryside. The woman, who is pregnant, is being pressured by her lover to have an abortion. As she looks out over some hills in the distance, she remarks that they look like white elephants. Her partner claims he sees no such resemblance. Suddenly, what had been simple geography assumes metaphoric importance, as Hemingway uses the hills to emphasize the different perceptions of both characters. They clearly represent the woman's fertility and, as white elephants, they also come to symbolize the unborn child the man wants his lover to get rid of.

At its basic level, setting need be nothing more than simple literal description — a word picture. In such cases setting functions little more than as a backdrop for the action. However, description can be shaped by a writer in such a way that the literal becomes infused with the symbolic. Setting now is asked to do double or triple duty. Take, for example, Thomas Hardy's description of Egdon Heath from the opening chapter of *The Return of the Native*:

> It was at present a place perfectly accordant with man's nature — neither ghastly, hateful, nor ugly: neither commonplace, unmeaning nor tame; but, like man, slighted and enduring; and withal singularly colossal and mysterious in its swarthy monotony. As with some persons who have long lived apart, solitude seemed to look out of its countenance. It had a lonely face, suggesting tragical possibilities [6].

Here Hardy invests description of place with human qualities by personifying the landscape. (Even the title of the chapter, "A Face on which Time Makes But Little Impression," reinforces the intended effect.) Setting here is no mere passive or static backdrop to the action that follows. Hardy presents it as a dynamic presence, alive in some fundamental way. It functions as a shaper of character as well as an implacable, indifferent force that underscores Hardy's view of man's tragic destiny.

Far more than a flavorful icing added to the cake, setting in *The Return of the Native* is an essential ingredient that gives the final product its distinctive flavor and texture. Hardy offers a good illustration of the point made by Gillian Tindall in *Countries of the Mind:* "There are indeed many writers for whom place is so important that the very word 'setting' carries for them a faint but distracting overtone of misunderstanding. Their novels are not just 'set' in Paris, Paraguay or wherever; they have grown there" (1).

Not all symbolic uses of nature are as obviously laid out as Hardy's. Here is a brief description of the town of Seney that opens Ernest Hemingway's "Big Two-Hearted River":

> The train went on up the track out of sight, around one of the hills of burnt timber. Nick sat down on the bundle of canvas and bedding the

baggage man had pitched out of the door of the baggage car. There was no town, nothing but the rails and the burned-over country. The thirteen saloons that had lined the one street of Seney had not left a trace. The foundations of the Mansion House stuck up above the ground. The stone was chipped and split by the fire. It was all that was left of the town of Seney. Even the surface had been burned off the ground [209].

At first glance, Hemingway's vivid description of place seems purely literal scene setting. However, as the story continues, the reader begins to sense a parallel between the young man, Nick Adams, and the place. Nick has returned to the woods of northern Michigan after suffering an unidentified trauma, probably in the war. He, it becomes increasingly clear, is very much like the town itself, burned out. As he makes his way from the town through the green forest to the shining river to fish for trout, the reader comes to understand his attempt to recapture something vital that has been lost. The physical journey from the burned-out town to the fresh and beautiful river comes to symbolize his own halting search for renewal.

Unlike Hardy, who left no doubt as to the importance he attached to place, Hemingway makes no explicit comments about the significance of the setting in his story. Rather, he lets the setting speak for itself, as it were. As he did in much of his writing, he counted on the attentive reader to make the necessary connection between setting and character.

In the preceding examples, the omniscient narrative voice was used to establish the setting and to suggest its significance in relationship to character. Another way of doing this is to filter description of setting through the subjectivity of first-person narration. This allows the writer to use setting to reveal important information about the person through whose eyes we see the scene. For example, when Raymond Chandler in "Red Wind" has Philip Marlowe comment on the hot desert winds that sometimes blow in L.A., we get not only a description of an atmospheric phenomenon characteristic of the location but also insight into Marlowe's distinctive way of looking at things:

There was a desert wind blowing that night. It was one of those hot dry Santa Anas that come down through the mountain passes and curl your hair and make your nerves jump and your skin itch. On nights like that every booze party ends in a fight. Meek little wives feel the edge of the carving knife and study their husbands' necks. Anything can happen. You can even get a full glass of beer at a cocktail lounge [*Trouble* 187].

As novelist Edith Wharton, an author whose own works illustrate the high value she placed on setting, observed, "The impression produced by a landscape, a street or a house should always, to the novelist, be an event in the history of a soul" (85).

Crime and mystery novels present an ideal opportunity to examine some of the artistic ways setting is used in fiction. For one thing, because of their essential subject matter — crime and its consequences — realism is fundamental to the genre and realistic depiction of setting is commonplace. Also, in realistic crime fiction, there is often an intimate connection between crime and its milieu, which thus comes to play a prominent thematic role in such novels. Finally, because crime novels are often published sequentially as part of an ongoing series, authors of crime fiction have multiple opportunities to create a distinctive sense of place. Only rarely do writers of non-genre fiction (Faulkner and Hardy, for example) make such an extensive use of one place over several novels. As a result, certain locations have become so indelibly associated with fictional detectives — Sherlock Holmes and London, Jules Maigret and Paris, Philip Marlowe and Los Angeles — that mystery readers can hardly imagine one without the other.

D.H. Lawrence boldly overstates the case when he asserts that "all creative art must rise out of a specific soil and flicker with a spirit of place" (334). But in those instances where writers deliberately make place an essential ingredient in their work, the added dimension has the power to create an indelible and lasting impression in the minds of their readers.

1

Georges Simenon

Paris

Few novelists have made better use of place than Georges Simenon. For one thing, as the setting for a long-running series of mystery novels featuring Chief-Inspector Jules Maigret of the Paris Police Judiciare Crime Squad, he had at his disposal one of the most picturesque cities in the world. Secondly, while many mystery writers have taken advantage of the multiple opportunities offered by a continuing series to create a strong sense of place, none has enjoyed a broader canvas than Simenon: the Maigret series spanned four decades and eventually numbered some seventy-five novels and twenty-eight short stories. The cumulative effect of this impressive oeuvre is a richly detailed portrait of a detective and the city he loved.

Simenon may very well be the most prolific and most widely-read novelist who ever lived. He published 192 novels under his own name and over 200 more under as many as eighteen pseudonyms, and his books have been translated into over fifty languages. To produce such a massive output, he developed a unique method of writing each book. As he rather offhandedly explained it, "Five or six times a year, at the very most, I retire into my own shell for eight days and, at the end of that time, a novel emerges" ("Mystery Man"). But the truth is more complicated than that. When the compulsion to write began to overtake him, he started jotting down names, birthdays, addresses, and other vital statistics about the characters he had been thinking about, always on a manila envelope. When these characters became so real to him that, as he described it, "they are jumping under my skin," he was ready to write (Mok 46).

Before shutting himself off from all distractions, like an athlete before a strenuous activity he would undergo a medical examination to ascertain his fitness for the demanding task that lay ahead. Then he would place a "Do Not Disturb" sign on the door of his office, line up his pipes and dozens of sharpened pencils, and write for the next eight to eleven days, no more. If he were interrupted for any reason, he would abandon that book entirely. He claimed to have lost as much as twelve pounds during these intense creative bursts.

The final result of this streamlined procedure was invariably a marvel of economy. Critic John Leonard has given an excellent description of the typically well-chiseled Simenon novel: "He [Simenon] selects a situation, clamps it like a hunk of pure carbon in a vise, notches and grooves it with details, applies the sharp edge of a steel plate to it, and with the single blow of a mallet, cleaves it. Behold: a diamond, each facet refracting the light in a different way." The impressive fact about Simenon's creative output is not the size of it but the artistic consistency he maintained.

Georges Simenon was born in Liège, Belgium, on 13 February 1903. At age nineteen he moved to Paris and soon began a writing apprenticeship cranking out pulp novels of adventure, crime, romance, and sex under several pseudonyms. In 1931, he began to focus his efforts in a new direction by trying his hand at a mystery novel. He wrote several novels in quick succession featuring Jules Maigret, a commissaire of the French Police Judiciare (the first of his novels to appear under his own name). Eleven Maigret novels were published in 1931. By 1934, eight more had appeared. He then abandoned Maigret temporarily before resuming the series in 1939. Between 1939 and 1972, when he ceased writing fiction, he turned out sixty-four more novels and dozens of short stories about Maigret. He died in 1989.

Maigret was conceived as a deliberate contrast to Edgar Allan Poe's C. Auguste Dupin, Arthur Conan Doyle's Sherlock Holmes, Agatha Christie's Hercule Poirot and the other brilliant detective figures that dominated the genre at the time. Unlike these heroes, Maigret was a professional policeman, not an eccentric amateur detective who prided himself on his intellectual superiority to the police. Unlike them, he possessed no superhuman deductive powers. Maigret is a common man of average intelligence. In many ways, he can be seen as a French counterpart to a revolutionary shift in the genre towards realism being undertaken in the U.S. at the same time by Dashiell Hammett, who had begun writing stories in *Black Mask* magazine about an overweight San Francisco private eye known as the Continental Op. (Hammett later named Simenon as his favorite mystery writer.)

There is nothing remotely hard-boiled about Maigret, but like the Op and the other fictional detectives who followed in his wake, he was defined by his ordinariness rather than his intellect. Despite a reputation as the legendary Maigret, he remains a modest, unpretentious man. Basically a country boy, like his creator he came to Paris as a young man. He lives with his doting wife in a cozy little apartment on Boulevard Richard-Lenoir. Except for occasional outings to the movies or to dinner with a doctor friend and his wife, the Maigrets exist in a cocoon of domestic bliss. At police headquarters at the Quai des Orfèvres on the Seine, Maigret has a second family, a small group of young officers who regularly assist him with his cases.

Maigret's characteristic method of investigation consists simply of soaking up the atmosphere of a crime scene and gradually immersing himself in the lives of people who previously had been strangers to him. Sooner or later, the solution comes to him "the way a bubble rises to the surface" (*Failure* 81). For Maigret, the mystery to be solved isn't the crime; it is the victim and his killer who interest him and his philosophy is, "I shall know the murderer when I know the victim well" (*Stonewalled* 134). His first publisher was initially so put off by Maigret's character and methods that he complained to Simenon, "Your detective is a man just like everyone else, not particularly intelligent, who sits for hours on end in front of a glass of beer. He's disgustingly commonplace. How do you hope to sell something like that?" (Dibdin "Introduction"). And yet out of the unassuming figure of such an ordinary man Simenon created one of the genre's most famous and enduring characters.

Given Simenon's highly disciplined method of composition, it isn't surprising that the Maigret novels, like the rest of his fiction, are short, well under two hundred pages. As he himself noted, "I will never write a big novel. My big novel is the mosaic of all my small novels" (Collins 160). And so rather than including lengthy passages of description of setting in any one of his Maigret novels — "One has to avoid the picturesque in one's writing," he insisted (Bresler 2) — he composed an elaborate portrait of Paris by using a mosaic technique. Each novel adds a small but distinctive bit or two of color, form, and texture to the overall design of the whole. The more Maigrets one reads, the more vividly detailed the mosaic becomes.

Like Ernest Hemingway (who as it happens was living in Paris and writing his groundbreaking short stories at the same time Simenon was creating the Maigret novels), Simenon understood the value of simple language and concrete diction. The best advice about writing he ever received came from Colette, who had served as literary editor for some of his early fiction: "Be simple," she advised him. "Never try for a literary effect. Leave out every word and syllable you can" (Gill 233). And so, like Hemingway, he scrupulously edited out all excess language; he also deliberately restricted himself to a vocabulary of some two thousand words in order to ensure a spare, unpretentious style. Like the best writers, he demonstrated that art doesn't come from the words you use but how you use the words you choose. In this regard, Simenon's remarks about the painter Paul Cézanne (an artist who also influenced Hemingway's simple style) are revealing: "A commercial painter paints flat; you can put your finger through. But a painter — for example, an apple by Cézanne has weight. And it has juice, everything, with just three strokes. I tried to give to my words just the weight that a stroke of Cézanne's gave to an apple" (Collins 158).

There are, of course, many different Parises. To the millions of people who live there, Paris is simply home. To countless others, Paris is a place largely defined for them by the picturesque images in travel brochures: the Eiffel Tower, Notre Dame, Sacré-Coeur, the Arc de Triomphe, the Champs-Élysées, etc. Because it's such a feast for the eyes, Paris has inspired many of the world's greatest painters, photographers, and writers to attempt to capture its allure. French artists like Renoir, Monet, Pissarro, Utrillo, Toulouse-Lautrec, et al., painted scenes of the city that fixed forever in the minds of many the visual splendor of the City of Light. Several of the world's most notable twentieth-century photographers (Henri Cartier-Bresson, Brassaï, Eugène Atget, André Kurtész, Robert Doisneau) are also known for their images of Paris, which have become commonplace thanks to countless reproductions on calendars, posters, datebooks, and the like.

"So seductive is the idea of Paris," Jennifer Lee notes in a collection of American writing about Paris she edited, "that even those who have never set foot in the city fall in love with it" (xvi). From Henry Miller's declaration, "When spring comes to Paris the humblest mortal alive must feel that he dwells in paradise" (61) to Anaïs Nin's description of Paris as a "magic city" (Kennedy 17) to Hemingway's celebration of it in his famous memoir as "a moveable feast," American readers have viewed the City of Light through the literary lens of writers who have come under its spell.

But as Gerald Kennedy reminds us, "all conceptions of place are inherently and inescapably subjective" (5) and the verbal portraits writers construct usually reveal as much about their consciousness as the place they are ostensibly describing. This is certainly true in the case of Simenon. Like many of those who wrote lovingly about Paris, Simenon was born elsewhere. But even though he left Paris in 1945 and lived in the U.S. for the next ten years and then spent the last thirty years of his life in Switzerland, Paris was never far from his imagination. Eighty percent of the Maigret novels are set in Paris; together they constitute one of the most vivid valentines to the city ever composed.

Though he acknowledged such literary influences as Gogol, Dostoyevsky, Balzac, Dickens, Conrad, and Stevenson, Simenon insisted that the strongest influence on his writing came from art. "All my life I've been closer to painting than to literature," he confessed. "My childhood was especially influenced by Impressionism and Pointillism (the gayest, happiest painting, where every spot of light is like a song) and I'll gladly admit that my novels reflected them" (*When* 258–259). So it isn't surprising that visual detail is as important to him as it was to the Impressionist painters: "I consider myself an impressionist," he once said, "because I work by little touches. I believe a ray of sun on a nose is as important as a deep thought" (Garis 22).

Simenon is the most atmospheric of writers. This is how crime novelist Nicholas Freeling describes that acute sensitivity to the world around him:

> A Simenon book is saturated in climate and weather, in the tactile sensual grip upon street, pavement, house, the sounds and smells of interior structure and furniture; creak of staircase, humidity of stone flags, mustiness of cupboard, dust in the fold of curtain. The nature and quality of the light: this painter, so Belgian and also so Dutch, tastes the texture of rain or the dust motes in a sunbeam [139].

In the following example — "The windows of the flat were wide open, letting in the smells from outside, the familiar noises from Boulevard Richard-Lenoir, and the air, already warm, was quivering: a fine vapor filtered the sunrays and made them almost tangible" (*Bides* 1)—Simenon shows his knack for getting the look, sound, smell, and feel of the city into a single sentence. The cumulative effect of such details is one of the most physical and sensuous portraits of the city any artist ever produced.

Simenon aims not simply to describe but to evoke atmosphere, and one highly effective way of achieving this is by detailing the weather. Observing that the weather is described "with such vigor and pleasure" in Simenon's books, Julian Symons argued that his "susceptibility to physical experience of this kind is greater than that of any other contemporary novelist" (147). From the bright promise of springtime, when Paris "was throbbing with youth and gaiety" (*Headless* 18) and the city is "as gay and colorful as a backdrop in an operetta" (*Madwoman* 15) through the sticky heat of August when life slows down and buses leave tracks in the overheated streets and on into the briskness of fall and bone-chilling cold of winter, Simenon gives us Paris in all its distinctive seasons. Even the air has its own delicious smell, taste and appearance that ranges from a "champagne sparkle" (*Pickpocket* 6) to a silvery haze "made up of thousands of tiny brilliant, living particles, peculiar to Paris" (*Pickpocket* 7).

Despite his disclaimer that, "If it rains, I write 'It rains.' You will not find in my books drops of weather that transform themselves into pearls, or I don't know what" (Bresler 2), the climate Simenon creates is unquestionably a poetic one designed to establish a mood for each book. Paris is often bathed in sunshine and like the Impressionists he admired, he artfully captures the play of light and shadow on the streets and buildings. When the sun is shining brightly, Paris glows with hopeful exuberance, which can be seen in such descriptions as, "The street was gilded by the sun" (*Burglar's* 80) and "The buildings of the Quai de Valmy were bathed in sunshine, golden, heart-warming sunshine, which made it hard to credit the sinister reputation of the place" (*Headless* 7).

But the sun doesn't always shine in Maigret's world and Simenon is a virtuoso when it comes to rain. No one describes a gloomy day, the kind that makes you wonder "why you came into the world and why you take so much trouble to stay in it" (*Montmartre* 23), better than Simenon. But as the following examples demonstrate, it isn't the simple fact of rain Simenon wishes to convey but its feel.

> The rain was soft, cheerless and hopeless, like a widow's tears. It could be felt rather than seen, although it spread over everything like a cold

layer of varnish and dotted the Seine with countless little vibrant cir-
cles [*Spinster* 115].

Paris still looked ghostly in the fine, misty drizzle, and the people in
the streets seemed as though they were moving through a kind of
aquarium, and hurrying to get out [*Montmarte* 93].

One could no longer say it was raining; one was actually living in a
cloud, with water everywhere, trails of it on the floors, and no one able
to utter three words without blowing his nose [*Failure* 9].

The dank gloomy atmosphere serves as a fitting backdrop to the sad tales
of unhappy people that Simenon tells so eloquently.

Nothing evokes a powerful sensory impression better than smell and
Simenon, who was especially sensitive to odors, fills the Maigret books
with distinctive fragrances. For example, "Maigret's nostrils were assailed
by a gust of fragrance which was forever to remain with him as the very
quintessence of Paris at daybreak: the fragrance of frothy coffee and hot
croissants, spiced with a hint of rum" (*Spinster* 4). Whether it's the aroma
of tarragon and chives from the kitchen of an inviting restaurant, the smell
of fresh fruits and vegetables in the market at Les Halles, the pungent odor
of beer and sauerkraut in a favorite brasserie, or simply the honeyed scent
of the chestnut trees on the Boulevard St-Germain, Simenon always finds
the precise olfactory detail to stimulate the reader's sensory memory and
place him immediately into the scene at the moment.

The reader also hears the hum of Paris life through Maigret's ears:

Outside, he could hear Paris gradually awakening — isolated noises,
more or less at a distance and separated at first, but mingling, as time
went by, into a kind of familiar symphony. The concierges began to
drag the dustbins to the edge of the pavements. He heard the little ser-
vant-girl from the dairy clattering upstairs to leave the bottles of milk
outside each door [*Young* 23].

Walking along the Parisian streets with Maigret, we hear the sounds of
women calling to each other from overhead windows, discordant radios
playing, whistles blowing and chains clattering as men work, and the endless stream of panting tugs on the Seine.

Paris for Simenon is not the tourist mecca, bohemian playground,
or fashionable City of Light celebrated by many. While there are fleeting
glimpses of notable local landmarks in the Maigret books, Paris is
portrayed as a city of ordinary people engaged in the daily business of

working, eating, drinking, and simply living in the beautiful city. In this respect, Simenon resembles the famous photographers of Paris more than the painters he admired growing up. Many of the most memorable of the timeless images captured by Cartier-Bresson, Brassaï, Atget, Kurtész, and Doisneau are not postcard views of the Eiffel Tower or Notre Dame but rather glimpses of everyday life, simple street scenes of Parisians going about their daily business.

The photographer whom Simenon most closely resembles is Robert Doisneau. Like Simenon, Doisneau avoided the Paris of the tourist brochures and instead sought to capture the casual intimacy of real life on the streets and in the cafes. (In 1962 Doisneau photographed Simenon, trademark pipe in his mouth, walking along a Paris street. His photographs of other famous figures like Orson Welles, Alberto Giacometti, and Simone de Beauvoir were also shot either on the street or in a cafe.) Whether it be a photograph of a shopkeeper, street sweeper, bookseller, flower vendor, or a gathering of fishermen along the Seine, Doisneau's images artfully isolate the perfect detail that brings the ordinary world of Paris to life. His style of documentary realism finds its parallel in the way Simenon similarly creates art out of the mundane in his own verbal snapshots of Parisian life.

There is a timeless quality to the Maigret books, with little mention of actual dates or important social or political events (including the Nazi occupation of Paris) that occurred during the forty-year run of the series. However, when it comes to place Simenon is scrupulously specific. He always names the actual Paris street Maigret visits, and these are usually the modest streets rather than the fashionable boulevards. When Maigret is called upon to investigate a murder at a fancy hotel on the Champs-Élysées, Simenon writes: "Maigret, plebeian to the core, to the very marrow of his bones, felt hostile toward the world that surrounded him here" (*Hotel* 104).

Unlike Sherlock Holmes, who made a deliberate effort to memorize the layout of London's streets, Maigret doesn't need to do the same with Paris. Like one of Baudelaire's *flâneurs*, he loves to roam the city soaking up impressions and information about the streets along the way. He's so at home in the neighborhoods, cafes, and brasseries of Paris that the city emerges less as a bewildering metropolis and more a small, intimate community. Here's a typical description, this one of Rue Notre-Dame-des-Champs (coincidentally the same street where Hemingway lived for a while in the 1920s):

> The street was quiet, country-like, with the sun on one side and shade on the other; in the middle of the road two dogs were sniffing each other, and behind the open windows some women were getting on with their housework. Three Little Sisters of the Poor in wide skirts, the wings of their coifs fluttering like birds, were walking toward the Luxembourg Gardens [*Black* 46].

In Simenon's world, the streets are seldom filled with tourists. Instead, they are usually populated by one or two familiar figures: a butcher's boy delivering meat, a postman on his rounds, a tramp doing his washing along the banks of the Seine. Simenon emphasizes neither the hustle and bustle of the big city nor the anonymity of the crowd. Instead he sees individuals, each one reminding us of the normality of everyday life. It is this "savoring of ordinariness" (70), as Dennis Porter called it, that is the key to Simenon's art.

Simenon's descriptions and impressions of Paris are more than window dressing. They emphasize the mundane reality of the city, which mirrors both the ordinariness of Maigret and the commonplace nature of most of the crimes he is called upon to investigate. Professional criminals and crazed serial killers are rare in his world. Those who commit murder in his books are ordinary individuals pushed by circumstance into killing other very ordinary persons.

Ordinary life, ordinary people, and ordinary crime are what interest Simenon. (One of his short stories is even titled "Death of a Nobody.") *Maigret and the Man on the Bench* is a typical example. Louis Thouret, a warehouse foreman, is found stabbed to death in an alley. But when Maigret delivers the news to his wife, she is surprised to learn that her husband was wearing brown shoes (which she says she never saw him wear in the twenty-six years they were married) and an uncharacteristically garish tie. The mystery deepens when it is revealed that Thouret had been out of work since his factory closed down three years earlier. Afraid to tell his wife that he had lost his job, he set off to work each day as usual but spent the time sitting on various benches in Paris. Who would want to kill such a man?

It is precisely people like Louis Thouret who interest Maigret so much, commonplace people "who were clean and decent and not in the least picturesque, and who fought day in and day out to keep their heads above water and to nurture the illusion, or perhaps the faith, that they were alive and that life was worth living" (74). Maigret knows that solving the mystery of the man's life will also solve the mystery of his death. Eventually he determines that while sitting on various benches, Thouret began to observe the habits of the various businesses in view. With the help of a fellow bench-sitter who would then rob the establishments they had cased out, he was able to maintain the charade that he was still employed. Unfortunately for him, the boyfriend of a woman he had met learned of his scheme and killed him for his money.

Maigret is especially interested in the unlikely victims of crime whose secrets are as important to him as finding their killers. In *Maigret and the Loner*, for example, the murder of a tramp with a neatly trimmed beard and carefully manicured hands whose body is found in the abandoned building in Les Halles where he has been living leads Maigret on a search for his identity and for an answer to the mystery of why he hasn't spoken to anyone in twenty years.

In *Maigret and the Bum*, a homeless tramp is bludgeoned and dumped into the Seine to die. He is rescued by a barge owner passing by. The mystery Maigret faces here is twofold: who would try to kill a harmless vagrant and what is the man's story? He digs up information that he is actually a respected doctor who abandoned his wife and daughter twenty years earlier and dropped out of society. The reason for the attack isn't so easy to figure out, especially when the prime suspect turns out to be the bargeman who rescued him. Nevertheless, Maigret's infallible intuition leads him to the solution: he concludes that the bargeman attempted to kill the vagrant because two years earlier, at a nearby spot on the Seine, the man had witnessed an incident where the bargeman tossed his drunken boss into the water and let him drown. Recognizing the vagrant, he sought to get rid of the only witness to his crime.

The problem is that Maigret has no proof and the victim stubbornly refuses to identify his assailant. The only clue to the reasoning behind his refusal is a comment he makes to Maigret that "Life's not easy for anyone.... What's impossible is to pass judgment" (*Bum* 148), apparently referring to his own understanding of the bargeman's reasons for wanting his boss dead. Maigret understands for he too seldom passes judgment, and arresting a suspect at the end of his investigation seldom gives him pleasure. Rather than an agent of justice for the state, he prefers to think of himself as a "mender of destinies" (*Failure* 44) and a "guide to the lost" (*Headless* 43). What little satisfaction he gets comes from solving the human mystery that led to the crime rather than the crime itself.

The key that unlocks the human mystery for Maigret is usually the victim's little world and in recreating the various milieus in which each lived, Simenon proved to be what John Raymond called a true "connoisseur of environment" (18). Any well-written novel is capable of transporting the reader to another world. Simenon's Maigret novels contain enough sensual detail and atmospheric texture to offer readers the next best thing to an actual trip to the City of Light.

2

Donna Leon

Venice

Venice, according to English writer Jonathan Keates, is "an extraordinary palimpsest on which everyone delights to scribble" (97). And scribble they have, scores and scores of writers. The list of authors who have used a Venetian setting reads like a literary Who's Who: Shakespeare, Jonson, Dickens, Byron, Shelley, Proust, Pound, James, Mann, Hemingway, to name but a few. Venice has been represented in fiction so often that, as Millicent Bell aptly notes, the city's canals "might be imagined to be black with literary ink" (124). This passionate love affair between literature and place has profited both parties. The literary works inspired by Venice have been enriched by the imaginative uses of that setting while the city itself has been elevated to a special place in the world's imagination.

It's not difficult to understand Venice's powerful attraction to tourists and writers alike. Unique among the cities of the world, it is romantic, picturesque, exotic, alluring. For writers, however, the attraction goes deeper. The physical characteristics of the city that lure tourists also lend themselves to symbolic interpretation: the confusing maze of streets that inevitably causes the visitor to become lost serves as an appropriate image of disorientation; the exotic buildings that appear to float on the water, subject to the constant shifting of light and shadow, seem unreal, ambiguous, a symbol of unstable meanings; the resplendent masks associated with the Venetian carnival make this a city of the masquerade, a place where deception rules; finally, as a city slowly sinking into the sea, its decaying beauty serves as an irresistible image of mortality. What richer territory could any writer, especially the mystery writer, hope for?

No writer has exploited the symbolic potential of Venice more effectively than Thomas Mann. His famous 1912 novella, *Death in Venice*, fashioned the template that has influenced writers ever since. *Death in Venice* tells the story of Gustav Aschenbach, a widely-respected German author whose life, like his work, is more a product of reason and self-discipline than passion or inspiration. One day, seized by uncharacteristic wanderlust, the aging writer decides abruptly to leave his familiar Munich surroundings in search of "someplace as out of the ordinary as a fairy tale" (13). His wandering soon takes him to Venice.

After first establishing Venice and its exotic delights as a polar opposite to the highly disciplined routine Aschenbach rigidly followed in Munich, Mann begins expanding upon Venice's symbolic suggestions. While Venice initially represents escape to the overly repressed Aschenbach, its mysterious allure also comes to represent something more ominous, i.e., the threat of death. This note is sounded early in the text by Mann's description of one of Venice's most picturesque trademarks, the gondolas that traverse her waters.

> This strange conveyance, surviving unchanged since legendary times and painted the particular sort of black ordinarily reserved for coffins, makes one think of silent, criminal adventures in a darkness full of splashing sounds; makes one think even more of death itself, of biers and gloomy funerals, and of that final, silent journey. And has anyone noticed that the seat of one of these boats, this armchair painted coffin-black and upholstered in dull black cloth, is one of the softest, most luxurious, most sleep-inducing seats in the world? [17].

Once settled in his hotel, Aschenbach becomes enchanted by a beautiful fourteen-year-old Polish boy named Tadzio, who is staying at the same hotel with his family. Intoxicated by the beauty of the boy "with the face of Eros," Aschenbach begins shadowing his every movement. Whether his obsession with the boy is understood as an aesthetic pursuit of the ideal of perfection or in sexual terms as the object of long-repressed homosexual love, the result is the same: self-destruction. Aschenbach succumbs to his obsessions and begins following the boy through the city: "Trailing the lovely boy one afternoon, Aschenbach had penetrated deep into the maze in the heart of the diseased city. He had lost his sense of direction, for the little streets, canals, bridges, and piazzas in the labyrinth all looked alike. He could no longer even tell east from west" (59). External details of the city mirror Aschenbach's inner confusion and his physical disorientation in the confusing city symbolizes his internal loss of bearings.

Mann employs other details of the landscape to mirror the various dualities he emphasizes in Aschenbach's character. Half land, half water, Venice itself embodies the notion of opposites. Mann balances references to the "wondrous, wonder-filled city" (35) with reminders of the "garbage-strewn water" (30) and "the stagnant-smelling lagoon" (29) that surrounds the city. In this way he uses Venice to symbolize the multiple dualities (reason vs. passion, Apollonian vs. Dionysian, classical vs. romantic, northern vs. southern Europe, east vs. west) that dominate the text.

Gondolas, canals, narrow, confusing streets, and other details of physical topography, of course, have no metaphoric significance in and of themselves. As Leonard Lutwack reminds us in *The Role of Place in Literature,* "Gibraltar is impregnable not because it is a rock but because people *think* a rock is impregnable.... Places are neither good nor bad in themselves but in the values attached to them, and literature is one of the agencies involved in attaching values to places" (35). If the gondolas represent death, it is because Mann employs language that directs the reader to see them as coffins. If a city built on water signifies duality, it is because Mann underscores the point by describing Venice, for example, as "half fairy tale and half tourist trap" (47). Mann simply endows the physical details of Venice with a significance that transforms them into powerful metaphors.

Mann's influence on later writers who also sought to exploit the symbolism of Venice cannot be overestimated. Thanks to Mann, in the minds of many authors death and Venice have become virtually synonymous. Two of the best-known examples — Daphne du Maurier's "Don't Look Now" (1971) and Ian McEwan's *The Comfort of Strangers* (1981) — both feature British tourists who meet fatal consequences in Venice. Other writers are more drawn to the romantic and picturesque elements of the setting. Whichever the case, Mann's telltale fingerprints can be found on virtually every literary work that has been set in Venice since the appearance of *Death in Venice.*

Venice might seem an unusual choice of setting for a crime series. The famed city is no hotbed of crime; it has the lowest crime rate in Italy and one of the lowest in all of Europe. Its population is small (70,000 or so), its citizens are law abiding, and criminals who come to Venice from outside, mostly thieves, are easily caught because they get lost and can't figure out how to get away. But what gives any crime novel set in Venice its special appeal is less the crime than the setting, the city itself.

2. Donna Leon

Among the many mystery novels set in Venice, a series of police procedurals by Donna Leon stand out and not simply because of their excellence. For one thing, she is one of only two mystery writers (the other is a fellow American writer, Edward Sklepowich) who have created a series of novels with a Venetian setting. But unlike Sklepowich and most other authors (mystery and otherwise), she is a rarity among foreign writers writing about Venice because her series character, Guido Brunetti, is Venetian to the core.

Brunetti is a commissario of police. His wife, Paola (like Donna Leon, an English professor at a local university), is the daughter of Count Orazio Falier, who can trace his illustrious family (which includes two doges) back to the tenth century. Paola's mother's family can trace its ancestry back to the Medici. In contrast to his wife's noble pedigree, Brunetti is a man of the people, an ordinary man more at home in the smoky neighborhood bars than at his father-in-law's magnificent palazzo on the Grand Canal. The frequent domestic scenes (usually involving tantalizing meals) Brunetti shares with his wife and two teenage children in their fourth-floor apartment near the Rialto Bridge emphasize the ordinary details of everyday Italian life.

Leon's challenge is to convince the reader of the authenticity of her Italian characters' views and attitudes as well as the ordinary details of a place which is to them merely home, not a tourist mecca. She effectively does this by evoking the Venetian setting from the inside, resisting the temptation to become overly caught up in descriptions of the many colorful tourist attractions. Thus, there are no atmospheric passages describing the beauty of San Marco, no moonlit gondola rides. When Brunetti crosses the Rialto Bridge or takes a boat across the Grand Canal, he is simply a man going about his job. As he makes his way through the narrow streets of Venice, the true flavor of the city emerges from the familiar sights, sounds, and aromas he experiences along the way.

Donna Leon was born in New Jersey in 1942. She left America for Italy at age twenty-three to continue her studies in Perugia and Siena. After eventually earning her Ph.D. (her doctoral dissertation was on Jane Austen), she taught English in Iran, China, Saudi Arabia and at American military bases near Venice, where she had located permanently in 1981. That Leon is not a native-born Italian has proven to be no impediment to her creating a believable portrait of Italian life. Raymond Chandler, for example, the most astute chronicler of L.A., grew up in England and did not move to Los Angeles until he was twenty-four. Leon has lived in Venice long enough to have assimilated many of the Italians' characteristic attitudes (a cynical distrust of all government agencies, a native-born inclination to see conspiracy everywhere) which she reflects through Brunetti. She generously sprinkles Italian words and phrases throughout the text as a reminder of Brunetti's nationality. She gives him a typically Venetian attitude toward tourists ("Why were they so slow and fat and lethargic? Why did they all have to get in his way?" [*Wilful* 236]). Finally, she clearly establishes his European viewpoint through his complaints about what seems to him to be the typical American "national sense of moral superiority, this belief so common among Americans that it had somehow been given to them to serve as a glistening moral light in a world dark with error" (*Strange* 34). Anti-American comments like these are rare, however, for with a few exceptions Americans hardly figure at all in the series.

Contrary to one critic's mistaken assertion that he is only a "tourist in drag as a detective" (Ghose 214), Brunetti is shown to be very much in tune with his native environment. He knows the walls and doors of his city "as other children could recognize the heroes of cartoons and television" (*Faith* 158). He recognizes the dogs that play in each local piazza, he knows which fruit vendor is the one who wears a wig. While certainly not blind to the many architectural splendors that draw tourists to his city, his concerns are those of the local citizenry rather than the visiting tourist: the high cost of housing, the tacky souvenir shops that are driving out local businesses, the pollution from the nearby industrial smokestacks whose poisonous clouds are slowly turning "marble into meringue" (*Fenice* 142). Though Leon makes an occasional slip — at one point she describes Brunetti jumping up "like a child at the sound of the bells of the ice cream truck in the street" (*Noble* 260), a sound that Brunetti likely never heard in the traffic-free streets of Venice — such lapses are exceedingly rare as she assiduously maintains Brunetti's identity as a true native of Venice.

Brunetti is a thoughtful man of considerable intelligence, a smart detective who is clever and imaginative in his methods. Outside of work he has few interests aside from his family and a fondness for classical authors like Tacitus and Herodotus. He is no crime-solver in the Sherlock Holmes tradition, no master of deductive reasoning. Nor does he have to be as tough as, say, Sam Spade to walk the streets of Venice. Since there are no cars, everybody walks the streets of Venice. And though it hosts over four million tourists a year, to those who live there Venice is just a small town, a "socially incestuous" place where gossip is "probably our richest source of information" (*Faith* 105). Brunetti's intimate knowledge of his city and the habits and manners of his fellow Venetians serves him well in his job. He always knows somebody — whether it's an old school friend or his aristocratic father-in-law — who might possess the information he needs, a valuable asset in a corrupt system where private connections are more useful than official police channels.

For Leon, Venice is more than just a colorful background. Instead of simply describing its famous landmarks, she goes deeper to capture its distinctive personality: "During the summer months," Leon writes, Venice "could remember her courtesan past and sparkle ... but in the winter she became a tired old crone, eager to crawl early to bed, leaving her deserted streets to cats and memories of the past." But like "many women of a certain age, the city needed the help of deceptive light to recapture her vanished beauty" (*Fenice* 32).

The first two books in the series resemble other Venetian novels written by non–Italians in that they deal with the deaths of foreigners. *Death at La Fenice* opens with the discovery of the body of a world-famous conductor (like Mann's Aschenbach, a German), poisoned during intermission of the opera he is conducting at La Fenice. The idea for the book, Leon's first attempt at novel writing, was inspired by a friend's comment during a rehearsal at La Fenice about a widely-hated conductor whom many felt deserved to be killed:

> So we thought what fun it would be to turn him into a crime novel,
> which I duly went off and wrote. But that's all it was meant to be, fun.
> I was lucky to be born without ambition, and I had none for this
> book. It sat in a drawer for a year and a half. Then I sent it off to a
> competition, and six months later they wrote back to say I'd won. I got
> a contract, and suddenly I had a purpose in life, a mission [White 14].

Death in a Strange Country concerns the murder of another foreigner, in this case an American soldier stationed at a nearby military base. Shortly afterwards, the apparent suicide of a second American, a female doctor who was the young soldier's commanding officer (and lover), deepens the mystery. But neither novel is about the threat to Venetian tourism prompted by the murders of foreign visitors to the city. The deaths of the two Americans, for example, turn out to be intimately connected to the larger issue of Italian political corruption: they had uncovered information about toxic chemicals being illegally buried near Venice.

Leon's main theme here is the high-level criminal complicity between politicians and prominent businessmen. Ultimately, Brunetti's investigation reveals that the tentacles of corruption come uncomfortably close to his own aristocratic father-in-law. Brunetti had originally sought his father-in-law's assistance in gathering information about a prominent contractor whose name surfaces during his investigation. However, he is surprised to learn just how much his wife's father knows. Left unanswered is the question about just how close he himself might be to the corruption that reaches the highest levels of business and government. As a fellow police officer reminds Brunetti, "Who can tell them apart anymore, Mafia and government?" (*Strange* 206).

As is the case with many of his fellow Italians, experience has taught Brunetti to harbor deep cynicism about any hope for improvement in the political situation. "The one thing he knew with absolute certainty was that nothing would change.... There'd be elections, there'd be new faces and new promises, but all that would happen would be that different snouts would go into the trough, and new accounts would be opened in those discreet private banks across the border in Switzerland" (*Judgment* 73). As an Italian, he is resigned to the fact that political scandal "had the same shelf life as fresh fish; by the third day, both were worthless; one because it had begun to stink, the other because it no longer did" (*Uniform* 169).

As a policeman, he has also learned that he must often fend off powerful forces aimed at undermining his job. When he is ordered by his superior to stop investigating a murder (a situation the Italians call *insabbiatura*, the burying of an inconvenient case in the sand), he can only speculate about the power behind the order: "The obvious candidates fell into the general categories of governmental, ecclesiastical, and criminal; the great tragedy of his country, Brunetti mused, was how equal they were as contenders" (*Blood* 138). Such a condition only makes him wonder, for example, why he should bother to put the boy who broke into a house in jail "when the man who stole billions from the health system is named ambassador to the country to which he had been sending the money for years?" (*Judgment* 73). Or why he should arrest anyone for murder when the man "who had for decades been the highest-ranking politician in the country stood accused of having ordered the murders of the few honest judges who had had the courage to investigate the Mafia?" (73).

Deception — evil hiding behind a beautiful facade — is a recurring theme in the series, and Venice itself provides an ideal example of how geography can embody duplicity. One's eye may initially be dazzled by the city's stunning beauty, but one cannot forget that all that splendor rests on the dark and muddy canals underneath it. Or, as Brunetti is reminded at low tide, "the stench of corruption ... always lurked beneath the water" (*Dressed* 93). In *Dressed for Death*, for example, the murder of a local banker whose body is found dressed in women's clothing eventually exposes a lucrative conspiracy hiding behind the cover of a prominent religious charity known as the *Lega della Moralita*. In *Death and Judgment*, the separate murders of three prominent local men, one a respected lawyer, the other two successful accountants, lead Brunetti to yet another conspiracy, this one engaged in the marketing of snuff films made in nearby Bosnia. Their killer turns out to be a former prostitute whose disgust at what she discovered about her associates' trade in the snuff films drove her to exact her revenge. She warns Brunetti that because of other high-level individuals also involved in the business (including the mayor of a town in Lombardy, the president of a pharmaceutical company, and an assistant minister of justice), she is now marked for death herself. Within hours of her arrest, she is found hanging in her cell, an apparent suicide. But Brunetti knows better. And he knows that with her death, the real reason behind the murders will never be revealed.

In *The Death of Faith*, Maria Testa, a former nun who once cared for Brunetti's ailing mother, comes to his office with her suspicions about a series of sudden deaths of elderly patients at the facility where she worked. Brunetti's investigations cause him to suspect the presence somewhere of Opus Dei, a secret society within the Roman Catholic Church:

> If any mystery was wrapped up in an enigma, it was Opus Dei. Brunetti knew no more than that it was some sort of religious organization, half clerical, half lay, which owed absolute allegiance to the Pope and which was dedicated to some sort of renewal of power or authority for the Church. And, as soon as Brunetti considered what he knew about Opus Dei and how he knew it, he was aware that he could not be sure of the truth of any of it [209].

Venice is a place of hidden secrets and covert power. Even though Brunetti is unable to penetrate into Opus Dei or in fact even to prove its existence, he does experience its power to hamper his investigation. But he is savvy enough to be able to tap into Venice's secret power and influence for his own purposes. During his investigation, he uncovers accusations of sexual molestation of young girls by his daughter's catechism teacher. Thanks to the influence of Brunetti's powerful father-in-law, the priest finds himself abruptly transferred to a chaplain position at an isolated prison in the middle of the Tyrrhenian Sea.

One of the best examples of Leon's skill in integrating story and setting is *Acqua Alta*. The action of the novel is set in winter, the season of "acqua alta," the high water caused by the southerly winds pushing the Adriatic waters into the city. The annoying flood of tourists has been replaced by the equally annoying Adriatic floods; the novel is filled with references to dripping rain, seeping water, and the sound of rubber boots being pulled on by anyone who ventures out.

But as evocative of Venetian climate as these details are, Leon is interested in something more than mere atmosphere. She employs the acqua alta as a symbol of a key concern in the novel. The novel begins with a brutal attack on Brett Lynch, a young American archaeologist whom Brunetti first met in *Death at La Fenice*. Her two assailants warn her not to keep a scheduled meeting with Dottor Semenzato, director of the museum at the Doge's Palace. Five years earlier, Brett had worked with Semenzato in arranging an exhibit of archaeological finds from her dig in Xi'an, China. Now suspicious that some of the original ceramics from the exhibit were replaced by fakes, she had planned to discuss the matter with Semenzato. Brunetti is called in and, following the subsequent murder of Semenzato, he uncovers evidence of a scheme to replace priceless art objects with well-executed fakes. Semenzato's partner in the fraud, he learns, was Carmello La Capra, a rich Mafioso art collector who had recently moved from Sicily into a palazzo on the Grand Canal.

Leon uses the cold Adriatic waters seeping into Venice from below the city as a symbol of the infiltration of the Mafia into northern Italy.

> For years, people in Lombardy and the Veneto, the wealthiest parts of the country, had thought themselves free from *la piovra*, the many-tentacled octopus that the Mafia had become. It was all *roba dal Sud*, stuff from the South, those killings, the bombings of bars and restaurants whose owners refused to pay protection money.... But in the last few years, just like an agricultural blight that couldn't be stopped, the violence had moved north: Florence, Bologna, and now the heartland of industrialized Italy found itself infected and looked in vain for a way to contain the disease [193].

La Capra's scheme to accumulate a private collection of great art led to the corruption of a respected museum director who paid with his own life for his complicity. In the end, however, La Capra proves to be slippery enough to escape any prosecution for the crime by shifting blame to his dead son, who was killed by Brett when he attempted to rape and murder her.

Some often-used Venetian symbols are impossible for Leon to use. For example, a native Venetian like Brunetti is not likely to become lost and confused while navigating the narrow twisting streets as outsiders do. So, using the labyrinth of streets as a symbol of mystery or disorientation won't work for Leon the way it does for writers describing a foreign tourist in Venice. But even native Venetians can become lost in the fog that often envelops the city, and Leon captures this image effectively in *Death at La Fenice:*

> A thick fog had appeared during the night, seeping up from the waters on which the city was built, not drifting in from the sea. When he stepped out of his front door, cold, misty tendrils wrapped themselves around his face, slipped beneath his collar. He could see clearly for only a few meters, and then vision grew cloudy; buildings slipped into and out of sight, as though they, and not the fog, shifted and moved [236].

Though it plays a crucial role in her books, the Venetian setting never dominates; Leon never indulges in scenic description for its own sake. In some novels, it scarcely figures at all. In *A Noble Radiance*, for example, the crime (illegal trafficking in nuclear materials and its tragic consequences for the prominent family involved) has nothing at all to do with Venice, or with Italy for that matter. Overall, however, Leon effectively weaves in rich atmospheric details which give her novels a powerful sense of place and also serve to embody several of the key issues and ideas in those books.

Leon's novels have enjoyed widespread international success: *Death at La Fenice* won Japan's Suntory Prize as best suspense novel of 1991 and *Friends in High Places* earned the 2000 British Crime Writers' Association Silver Dagger Award. They have been translated into nineteen languages (though not Italian at her choice; she simply prefers to live anonymously in a place where she isn't well known) and are hugely popular in Europe, especially in England, Austria and Germany. Several of the books have been filmed for a German television mini-series, which is ironic considering that Leon confesses that she has never owned a TV. For many years, only the first five books in the series were available in the U.S., but that situation has now been rectified and American readers are able to enjoy the company of Guido Brunetti and experience with him the many pleasures and frustrations of this beautiful yet fragile city.

To better appreciate the way Leon uses Venice, it is useful to briefly consider how two other mystery writers use the same setting. Edward Sklepowich, an American like Donna Leon, launched a series of mystery novels set in Venice in 1990 with *Death in a Serene City*. The books feature amateur sleuth Urbino Macintyre, an American writer who, like many, fell in love with Venice on his first visit. Now, thanks to the inheritance of a palazzo from his grandfather, a Venetian, he lives in the city, though it would it be inaccurate to describe him as Venetian. He remains a tourist at heart.

In every way imaginable, Urbino is a direct opposite to Brunetti. By profession a biographer (of Ruskin, Browning, and Proust, all, like himself, visitors to Venice), he solves crimes the way he writes his books: by sitting in his palazzo, weaving loose strands into a coherent narrative that eventually clears up the mystery. Fashionably dressed in an Ermenegildo Zegna suit and Gucci shoes, he favors glitzy establishments like the Chinese room at Florian's (at his usual table by the window) or Harry's Bar or the terrace at the Gritti Palace, touristy places Brunetti avoids at all cost. His closest friend (and the person who usually seeks his assistance in solving a crime) is the Contessa da Capo-Zendrini, owner of a palazzo on the Grand Canal. Unlike Brunetti, who is uncomfortable around his aristocratic in-laws, Urbino delights in his close association with the contessa's lofty circle.

Brunetti is scornful of the way his beloved city has been transformed into a kind of Disneyland for art lovers; Urbino, on the other hand, is one of those very people for whom art is the measure of his passion for Venice. He routinely describes people in terms of his favorite paintings: an old woman reminds him of the toothless figure in a Giorgione painting at the Accademia; the expression on another woman's face reminds him of a figure in the Bronzino portrait that hangs above his sofa. Even the Venetian weather largely serves only to prompt artistic references: a pearly gray day brings to mind a Singer portrait of Venice; a hot summer day reminds him of a Dali painting. For Brunetti, Venice is simply home, the place where he lives and works; he takes its beauty in stride. Urbino, on the other hand, remains goggle-eyed at its beauty. Equally important to him, it's the place where famous writers and artists have lived. Thus the reader is treated to an obligatory visit to Diaghilev's grave (with a ballet slipper atop the tombstone) and pauses with Urbino to gaze admiringly at the building where Tintoretto's daughter lived and the palazzo where a friend of Henry James jumped to her death.

In Leon's series, Venice is integrated naturally into the novels thanks to her strategy of using Brunetti to provide an insider's point of view. In Sklepowich's books, the setting is like a decorative facade on a beautiful building; more exotic than functional, it simply adds a glossy surface to each of the novels. Where both Thomas Mann and Leon drew upon elements of the natural Venetian setting to symbolize confusion and disorder (Mann used Venice's twisting streets, Leon its pervasive fog), Sklepowich by contrast compares Urbino's confusion to the amorphous forms of an Yves Tanguy painting that happens to hang in the Peggy Guggenheim Museum. Urbino is a knowledgeable (and upscale) tourist guide who provides ample information about Venice's cultural history. However, a reader seeking to learn something of the city's personality and character will better find it in Leon's novels.

One other novel worth examining for its evocative use of Venice is Michael Dibdin's *Dead Lagoon* (1994). Born in England and raised in Northern Ireland, Dibdin lived in Italy for five years, an experience he has put to good use in a series of mystery novels featuring Aurelio Zen, a member of Italy's elite Criminopol police agency. Dibdin has taken on an unusual and ambitious project of using all of Italy as his canvas in the Zen series. Each of the novels is set in a different location: Perugia (*Ratking*), Rome (*Cabal*), Sardinia (*Vendetta*), Naples (*Cosí fan Tutti*), Asti (*A Fine Finish*), Sicily (*Blood Rain*) and Bologna (*Back to Bologna*). *Dead Lagoon*, one of the finest in the series, is set in Venice.

Dibdin's use of Venice much more closely resembles Leon's than Sklepowich's. Like Brunetti, Zen is a native-born Venetian and a police detective. Venice is his home (or at least his former home, as he now lives in Rome) and he has no interest in the famous touristy locations that are so appealing to Urbino Macintyre. Dibdin also resembles Leon in the highly effective way he uses the Venice setting symbolically.

In *Dead Lagoon*, Venice is a dying city. The novel opens with a scene set on Sant' Ariano, the ossuary island littered with the bones of thousands of dead Venetians. A body, half eaten by rats, is found among the bones. This morbid note is reinforced by several other images of death, including a seagull with a piece of bloody liver in its mouth and a cat with a half-eaten fish dangling from its teeth. The air is also filled with a "noxious miasma" rising from the canals and "gobs of slush" that fall from the winter sky. This is not *La Serenissima,* the picturesque Venice so lavishly promoted in the glossy travel brochures; it is a picture, however, that, as is the case in Leon's books, underscores the novel's portrait of corruption.

Dibdin weaves a variety of serious issues — heroin trafficking, Serbian war crimes, the deportation of Jews from Venice during the Holocaust, the Venetian separatist movement — into an intricately-spun web that, like many of the novels in the series, leaves Zen weary and disillusioned at the end. As he peels away layer after layer of deception, Venice itself seems to embody his difficulty in getting to the truth: "If Rome was a labyrinth of powerful and competing cliques, each with its portfolio of secrets to defend, here everything was a trick of the light, an endlessly shifting play of appearances without form or substance. What you saw was what you got, and all you would ever get" (254). Like Leon, Dibdin also uses the perennial Venetian fog (which one character describes as "thick as snot") and the characteristic play of light and shadow on the lagoon ("the hazy light and the pervasive instability of water defeated every attempt at clarity or precision" [41]) as apt symbols for the elusive mysteries Zen is trying to untangle.

As far back as 1882, Henry James complained, "Venice has been painted and described many thousands of times, and of all the cities of the world is the easiest to visit without going there.... There is notoriously nothing new to be said about her" (1). The works of gifted writers like Donna Leon and Michael Dibdin prove him wrong and convincingly demonstrate that the artistic possibilities of this great and beautiful city can never be fully exhausted.

3

Tony Hillerman

The American Southwest

In a widely-acclaimed series of mystery novels featuring a pair of Navajo tribal policemen, Tony Hillerman employs a vast setting — the Four Corners area of the American Southwest where Arizona, New Mexico, Colorado, and Utah meet. Thanks to countless Hollywood films and television shows, it's a very familiar setting. But by employing an unusual point of view (i.e., that of his Navajo cops), Hillerman defamiliarizes the landscape and presents it from a fresh perspective. And though the land may appear empty, in the hands of a writer who makes it the center of his fictional universe, it is rich with promise.

Hillerman's interest in Indian cultures began at an early age. Born in 1925 to German-American parents, he grew up in the tiny town of Sacred Heart, Oklahoma, where his father ran a crossroads store and worked a small farm. He attended St. Mary's Academy, a two-room boarding school for Indian girls run by the Sisters of Mercy. There he enjoyed a close kinship with his Seminole and Pottawatomie friends; like him, they were looked down upon as country bumpkins by the town kids. Following his return from World War II in 1945 (on convalescent furlough due to injuries that included a crippled leg and a damaged eye suffered when he stepped on a land mine), he happened upon a group of Navajos in Crownpoint, New Mexico, dressed in ceremonial dress. Curious, he learned they were performing an Enemy Way ceremony to purify and restore to harmony with their people two young Navajo soldiers returning from fighting the Japanese. Hillerman was deeply moved by the experience: "To see people with a living culture still affecting how they live — that interested me. I'm drawn to people who believe in something enough that their lives are affected by it" (Breslin 57). Twenty-five years later he would feature the ceremony prominently in his first novel, *The Blessing Way*.

But Hillerman's interest in the Navajo was fueled by more than simple curiosity:

> I identify with the Navajo. I like them. I like their philosophical position. The Navajo as much as anything is a product of his environment. I came out of the same kind of environment, poverty, trying to make a living from the land, hoping the hell it would rain and it wouldn't, always being at the bottom of the pecking order, socially. Not only were we poor, we were Catholic, living in Oklahoma and surrounded by Fundamentalist Protestants, which really set us apart. So when I see these Navajos, I know where they're coming from. I can sympathize [Bernell 46].

After his return from the war, Hillerman graduated from the University of Oklahoma, settled in the Southwest and began a career in journalism. In 1952 he became the United Press International bureau manager in Santa Fe and later served as editor of the *Santa Fe New Mexican* newspaper. In 1963 he and his family (wife Marie and five children) moved to Albuquerque where he began studying for his M.A. in English at the University of New Mexico. While there, he worked as an assistant to the president of the university and later joined the journalism faculty, eventually serving as department head. But in his early forties, after two decades in journalism, he decided to satisfy a longtime desire to try his hand at fiction. Given his interests, it's no surprise that his first novel, *The Blessing Way*, featured a Navajo character and was set in the desert Southwest.

Growing up in an isolated town with no library, Hillerman as a boy depended on the packages of books he would regularly receive from the state library. Included would often be books he had not ordered. One such author he remembers reading was Arthur W. Upfield, who wrote mysteries about a half-breed Australian aborigine policeman who solved crimes in the desert Outback. What struck him most (and would one day powerfully influence his own writing) was Upfield's descriptions of the magnificent landscape and the sense he gave of desert isolation and tribal cultures. Other writers he would cite as influences — Raymond Chandler, Eric Ambler, Graham Greene — he admired for their skill in using the mystery form for something more than just the puzzle. In addition, they also shared in common a powerful sense of place.

When he decided to make the plunge from journalism to fiction,

Hillerman concluded that instead of trying to write something big and important like *War and Peace, American Style*, he should attempt something shorter, like a mystery. He also realized that if he wanted to make a story about an unfamiliar subject like the Navajos believable, he needed to make the setting as real as possible. To insure the topographical accuracy of the places he features in his novels he pays close attention to the framed copy of the Southern California Auto Club "Guide to Indian Country" map he keeps on the wall above his desk. He also makes it a point to physically visit the locales he uses in each book. "It is my habit to visit the places where I want my fictional events to happen, to stand in the dust, breathe the air, consider the sounds and the smells, watch the light change when the sun goes down" (*Hillerman Country* 143).

(Though he strives for scrupulous accuracy, he does make an occasional error, like putting limestone caves where none exist in *Listening Woman*. Sometimes, he deliberately fudges things; for example, he liked the name of the town Burnt Water so much, he relocated it to fit the plot requirements of *The Dark Wind*. Overall, however, a traveler to Indian Country might well use Hillerman's books as a rough guide to the territory.)

What above all inspires the powerful sense of place in Hillerman's fiction is simply his love for the desert Southwest:

> One of the key reasons I opted to set my first book on the Navaho reservation was my love of that huge, high, dry, mountain-rimmed landscape and the immense sky which looks over it. It is open, empty country, and the great storm clouds which rise above its mountain ranges remind me of the Glory of God [Shoup 159].

The deserts, canyons, and mesas of the Navajo reservation and its surrounding area, some 25,000 square miles (larger than New England), might on the surface appear barren and desolate. But to Hillerman, this is a place of infinite variety and subtle beauty, which his novels celebrate in diverse ways.

The Blessing Way introduced Navajo tribal policeman Joe Leaphorn, though the novel was not envisioned as the first in a series. In fact, Leaphorn originally was only a minor character in the book. The central character is an anthropology professor named Bergen McKee, whose encounter with the villain dominates the action. Hillerman said he set the novel on the Navajo reservation because "I thought the Navajos were so interesting, and their reservation was so interesting, that it would make a captivating setting for a mystery novel, which otherwise might not be very good, because I didn't know if I was going to be a good mystery writer" (Breen 53). Leaphorn was intended to be little more than a device for passing along information to the reader. The name Leaphorn isn't even Navajo (the name was inspired by Mary Renault's *The Bull from the Sea*, which describes young boys in ancient Crete leaping over the horns of bulls), and Hillerman admits he wouldn't ever have given his character that name if he'd intended him to be an important character.

A literary agent who read the novel advised Hillerman, "If you insist on rewriting this, get rid of all that Indian stuff" (Breslin 58). Rather than heeding her advice, Hillerman revised the manuscript, significantly increasing Leaphorn's role, though he did not become the main character until Hillerman decided to write a follow-up novel to *The Blessing Way*.

Dance Hall of the Dead and *Listening Woman* both featured Joe Leaphorn, who gradually became fleshed out as a character. But with his fourth novel set in Navajo country, *People of Darkness,* Hillerman introduced a new protagonist, Jim Chee. Two primary reasons dictated the change. Hillerman felt that Leaphorn "was too old, too sophisticated and knowledgeable of the white man's world to ask the kind of questions I wanted him to ask" in the new book (Bernell 47). He needed a younger character and a more traditional Navajo. He also learned to his chagrin that because of the sale of TV and movie rights to *Dance Hall of the Dead,* a Hollywood producer now owned the rights to the character of Leaphorn. (He later bought them back for $20,000). Consequently, Leaphorn is mentioned only once in the novel (he leaves a phone message for Chee). Chee would go on to be featured in Hillerman's next two novels, *The Dark Wind* and *The Ghostway.*

Then, bothered by one reader's complaint that she couldn't tell Chee and Leaphorn apart, Hillerman decided to resurrect Leaphorn and feature both characters in his next novel, *Skinwalkers.* Hillerman's move added a new level of depth and interest to the series, which has since continued to feature both characters.

Lt. Joe Leaphorn has spent his entire career as a member of the Navajo Tribal Police. Holder of a B.A. and an M.A. in anthropology from Arizona State, he shares few of the traditional Navajo beliefs. He has nothing but contempt, for example, for everything related to the Navajo belief in witchcraft. "Leaphorn was not a believer. Those who were were the bane of his police work" (*Thief* 29).

Jim Chee is a much younger, far less experienced member of the Navajo Tribal Police. Like Leaphorn, he too has a degree in anthropology (from the University of New Mexico), but unlike Leaphorn, he professes a deep belief in the religion of his people. He begins each day with a dawn chant and when his police work brings him into contact with the bones of the dead (a Navajo taboo), he feels obliged to take a sweat bath to purify himself. He is studying to become a *yataalii,* a Navajo singer or shaman. He is also struggling to find his place in the world as a Navajo. Though he once qualified for the F.B.I. academy, he fears that accepting that job would threaten his identity as a Navajo.

While Leaphorn works out of central headquarters in Window Rock, Chee is just a foot soldier out in distant Shiprock doing the routine stuff. Chee's a bit too romantic and idealistic to suit Leaphorn; Leaphorn's too rigid and logical to suit Chee. Chee admires and respects Leaphorn (known throughout the department as the "Legendary Lieutenant"), but a meeting with him always makes him feel uneasy and incompetent, "like a rookie reporting for basketball practice with Michael Jordan" (*Hunting* 134). Despite a sometimes prickly relationship, the two eventually come to understand and respect each other. Though not officially partners, they work closely together, even after Leaphorn retires from the force.

Having had over three decades in which to develop his characters, Hillerman has used the opportunity to explore his two main protagonists in interesting ways. Chee, the more conflicted of the two, constantly struggles to find a balance between the traditional and the modern sides of his personality. Can he be a Navajo singer and a policeman at the same time? His struggle is represented by his relationships with the women in his life. Mary Landon is a blonde, blue-eyed schoolteacher from Wisconsin he first meets in *People of Darkness.* They fall in love, but Chee's constant worries about whether marrying her would threaten his Navajo identity eventually doom the relationship. In *Skinwalkers* he begins a long-term relationships with Janet Pete, a Navajo public defender. Though her father was Navajo, her background is Stanford sorority girl, Maryland cocktail circuit and tickets to the Met. For a time Chee entertains hopes that their love could "blend oil and water," but eventually he realizes that neither can compromise enough to escape their different value systems. In the most recent books, Chee takes his first halting steps towards a relationship with Bernadette Manuelito, a rookie Navajo cop, which finally culminates in marriage in *Skeleton Man*. Maintaining Navajo identity is not an issue with her.

Leaphorn is a different case. For him the problem is personal rather than cultural. He is much more assimilated and at ease with who he is than Chee. But when Emma, his wife of thirty years, suddenly dies, he is cast adrift. For several books in the series, he grapples with loneliness and grief over her loss. His retirement from the Navajo police force presents him with another reason to feel isolated, though "like an old retired fireman who can't stay away when something's burning" (*Wailing* 57), he continues to become involved in cases. Eventually he develops a relationship with Louisa Bourbonnette, a professor of American Studies at Northern Arizona University, which helps lessen his loneliness. Hillerman isn't writing romances, nor are there any titillating sex scenes in his novels. Instead he looks for ways to humanize his two cops by exploring different ways of finding harmony in accommodating to the modern world.

Conveying Navajo beliefs and customs through the eyes of two characters with contrasting views allows Hillerman to present a complex and balanced picture of Navajo culture. Despite their differences in beliefs, the two share the same fundamental Navajo desire for harmony with nature and a deep appreciation of the beauty of their surrounding world. Immensity of space in a forbidding landscape can either be intimidating or comforting, depending on one's point of view. For Leaphorn and Chee, it is the latter. For them, appreciation of nature is more than a simple aesthetic experience; it plays a spiritual role in their lives. Chee, for example, looking over the landscape near Shiprock, "drank in the view, letting the grandeur of immense space lift his spirits" (*Ghostway* 24). Leaphorn shares the same love of open space and, on the occasion of flying over America's Heartland, silently rejoices in being spared a life lived in "bleak, featureless landscapes closed in by a sky no more than six feet above one's forehead" (*Thief* 225).

Hillerman effectively captures both the geographical emptiness and the metaphysical plenitude of his desert setting. He impresses upon the reader the immensity of open space that, for example, allows one to see a mountain a hundred miles off into the distance. Human settlements are so scattered that it isn't uncommon for children to have to ride a bus to a school sixty miles away. But Hillerman also aims at capturing the spirit of the place and few places on earth are as imbued with spirits as the American Southwest. For the Navajo, the land which Hillerman has called "America's very own Holy Land" (*New Mexico* 101) is spiritually charged and alive with ancient deities as well as *chindi*, the spirits of the departed. This haunted presence permeates the books and gives them a sense of mystery that transcends the question of who is guilty of whatever crime is being investigated.

Hillerman evokes the harsh beauty in this empty landscape in many ways. With a journalist's economy of language and eye for telling detail, he paints the subtle colors that enliven this brown landscape, as the following two brief passages illustrate:

> The San Francisco Peaks made a dark blue bump against the yellow glare of the horizon. The cloud over Navajo Mountain was luminescent pink and the sandstone wilderness through which Leaphorn walked had become a universe of vermilion under this slanting light [*Listening* 37].

> The sage was gray and silver with autumn, the late afternoon sun laced it with slanting shadows, and everywhere there was the yellow of blooming snakeweed and the purple of the asters [*Talking* 21].

Desert colors are as integral to the mood Hillerman aims to create as neon lights are to a noir writer.

Usually relying on straightforward description, Hillerman seldom employs similes or other kinds of figurative language for effect. The only time he uses similes is to describe Ship Rock, which he variously compares to a "surreal Gothic cathedral," "an oversized, free-form Gothic cathedral" and a "Gothic cathedral for giants." Instead, he simply describes what his two Navajo cops see and what they are conditioned to see is the beauty all around them.

Nature is seldom seen as threatening even though storms, while rare, are also a defining feature of this landscape. Chapter 13 of *Listening Woman*, for example, opens with a lengthy description of a gathering storm that soon explodes into falling ice and water. What might seem like an unnecessary intrusion in another book serves a useful function here: it reminds us of how unusual a phenomenon rain is in the parched desert environment; it illustrates the explosive power of nature; and as Leaphorn sits trapped in his carryall, it also emphasizes his isolation and vulnerability.

A storm like this can be a real danger to someone who is miles away from another person if he should need help.

The storm also illustrates Hillerman's ability to infuse a scene with vibrant sensory details. From the "plong-plong" sounds of the rain crashing down on the roof of Leaphorn's carryall to the picture of the droplets reflecting the sun "like a rhinestone curtain," the reader feels the storm. The silence after the brief storm also serves to highlight the rare sounds of the desert: the song of insects, the chirping of crickets, the call of an owl. Normally the thin dry air of the desert carries few smells, but Leaphorn can now detect the smell of wet sand, the faint aroma of cedar, and the perfume of piñon needles.

Specific features of the setting also serve to symbolize the mysteries Chee and Leaphorn must solve. Where Donna Leon's mysteries utilize Venice's confusing streets and canals to represent puzzlement, Hillerman uses the many narrow and twisting canyons which dot the landscape:

> To the north, northwest and northeast, the ground fell away into a labyrinth of vertical-walled canyons which he [Leaphorn] knew drained, eventually, into the San Juan River. The track he had taken circled in from the south, through a wilderness of eroded stone.... A reasonably agile man could climb down off this bench to the canyon floor, but canyons would lead him nowhere. Only into an endless labyrinth — deeper and deeper into the sheer-walled maze [*Listening* 136].

Even the skilled have to remain alert to avoid getting lost on their journey to the truth.

To be successful, a good detective must have intimate knowledge of his world. As products of their environment, both cultural and geographic, Leaphorn and Chee have developed attitudes and learned skills that make them especially good detectives. Among the specific Navajo habits each possesses are patience and a suspicion of coincidence, which combine to make them persistent investigators. In *The Dark Wind*, for example, Jim Chee is confident that he will eventually find the answer to who is vandalizing windmills on the Navajo reservation:

> Sooner or later he would understand this business. He'd find the cause. Senseless as it seemed, there'd be a reason behind it. The wind did not move, the leaf did not fall, the bird did not cry, nor the windmill provoke such violent anger without a reason. All was part of the universal pattern, as Changing Woman had taught them when she formed the first four Navajo clans. Jim Chee had ingested that fact with his

mother's milk, and from the endless lessons his uncle taught him. "All is order," Hosteen Nakai taught him. "Look for the pattern" [*Dark* 40].

Leaphorn shares the same belief that an underlying pattern can always be found amidst the chaos:

> Too much coincidence. Leaphorn didn't believe in it. He believed nothing happened without cause. Everything intermeshed, from the mood of a man, to the flight of the corn beetle, to the music of the wind. It was the Navajo philosophy, this concept of interwoven harmony, and it was bred into Joe Leaphorn's bones [*Listening* 137].

Knowledge of their fellow Navajos also gives Chee and Leaphorn a distinct advantage over their white counterparts when it comes to interviewing witnesses and suspects. They understand the Navajo respect for silence and know that politeness demands that they not interrupt a speaker. In *Listening Woman*, for example, Leaphorn is able to obtain vital information from a woman a white policeman had previously questioned by telling her, "I listened to the tape recording of you talking to the white policeman.... But I noticed, my mother, that the white man didn't really let you tell about it. He interrupted you" (*Listening* 94).

As individuals shaped by their desert environment, Leaphorn and Chee have learned to become skilled readers of signs. Faint footprints in the sand are far more important sources of information to them than ballistic tests and fingerprints. Other signs, like the movement of birds in the air, can lead them to water, or alert them to the presence of someone hiding in the brush nearby. Chee is also able to track down a trailer parked next to some cottonwoods he saw in a photograph because he knows the rare places with enough water to produce cottonwoods.

Detectives — whether private or police — solve crimes for a variety of reasons. For Hillerman's tribal policemen, one compelling motive is the Navajo desire for harmony. In "The Guilty Vicarage," his famous essay on mystery fiction, poet W.H. Auden observed that a crime like murder is an offense to society itself, a violation of what he termed "The Great Good Place"; it is the task of the detective to solve the crime and to restore "the state of grace" to society. Chee and Leaphorn are crime solvers whose motives are as much spiritual as professional.

For the Navajo, the goal of life is *hozro* or *hozho*, described as "a sort of blend of being in harmony with one's environment, at peace with one's circumstances, content with the day, devoid of anger, and free from anxieties" (*Ghostway* 219). Crimes like murder disrupt this balance and must be solved so harmony can be restored. Chee is learning to be a singer so he can bring harmony to the individual who needs it; as a policeman, his task is to bring harmony to the larger community. Sometimes, Chee and Leaphorn not only risk their lives as law enforcement officers, as Navajos they risk contamination by the powers of evil. When Chee feels tainted after walking among the bones of the dead, he undergoes a purifying ceremony. Even the non-believer Leaphorn is prompted to ask Chee to perform a Blessing Way purification ceremony for him at the end of *A Thief of Time*. Chee and Leaphorn risk such violations of their own personal sense of harmony in order to achieve a greater purpose, i.e., doing what they can to restore cosmic orderliness.

One part of his job that bothers Chee is having to track down criminals only to see them put in jail rather than returned to harmony. At times, he is even willing to jeopardize his career by choosing harmony over the *belangaana*, or white, system of justice. In *Sacred Clowns*, for example, he is assigned a hit-and-run case which, he is led to believe, will result in his promotion to sergeant if he can solve it. He does, but he also discovers circumstances which create a conflict between his police duty and his Navajo upbringing which puts more value on curing than punishment. He learns that the guilty driver is sole guardian of his grandson, a teenage boy afflicted with Fetal Alcohol Syndrome. What should Chee do? Because the man has publicly acknowledged his crime (over the airwaves during an open-mike session at the local radio station) and is sending money to the family of the man he killed, Chee decides to protect his identity so he can continue to care for his grandson. Chee's reasoning goes like this: "He [Chee] was a big boy before he heard about 'make the punishment fit the crime' or 'an eye for an eye, a tooth for a tooth.' Instead of that he was hearing of retribution in another way. If you damage somebody, you sit down with their family and figure out how much damage and make it good. That way you restore *hozho*. You've got harmony again between two families" (*Sacred* 271). Chee won't get his promotion, but he will take satisfaction from knowing that he acted to restore harmony in accordance with his religious beliefs.

Most crimes committed on the Navajo reservation are minor: drunkenness, auto theft, witchcraft complaints, and various other social problems that occur among people "turned eccentric by an overdose of dramatic skyscrapes, endless silence and loneliness" (*Hunting* 80). Most of the murders, on the other hand, given the Navajo attitude toward death — "Navajos were conditioned almost from infancy to avoid the dead and to have a special dread of death" (*Thief* 76) — and the lack of such drives as revenge and greed among the people, are committed by whites. Because of its isolation, canyon country is also an ideal spot for crimes like the transportation of drugs (*The Dark Wind*) and its fatal consequences. Because the land is a rich depository of archaeological treasures, it also produces such killers as the anthropologist who murders to cover up his salting of sites to prove a disputed theory about Folsom man in *Dance Hall of the Dead* and the one who kills to cover up his illegal digs of Anasazi sites in *A Thief of Time*. In the rare instance when an Indian is revealed as the killer, as in *Coyote Waits,* the crime can be traced to the alcohol which was given to the aged Navajo by a white man trying to obtain information from him by getting him drunk.

Though Hillerman paints an impressive picture of the stunning beauty of the landscape, not everything is perfect in this desert paradise. It is, after all, a landscape "that offered nothing but beauty and poverty" (*Wailing* 249), and Hillerman offsets descriptions of the beauty with reminders of the hard life lived by many who inhabit the land. There are also human threats to the majestic environment, as the aptly titled *The Fallen Man,* with its Edenic overtones, reminds us. The plot of that novel involves a legal battle over property that certain individuals wish to lease for strip mining of molybdenum. Leaphorn is dismayed to learn about the devastating effects of such mining, which involves ripping up the land and poisoning rivers with the cyanide used in the operation.

Defilement of the landscape takes a different form in *The Fallen Man.* Jim Chee becomes angry at some white rock climbers who, in his view, are guilty of desecrating Ship Rock, sacred in Navajo legend for flying from the North and bringing the first Navajos on its back. To him, scaling the rock is as sacrilegious as climbing St. Patrick's Cathedral or the Wailing Wall would be. Equally offensive to a Navajo like Chee is the idea that people feel they need to climb places like Ship Rock simply to prove that man is the dominating master of the universe.

Setting, of course, involves much more than simple geography. A critical element in Hillerman's depiction of place is the Navajo culture that is so closely identified with the landscape. Hillerman immerses his readers in the religion, social customs, codes and taboos of a people who have inhabited the land for centuries. Though he modestly makes no claim as an authority on Navajo culture, Hillerman does extensive research on his favorite subject. He reads everything from books on Navajo history to the local Navajo newspaper and minutes of tribal council meetings. He also confesses to hanging around trading posts, police substations, rodeos, rug auctions, and sheep dippings soaking up material that often makes its way into his novels.

Using the West as setting for a novel is nothing new. Western novels and films have long been a staple of American popular culture, beginning with the publication of Owen Wister's *The Virginian* in 1902. What distinguishes Hillerman's books is their point of view. In most Westerns, the land and its Indian inhabitants are seen as alien to the white visitors from the East. The harsh land has to be tamed and the intractable Indians must be subdued and conquered so that the demands of Manifest Destiny can be fulfilled and the westward expansion of the American empire be completed. Hillerman subverts this myth by presenting the land and its people through the eyes of his two Navajo cops. To them, the land is a comfort and the whites are the aliens.

The heroic myths celebrated in the classic Western are notably absent from the pages of Hillerman's books. No *Gunfight at the O. K. Corral,* no *High Noon* heroes standing tall. Among the few nods made to the Western tradition is a search for the bones of Butch Cassidy, which figures in the plot of *Coyote Waits,* and a viewing at a drive-in of John Ford's classic *Cheyenne Autumn* in *Sacred Clowns.* Ford's 1964 film tells the story of the Cheyenne's attempt to return from an Oklahoma reservation to their Wyoming home. Chee and his Navajo friends enjoy the film because it gives them a chance to see their relatives, who play the Cheyenne in the film, and to hear them, speaking in Navajo, make fun of the white folks in the movie who don't understand what they are saying. There is no room for nostalgia for a lost heroic past in Hillerman's contemporary look at the land and its inhabitants, just an honest depiction of the strengths and problems of the Navajo people.

One telling illustration of the key role setting plays in Hillerman's books is to consider what happens when he moves the action off the reservation, as he does in *Talking God.* Much of the novel is set in Washington,

D.C., where Chee and Leaphorn end up purely by chance (Leaphorn is working on a case that has a possible Washington connection while Chee is using vacation time to visit Janet Pete who is living there). Uprooting the two Navajo cops from their natural setting not only disorients them, it places them in the implausible situation of working to foil a plot by a Chilean terrorist to set off a bomb in the Museum of Natural History. The whole novel has an uncharacteristic forced and artificial feel to it. Wisely, Hillerman returned Chee and Leaphorn to their familiar native environment in his next novel and has kept them there through the rest of the series.

Hillerman's a storyteller, not an anthropologist, and though he confesses he's always looking for an opportunity to teach the reader something informative about the Navajo, he's very careful to work it in without slowing the pace of the story:

> The people who read me have had a hard day at the office; they've got all kinds of problems; they're worrying about God knows what; and they want to be entertained. They don't want some guy out in Albuquerque preaching to them about the sins of their fathers. They don't want me trying to retrain them in American history. They don't want me sermonizing on religion to them. They want to be entertained. I've gotta keep that in mind all the time, remind myself who I am and what I'm doing. I'm writing what Graham Greene called an entertainment [Herbert 90].

The discovery of a body, for example, offers Hillerman an opportunity to include information about Navajo attitudes toward the dead. When Jim Chee concludes that footprints surrounding a corpse must have been made by a Navajo because only a Navajo would shuffle his feet that way to erase snake tracks in the sand, we learn about certain tribal taboos.

Hillerman also uses his plots as a way of incorporating Navajo material; central to the plot of *The Dark Wind,* for example, is a crime motivated by revenge, which allows him to introduce information about the lack of value the Navajos place on revenge. Chee and Leaphorn's investigations also frequently bring them to tribal ceremonies, where the reader learns about certain religious practices. Describing differences between Navajo and Zuni or Hopi ceremonies also enables Hillerman to remind the reader that Indians are not all alike, that there's a greater difference between the Hopi and the Navajo than between the Hopi religion and Judaism or Christianity.

3. Tony Hillerman

The key to Hillerman's success in working this material in unobtrusively is that he presents everything through the eyes of his two Navajo cops. However, a white writer like Hillerman representing Navajo Indians operates in what can be described as a cultural and political minefield. But aside from the rare complaint — in one strongly-worded polemic, Indian activist Ward Churchill castigated Hillerman's novels as "dangerous" and "the very quintessence of modern colonialist fiction in the United States" (279) — Hillerman's novels have been well received, especially among the Navajo. They are read widely in Navajo schools, and in the words of one Navajo librarian, "Like the stories our grandmother used to tell us, they [Hillerman's novels] make us feel good about being Navajo" (Hillerman *Talking* 43). Especially cherished among the many awards Hillerman has received is one given to him by the Navajo Nation expressing appreciation for authentically portraying the strength and dignity of traditional Navajo culture.

Non-Indian readers can expect to come away from Hillerman's novels with a greater understanding and respect for a people and a culture that may not be widely known to them. All readers, Indian and otherwise, thanks to Hillerman's vivid portrayal of the setting, can also expect to gain a deeper appreciation of the landscape of the Southwest and a powerful reminder about the value of striving to live in harmony with the land we inhabit.

4

Walter Mosley
South Central Los Angeles

Thanks to Raymond Chandler, Ross Macdonald, and a host of crime writers up to and including such popular contemporary favorites as James Ellroy, Jonathan Kellerman, and Michael Connelly, Los Angeles has become a staple of the American crime novel. The city has also been appropriated artistically by mainstream novelists ranging from Nathanael West and F. Scott Fitzgerald to Joan Didion, Thomas Pynchon, and Bret Easton Ellis. Capitalizing on its amorphous nature, multiple identities, and rich metaphoric associations (L.A. as Dream Factory, as Lotus Land, as El Dorado, as Sodom and Gomorrah, etc.), each of these writers has made L.A. his or her own, stamping a unique style and perspective on the malleable setting. Consequently, according to Michael Sorkin, "L.A. is probably the most mediated town in America, nearly unviewable save through the fictive scrim of its mythologizers" (Davis 20).

The most interesting contemporary writer to lay artistic claim to this well-trampled territory is Walter Mosley. Mosley doesn't attempt, as many writers do, to explain the city, nor does he concern himself with what David L. Ulin describes as the "all sun and celluloid" image of Southern California (xv). In a series of crime novels featuring reluctant private detective Ezekial "Easy" Rawlins, Mosley instead mines a largely unexplored part of the terrain to tell the previously overlooked story of African Americans in L.A. from the late 1940s up to the 1960s.

Mosley, of course, is not the first black writer to employ the crime novel to depict the African American experience in America. Chester Himes's Coffin Ed Johnson and Grave Digger Jones series of mystery novels was set in Harlem in the 1950s and '60s. Mosley's novels are far less violent and polemical than Himes's books. Also, as Stephen F. Soitos observed in *The Blues Detective: A Study of African American Detective Fiction,* Hines recreates Harlem as a "mythical cityscape" whose truth exists "on a metaphorical rather than a historical level" (143). Mosley, by contrast, aims at historical rather than metaphorical truth in his depiction of place.

Mosley is not the only contemporary crime writer to find inspiration in the L.A. of the past. James Ellroy shares a similar interest in the postwar years, most notably in his L.A. Quartet: *The Black Dahlia* (1987), *The Big Nowhere* (1988), *L.A. Confidential* (1990), and *White Jazz* (1992). These dates of publication overlap with Mosley's books, as does the time period covered. Ellroy admits that setting his novels in the past allows him to "swim in L.A.'s historical gutter" and to re-create the city he calls, among other things, a "Multicultural Hellhole" (49). His purpose in revisiting the past is to subvert the myth of L.A. perpetuated in such popular 1950s television programs as *Dragnet*. In characteristically manic prose, Ellroy maps the history of modern Los Angeles, according to Mike Davis, as a "secret continuum of sex crimes, satanic conspiracies and political scandals" (45). Mosley's primary concern, by contrast, is not to rewrite the past but to rescue it by mapping out previously hidden or overlooked history.

Mosley was born in L.A. in 1952, the son of a black father and a white Jewish mother. His father, Leroy, had migrated from Houston, Texas, to L.A. after World War II in search of a better life. He got a job as a school custodian and met his wife, Ella, who was a personnel clerk at the same school. Mosley grew up in Watts until the age of twelve, when his family moved to a middle-class neighborhood in West Los Angeles. After graduating from high school, he left L.A. to attend Goddard College in Vermont and later settled in New York, where he worked as a computer programmer before beginning to write fiction in his mid-thirties. In re-creating the past in the Rawlins books, Mosley drew upon childhood memories as well as stories he remembers his father and his friends telling of life in L.A. in the late 1940s. "He lived a long-suffering life," Mosley has said of his father, "so that I could tell his stories" (*What Next* 65).

Devil in a Blue Dress is set in 1948. Easy Rawlins has just been laid off from his job at Champion Aircraft and is worried about making the upcoming mortgage payment on his house. A white man named DeWitt Albright (the name is obviously significant) is looking for someone to track down a missing young white woman named Daphne Monet who he claims has "a predilection for the company of Negroes" (19). He knows a black person like Rawlins can gain access to places a white man like himself can't. Needing some quick cash, Rawlins takes the job and sets out to discover the whereabouts (and uncover the secrets) of the missing woman.

The opening scene of *Devil in a Blue Dress* is set in Joppy's bar, located on the second floor of a butcher's warehouse on 103rd Street in Watts. The scene self-consciously mirrors the opening pages of Raymond Chandler's *Farewell, My Lovely.* That novel begins with Philip Marlowe following Moose Malloy into Florian's, a bar and gambling joint on Central Avenue which in the eight years since Malloy last visited the place has changed from a white to a black establishment. What differentiates the two scenes is the perspective.

In Chandler's novel, the action is viewed through the eyes of Marlowe, whose famous description of the gaudily dressed Moose Malloy ("He looked about as inconspicuous as a tarantula on a slice of angel food" [3]) echoes his own sense of displacement. As he and Malloy enter Florian's, the customers, all black, suddenly become quiet: "There was a sudden silence as heavy as a water-logged boat. Eyes looked at us, chestnut colored eyes, set in faces that ranged from gray to deep black. Heads turned slowly and the eyes in them glistened and stared in the dead alien silence of another race" (5). The setting is indeed presented as an alien place, but from Marlowe's point of view it is the black customers at Florian's who are alien. In Mosley's version of the scene, the perspective is reversed. Seen through Rawlins's eyes, what had been alien in Chandler's world is now the familiar, the world of South Central L.A. now the norm. In this way Mosely effectively signals to the reader that while L.A. is still the setting, it is an L.A. that has previously been overlooked or marginalized in the pages of the crime novel.

As conceived by Chandler and his successors, the private eye is usually an outsider who can freely range across social classes, moving through the neighborhoods of both rich and poor alike. A member of an oppressed minority like Easy Rawlins is even more of an outsider than his white counterparts. But as a veteran of the Normandy invasion and the Battle of the Bulge, he also possesses an advantage denied his white private-eye brethren: five years spent eating, sleeping and killing with whites has given him knowledge and experience that enables him to range over both social *and* racial borders, which makes him an especially effective private detective.

Mosley describes Rawlins as "the voice of a million people who moved out of their sharecropping days and came into Southern California" (Lomax 32), and he embodies both the dream and the harsh reality of that experience. Like many of the other African American characters in the novel, Rawlins settled in L.A. from Houston after the war. "California was like heaven for the southern Negro," Rawlins notes. "People told stories of how you could eat fruit right off the trees and get enough work to retire one day"(27). As a proud homeowner whose house "meant more to me than any woman I ever knew" (11), he has staked out his claim to the American Dream.

But in many ways, L.A. turned out to be simply an extension of the plantation life Southern blacks thought they had left behind when they moved to California. After losing his job at Champion Aircraft because he wouldn't kowtow to his white boss, Rawlins concludes that "a job in a factory is an awful lot like working on a plantation in the South. The bosses see all the workers like they're children, and everyone knows how lazy children are" (*Devil* 62). He recognizes that his white boss "needed all his children to kneel down and let him be the boss. He wasn't a businessman, he was a plantation boss; a slaver"(66). Rawlins also learns that simply owning a home doesn't exempt him from police harassment, as he gets roused from his own front yard by two policemen playing what he calls "the game of 'cops and nigger'" (69). Nevertheless, owning his own home and working for himself gives him a sense of pride and autonomy he can find nowhere else: "It was as if for the first time in my life I was doing something on my own terms. Nobody was telling me what to do. I was acting on my own" (124).

Rawlins's story continues in *A Red Death,* set in 1953, five years after the events in *Devil in a Blue Dress.* More economic success has come Rawlins's way, thanks to the $10,000 he kept as his share of the $30,000 Daphne Monet had stolen from her wealthy lover. Rawlins now owns three apartment buildings, though he is unable to enjoy his new status publicly. He feels compelled to keep his ownership of the properties secret and instead poses as a maintenance man in one of the buildings. In this respect, he is simply a product of his environment. As Mosley explains it, "He learned when he lived in the Deep South that anything you had, could be taken away from you, and there was no recourse. White people could take it from you. Black people could take it from you. If you told somebody you had some money, they were gonna come in and they were gonna get that money away from you. So he keeps everything a secret, even when he doesn't have to" (*Maidment* 72). Despite Rawlins's efforts at secrecy, the IRS begins investigating his finances, which poses yet another threat to his property. When an FBI agent offers to fix his tax problems in return for whatever information he can turn up on Chaim Wenzler, a suspected communist working in a local black church, Rawlins once again reluctantly assumes the role of detective.

White Butterfly is set in 1956 and in the three years since his last case, Rawlins has married a nurse named Regina and is father to two children: a daughter, Edna, by his wife and a son, Jesus, a young mute Mexican boy whom he rescued from a sexual predator who had been molesting him in *Devil in a Blue Dress*. The tokens of his economic success are multiplying as well, as he now owns seven buildings. However, he still is unwilling to share his success with anyone, including his wife, which is one of the reasons she leaves him at the end of the novel.

Three young black women have been killed and disfigured by the same assailant in Watts. When a fourth victim — a white UCLA coed named Robin Garnett, who has been working as a stripper in Watts under the name of Cyndi Starr — is also murdered in similar fashion, the police develop a greater sense of urgency to catch the killer. They enlist Rawlins's help, arguing as DeWitt Albright did that he has access to places they don't. "I was worth a precinct full of detectives when the cops needed the word in the ghetto," he notes (2). Although Rawlins never feels comfortable having to "run down a black man for the law" (10), circumstances often force his involvement. This time the incentive comes in the form of a threat by the police to jail Rawlins's best friend, Mouse. And once again the reluctant detective proves he is more than capable of solving a crime the police can't on their own.

Black Betty skips ahead to 1961. Rawlins is hired to find a wealthy family's missing black housekeeper, a woman he knew in Houston when he was twelve. Easy's investigation, as is usually the case, soon widens into a larger picture. There's a new young Irish president in the White House and Martin Luther King, Jr., is marching for Civil Rights in the South. "The world was changing," says Rawlins, "and a black man in America

53

had the chance to be a man for the first time in hundreds of years" (11). But his cheery optimism is undermined by his own financial predicament: he's almost bankrupt and he and his family (which now also includes adopted daughter Feather, child of the murdered Robin Garnett from *White Butterfly*) live in a rented house and eat beans and rice three times a week. He also notes somberly that the world he feels so hopeful about is being rocked almost daily by underground nuclear explosions and the ongoing threat of war.

A Little Yellow Dog jumps ahead two years to 1963. Easy has been off the streets for two years, happily enjoying an ordinary working life as chief custodian at Sojourner Truth Junior High School. But a request from Idabell Turner, a teacher at the school, that Rawlins take care of her dog Pharaoh, whom her husband has threatened to kill, soon changes all that. First, both Idabell's husband and his twin brother turn up dead, then Idabell herself is murdered. Inevitably Rawlins finds himself back in the detective business once again.

Life on the streets of Watts is often a dangerous activity for Rawlins, but it is his old friend Mouse who ends up dead, gunned down as he (as usual) tries to bail Rawlins out of trouble. (Mouse is later, without explanation, miraculously resurrected in *Little Scarlet*, though he plays only a minor role in that novel.) The close friendship between Rawlins and Raymond "Mouse" Alexander goes back to their boyhoods. Their early history is recounted in *Gone Fishin'*, Mosley's first novel, written in 1988 but not published until 1997, following the appearance of the first five Rawlins novels. A coming-of-age story rather than a mystery, *Gone Fishin'* tells the story of a trip in 1939 that nineteen-year-old Easy and Mouse make from Houston, where they live, to a small Texas bayou town. During their visit, the volatile Mouse murders his stepfather in a dispute over money. Rawlins, who witnesses the killing, learns some important lessons about mortality, the demands of friendship, and the painful burden of guilt. At the end of the novel, Easy leaves Houston for L.A., though his life will continue to be haunted by the dangerous presence of Mouse, who soon follows him there.

Rawlins considers Mouse both "the truest friend I ever had" and "true evil" (*Red* 57). The recklessly violent Mouse lacks all sense of morality. His propensity for violence poses a constant threat to everyone, including Easy, though it also makes him an invaluable companion on the mean streets of L.A. Easy often relies on Mouse to bail him out of a dangerous situation. While Rawlins represents one kind of black male hero, a flawed man trying to do his best in an uncertain world, Mouse can be seen as a different type of hero. According to Mosley, "For a group of oppressed people a man like Mouse is the greatest kind of hero. He's a man who will stand up against bone-cracking odds with absolute confidence. He's a man who won't accept even the smallest insult. And for a people for whom insult is as common as air, that's a man who will bring joy" ("Black Man" 239).

The news of Mouse's (apparent) death comes on the same day that JFK is murdered in Dallas and the twin tragedies leave Rawlins shattered. On a personal level, Mouse's death haunts Rawlins with feelings of guilt; on another level, JFK's death represents a setback to Rawlins and his people's hopes for improvement in America. His experience of false hopes and dashed promises even affects his personal relationships. Though he finds himself strongly attracted to Bonnie Shay, a friend of Idabell's, he remains wary. Her soft and caring voice "had the promise of daylight and love," but he cautions himself that "it was like the lie of peace and brotherhood that had hoodwinked so many of my kind" (294).

Though six years would pass before Rawlins's next appearance, the action in *Bad Boy Brawly Brown* takes place only three months after *The Little Yellow Dog*. Bonnie Shay has moved in with Easy and his children and life has settled once more into a quiet routine. That is, until an old friend requests Easy's help in tracking down Brawly Brown, son of his girlfriend Alva. On the surface, the case is a typical missing-person investigation. But as is usual in Mosley's novels, the situation leads to much more, this time a glimpse into disturbing signs of growing anger and frustration in the Watts community. Rawlins learns that Brawly Brown has joined the Urban Revolutionary Party, a group demanding better rights and opportunities for blacks in America. A local policeman, head of a unit that is monitoring potentially subversive groups, seeks Rawlins's help in keeping an eye on the activities of the radical group, which he fears will become violent. As he explains to Rawlins, "There's blood boiling under the surface of Watts.... The Negroes are getting anxious for some changes.... They want to end de facto segregation. They want better jobs" (104). Rawlins learns from a police informer that members of the radical group (including Brawly Brown) are planning a bank robbery to get cash to finance their activities. Easy shoots Brown in the leg to prevent him from participating, which saves his life as the other bank robbers are all gunned down by the police in a shootout. But readers with a knowledge of history know that the boiling blood in Watts will within the year erupt into the devastating riots that will leave the neighborhood shattered.

"The morning air still smelled of smoke," reads the pungent opening line of *Little Scarlet,* which is set during the Watts riots of August 1965 (3). Buildings are burning, shops are being looted, and the death toll numbers thirty-four. In this volatile atmosphere of violence and hatred, the police once more come to Rawlins for help, this time in solving the murder of Nola Payne, a young black woman nicknamed Little Scarlet because of her red hair. She was last seen in the company of a white man and the police are worried that if it turns out she was killed by him, racial tensions will become even more inflamed.

Rawlins's search for the killer gives Mosley an opportunity to sketch a chilling of picture of the destruction in Watts:

> On Avalon and Central and Hooper the burned buildings outnumbered the ones still intact. There was at least one torched car hunkered down at the curb on almost every block. Debris was strewn along the sidewalks and streets. Smoke still rose here and there from the wreckage. Furtive shadows could be seen sifting through the debris, searching for anything of value that had been overlooked [51].

Mosley explores both the roots and the consequences of the riot. The main cause is obvious — pent-up rage over racism. Rawlins himself nearly succumbs to that "angry voice in my heart that urged me to go out and fight after all the hangings I had seen, after all of the times I had been called nigger and all of the doors that had been slammed into my face" (18). But he is also devastated by the mindless destruction and looting that victimizes innocent shopkeepers: "Why would somebody want to burn shoes," he wonders (11).

Rawlins also detects the first glimmer of hope amidst the horrors as racial barriers seem to be breaking down. One indication of that is the way the police now begin to treat him differently. He is given a letter of authority by an LAPD deputy commissioner that works like a get-out-of-jail card. At the end of the novel he is even recommended for an official investigator's license by the L.A. police. Things are also changing on a personal level. When his finger accidentally brushes against that of a white woman from Tennessee as she hands him a pencil, he observes, "I think we both got a shock. It wasn't a sexual thing but the breaking of a taboo that had governed her people and mine for hundreds of years" (35).

Rawlins's solution to the murder of Nola Payne exposes yet another side to the complexity of the issue. It turns out that she was the victim of a black man who, thanks to the indifference of the white police to the murders of black women, had already killed over a dozen black women. Each woman was killed because he saw her with a white man. Rawlins learns that the killer is the son of a black woman who successfully managed to pass for white. Embarrassed by her son's dark skin, she pretended that he was the son of her black housekeeper. Mosley shows how, in the manner of a Faulknerian tragedy, the son's feelings of betrayal and rejection resulting from his mother's racial self-hatred produces deadly consequences. Rawlins's meditations about the killer's mother lead him to an important insight that sheds light on the riot itself:

> If everybody in the world despises and hates you, sees your features as ugly and simian, makes jokes about your ways of talking, calls you stupid and beneath contempt; if you have no history, no heroes, and no future where a hero might lead, then you might begin to hate yourself, your face and features, your parents, and even your child. It could all happen and you would never even know it. And then one hot summer's night you just erupt and go burning and shooting and nobody seems to know why [255–56].

Rawlins is at times uncharacteristically preachy in *Little Scarlet*—a consequence perhaps of Mosley's recent foray into political commentary in *Workin' on the Chain Gang: Shaking Off the Dead Hand of History* (2000) and *What Next: A Memoir Toward World Peace* (2003). Nonetheless, his insightful observations about race in America certainly bear repeating.

Cinnamon Kiss takes up Rawlins's story less than a year after the riots. Still devastated by the violent upheaval in Watts, he is even more distraught over a personal crisis: he desperately needs $35,000 to pay for treatment at a Swiss clinic for a rare blood disease his adopted daughter Feather has contracted. Rejecting a plan suggested by Mouse (now fully recovered from the apparent death he had suffered in *A Little Yellow Dog*) that they knock off an armored car, Easy instead takes a high-paying job for a San Francisco private eye (with the improbable name of Robert E. Lee). His task is to track down a briefcase filled with important documents stolen by a lawyer and his female associate named Philomena Cargill, a cinnamon-skinned black beauty whose kisses (and more) Easy will soon come to enjoy.

Plotting has never been Mosely's greatest strength, but the creakiness of this plot (which also involves secret Nazi business connections and a psychopathic hitman) is extreme. What excuses the plot weaknesses in his earlier novels was the way Mosley used the action to explore issues of consequence. But except for a passing comment about the aftermath of the Watts riots ("The economy of Watts was like Feather's blood infection. Both futures seemed devoid of hope" [28]) and brief encounters with some budding hippies in San Francisco and a man who reportedly singlehandedly wiped out an entire village in Viet Nam, the real world isn't integrated into the fabric of this book. Removing Easy from his home turf of L.A. and sending him off on a preposterous job-for-hire leaves him (and Mosley) far too detached from the kind of serious engagement with vital issues of race and class that informed the previous books in the series.

Recurring phrases like "way back then" and "in those days" scattered throughout the books remind us that Rawlins is narrating events some time after the action he describes. For example, in *A Red Death*, set in 1953, Rawlins mentions having received postcards for over thirty years from a woman he meets during his investigation, which places the time of narration of that novel in the mid-eighties. This thirty-year perspective on events allows Mosley to reconstruct the past from a point of view that includes knowledge of later events ranging from the optimism of the Civil Rights movement to the tragedy of the Watts riots.

According to Mosley, postwar L.A. was a time of great hope and possibility for blacks in America:

> It's when people started to flood into Southern California, and it's when Black people in the Deep South realized that they didn't have to live the kind of lives they were living in the Deep South. They could get away from that, they could go get a good job and buy property and live with some measure of equality. So that was the beginning of a period of transition and hope that didn't quite work out. I want to provide a map through the years of how it didn't [Maidment 68].

Mixing nostalgia with regret, Rawlins's narratives often sound an almost elegiac note: "There was a peaceful feeling about the streets of Los Angeles in those days" (*Red* 4), he notes sadly. But there's nothing nostalgic about the many hurtful experiences he also includes that characterize daily life for African Americans encountering the widespread racism of the day.

Mosley's novels vividly bring to life the African American community in South Central L.A. in the late 1940s and '50s "before the general decline of the neighborhood" (*White* 7). Smoky juke joints, soul-food diners, churches, poolrooms, bars, brothels, barbershops and assorted other neighborhood gathering places paint a picture of a vibrant community. None of these places is presented as an exotic locale or alien environment, as Florian's was in *Farewell, My Lovely.* These are simply locations where residents gather and life is lived in this part of L.A. Several brief vignettes also emphasize the communal aspect of life for the transplanted southern blacks in Watts:

> At Central and Ninety-ninth Street a group of men sat around talking — they were halfheartedly waiting for work. It was a habit that some southerners brought with them; they'd just sit outside on a crate somewhere and wait for someone who needed manual labor to come by and shout their name. That way they could spend the afternoon with their friends, drinking from brown paper bags and shooting dice. They might even get lucky and pick up a job worth a couple of bucks — and maybe their kids would have meat that night [*Red* 7].

The neighborhood women are also a picture of group activity, as the following description of their labors in the basement of a local church illustrates:

> There I saw a scene that had been a constant in my life since I was a small boy. Black women. Lots of them. Cooking in the industrial-size kitchen and talking loud, laughing and telling stories. But all I really saw was their hands. Working hands. Laying out plates, peeling yams, folding sheets and tablecloths into perfect squares, washing, drying, stacking, and pushing from here to there. Women who lived by working. Brushing the hair of their own children, or brushing the hair of some neighborhood child whose parents were gone, either for the night or for good. Cooking, yes, but there was lots of other work for a Negro woman. Dressing wounds of the men they started out being so proud of. Punishing children, white and black. And working for God in His house and at home [*Red* 87–8].

As Andrew Pepper has noted, the various black neighborhoods in Mosley's books "though poor and at times dangerous, are not represented as unremittingly bleak ghettos. Mosley's setting is neither romanticised nor demonized" (129). While it is true that many of the streets Rawlins walks are dangerous, other streets paint a brighter picture. Alaford Street, for example, is described as "a quiet block of one-family homes behind a row of well-kept lawns and trimmed bushes" (*Red* 190). On Bell Street, "a short block of large houses with brick fences and elaborate flower gardens" (*Red* 169), people line up in their cars at Christmas time to see the thousands of colored lights the residents display on their trees and bushes. Such scenes help Mosley achieve his stated aim of writing "about Black people as Black people. Not as Black people in relation to White people, not as Black people as victims of whatever, but Black people living their lives" (Whetstone 112).

Watts also serves as the setting for two volumes of short stories (*Always Outnumbered, Always Outgunned* and *Walkin' the Dog*) about an ex-con named Socrates Fortlow, set in the present, and a second series launched in 2001 with the publication of *Fearless Jones,* set in the 1960s. Described by Mosley as "comic noir," the novels are narrated by Paris Minton, owner of a small used bookshop. A bookworm and self-proclaimed coward, Minton gets dragged into dangerous situations by his best friend, Fearless Jones, whom he describes as "more trouble than a white girl on the prowl in Mississippi" (*Fear* 46). Minton and Rawlins even cross paths on occasion. In *Little Scarlet,* for example, Rawlins encounters Minton protecting his bookshop against arsonists looking to torch businesses during the Watts riots. Though time and place figure less prominently in the Fearless Jones books than in the Rawlins series, Mosley provides a valuable picture of small-time business owners like Paris Minton who migrated to L.A. seeking to capitalize on the economic opportunities becoming available to blacks in the postwar years. Business ownership was important, Mosley notes, for it made an ordinary black man like Paris "feel like I was somebody; not just passing through but having a stake in the world I lived in" (*Fear* 18).

One of the biggest challenges Mosley faces in writing realistically about the lives of African Americans is that "it's very hard for those outside to understand our life because the way the media deals with us: we're drug addicts, we're welfare people" (Silet "Other" 13). Mosley's effort to get beyond the stereotypes brings to mind to the work of noted New York photographer Weegee, a volume of whose photos Paris Minton examines in *Fear Itself.* Weegee roamed the city at night, taking pictures, "getting behind all of the lies we tell" in order to reveal a side of the city that few tourists ever saw "even though it was right there under their toes and noses"

(94). Mosley aims to do the same by transporting his readers to an unfamiliar world "populated by lost peoples that were never talked about in the newspapers or seen on the TV" (*Yellow* 32).

Setting for Mosley is more than a simple matter of place and time; it is also marked by the pervasive presence of racism. For many, L.A. is characterized by the smog that poisons the air above the city. For the African Americans of Watts, the atmosphere they live in is also poisoned by something equally toxic, racism. "The air we breathed was racist," complains Rawlins (*White* 50). Mosley is no polemicist, railing at the injustices heaped upon African Americans by a racist white population. Yet he pointedly reminds his readers of the painful consequences of racism, as this description of the passengers on a Central Avenue bus illustrates:

> Most of them were black people. Dark-skinned with generous features. Women with eyes so deep that most men can never know them.... And there were the children, like Spider and Terry T once were, with futures so bleak that it could make you cry just to hear them laugh. Because behind the music of their laughing you knew there was the rattle of chains. Chains we wore for no crime; chains we wore for so long that they melded with our bones. We all carry them but nobody can see it — not even most of us.
> All the way home I thought about freedom coming for us at last. But what about all those centuries in chains? Where do they go when you get free? [*Yellow* 199].

Throughout the series, Mosley paints a disturbing picture of the daily indignities that a black man like Rawlins faces, ranging from job discrimination to brutal treatment at the hands of racist cops.

Despite his black skin, Rawlins feels he has an equal right to make it in America. Owning his own house is a start, giving him the respect he longs for. However, despite feeling at home in the familiar environs of Watts, he can never fully enjoy that same sense of belonging in the larger (white) world. "I wondered at how it would be to be a white man," Rawlins says, "a man who felt that he belonged" (*White* 45).

Mosley's novels are fraught both with the weight of history and the sense of personal burden. As Mosley puts it, "There's a lot of weight put on a black man. And the weight is: You shouldn't have been born. This is your problem" (Sherman 35). Through the character of Easy Rawlins, Mosley charts the daily struggle to survive and to prosper against considerable obstacles, some imposed by the racism of the outside world, some self-imposed by the sense of limitation within themselves poor blacks from the South carried into postwar L.A.

Mosley's novels have received high praise; one critic even went so far as to proclaim the Easy Rawlins books "the finest detective oeuvre in American literature, surpassing even that of card-carrying formalist Hammett and dwarfing Chandler and Leonard and Macdonald" (Christgau 31). And so a comparison between Mosley and noted American novelist John Updike might not be farfetched. In a quartet of novels published over a thirty-year period — *Rabbit, Run* (1960), *Rabbit Redux* (1971), *Rabbit is Rich* (1981), and *Rabbit at Rest* (1990) — Updike chronicled changing attitudes in American life as reflected through the experiences of Harry "Rabbit" Angstrom. Unlike Mosley's novels which re-create the past, each of Updike's novels mirrors the specific decade in which it was written. Yet both writers share a similar desire to record the changing mood of the country through the perspective of their protagonists. Though white small-town Pennsylvania Toyota dealer Harry Angstrom and black L.A. private eye Easy Rawlins share little in common as individuals, their creators have both produced a series of novels that offer an illuminating fictional travelogue through some crucial decades in recent American history.

5

George P. Pelecanos
Washington, D.C.

Although Washington, D.C., has often been featured as background setting in novels, it is usually the nation's capital that is the primary focus. The city of familiar landmarks — the White House, Capitol Dome, Lincoln Monument and Jefferson Memorial — has been employed almost exclusively in novels about Washington power and politics. However, just a stone's throw from the marble monuments and imposing corridors of power is quite another city. That other Washington — residential Washington — is a city of over half a million residents with a distinctive character, history, and atmosphere that is largely absent from the pages of popular fiction. Washington-born-and-bred novelist George P. Pelecanos felt the time had come to rectify the situation:

> When I started out, I didn't feel as if Washington D.C. had been fully represented in literature. And by that I mean the real, living, working class side of the city. The cliché is that Washington is a transient town of people who blow in and out every four years with the new administrations. But the reality is that people have lived in Washington for generations and their lives are worth examining, I think ["An Interview"].

Pelecanos adopts a two-fold approach to the use of Washington in his fiction. One of his goals is to celebrate the city he loves but that few know, thanks to its being overshadowed in the popular consciousness by the nation's capital. To accomplish this, he sets the action of several of his novels in the past in an effort to tell the story of a lively working-class city inhabited by transplanted Southerners and Greek, Irish, and Italian immigrants. This Washington even today remains a small town where residents still identify themselves by the high school they attended, and this strong sense of community is a defining feature of the city Pelecanos describes so vividly.

But Pelecanos is also something of an urban anthropologist coolly analyzing the sad state of the current city, examining how it shapes (and distorts) the lives of its residents, especially its young. Grinding poverty, substandard housing, poor schools, lack of opportunity and assorted other urban maladies have combined to produce a culture of crime — especially drug-dealing — that has had dire consequences for the city and its people. Pelecanos the anthropologist is unable to celebrate the city's present the way he can its past, though he does honor the heroic efforts of some who amidst the blight are trying to make it a good place to live again.

Unlike the other writers included in this book, Pelecanos hasn't built a series around a single character. He has published a trio of novels about a private eye named Nick Stefanos; a quartet of novels featuring a pair of characters, Dimitri Karras and Marcus Clay, one black and one white; and a trilogy of novels with another salt-and-pepper duo, ex-cops Derek Strange and Terry Quinn. Most of his novels are set in the present, but some focus on past decades. Despite all this variety, there are several consistent features in style and theme. But the single most important organizing feature of all Pelecanos's fiction is setting. Just as William Faulkner used Yoknapatawpha County as the unifying element for a range of diverse novels, Pelecanos makes Washington the center around which all his novels revolve.

Pelecanos was born in Washington, D.C., on 18 February 1957. His grandfather had emigrated from Greece with his young son (Pelecanos's father) after World War II. In 1965, Pelecanos's father purchased his own business, the Jefferson Coffee Shop on 19th Street between M and N in Washington. The young Pelecanos first began working there as a delivery boy when he was eleven. In 1976, he entered the University of Maryland, then dropped out for a year to run his father's coffee shop, finally graduating in 1980.

Like many crime and mystery writers, Pelecanos got a late start; he didn't write his first novel until he was thirty-one and suffering from an early midlife crisis. At the time he was general manager of a $30 million appliance chain in Washington, D.C. But he hated the job. According to his wife, Emily, "At night, he came home and said he felt like someone was standing on his chest all day" (Mason). Inspired by the punk rock movement, where untrained musicians simply picked up guitars and played, he quit his job and began to write: "I spent the next year in a dark room, writing in longhand, filling notebook after notebook, not knowing if I was writing for anyone other than myself" (Pelecanos "Between"). Lacking an agent, he naively sent the completed manuscript of *A Firing Offense* off to St. Martin's Press. There it languished for a year until it was plucked out of the slush pile by a twenty-four-year-old associate editor who called to say he wanted to publish it. Not bad for someone who had no formal training as a writer, had never taken a writing class nor had grown up with dreams of being a writer. "I thought writers were Waspy guys with Harris tweeds and suede patches on their elbows," he said, "not Greek kids like me who worked in carryout shops" (Schuessler 53).

Pelecanos does remember writing one book, a story entitled *The Two Wars of Lieutenant Jeremy* when he was ten years old. He also began to develop a storytelling talent as a youngster delivering food from his father's coffee shop to offices in the Dupont Circle area: "I listened closely to the rhythms of the speech and the unique slang of the street. I became familiar with every alley. On my runs I made up stories, serial-style, complete with music, to pass the time. I would space the stories out so that they would climax at the end of the week. I thought I was making movies, but I was writing my first books" ("Between" 86).

A film major in college, Pelecanos happened to take a course in crime fiction. Turned on to the hard-boiled novels of Raymond Chandler, Dashiell Hammett, Ross Macdonald and David Goodis, Pelecanos saw how crime stories could also be serious novels that dissected American society. "For the first time I knew," he said, "with the shock of recognition that only the most fortunate experience, what I wanted to 'do'" ("Between" 87).

Action films — especially those of directors like John Sturges, Robert Aldrich, Sergio Leone, and Sam Peckinpah — also played an influential role in Pelecanos's life. "If it weren't for the crime and action films I saw over thirty years ago," he confesses, "I wouldn't be a novelist. Big-balls movies goosed my flesh and blew up my worldview, stoking me to the degree that I knew I would someday make my living telling stories" ("Action" 318). Pelecanos later worked for Circle Films, a Washington production company which produced the first three Coen Brothers films and was the U.S. distributor for John Woo's *The Killers*. More recently, he has also served as writer, story editor, and producer of the popular HBO crime series *The Wire.*

A Firing Offense, self-consciously modeled on the hard-boiled examples of Chandler and Hammett, introduced readers to Nick Stefanos, advertising manager for Nutty Nathan's, a chain of Washington, D.C., area electronics stores. When a young employee at one of the stores turns up missing, his grandfather enlists Stefanos's help in finding him. The part-time sleuth finds the youth, but ends up getting fired from his job for drinking and smoking dope in one of the stores during business hours; at the end of the novel, however, his application for a private detective license is approved, and he sets off on a new career.

Pelecanos doesn't use Washington as extensively here as he does in his later books; the city is simply described in broadly contrasting terms. D.C. is characterized on the one hand as "Murder Capitol," a dangerous place "where the only common community interest was to get safely through another day" (106). On the other hand, we are also treated to brief glimpses of the White House, the Capitol Dome and other familiar monuments and also gaze with Stefanos over the majestic cityscape from the Bell Tower of the Old Post Office, the best view of D.C.

Pelecanos's second novel, *Nick's Trip,* is richer in plot, characterization, and use of the Washington setting. Though he's had his private eye license for a year, Stefanos hasn't seen much business. So he takes a job at the Spot, a "shitty little bar" where he's a regular customer. One day, Billy Goodrich, a childhood friend he hadn't seen in fifteen years, shows up and asks him to find his missing wife. Also missing he learns is $200,000 that Goodrich's wife stole from a gangster boyfriend. Stefanos discovers the truth, but in the process realizes he has been duped by his old friend, who has been using him to get to the money. (The thematic similarity to Chandler's *The Long Goodbye* is far from accidental.)

Washington begins to come into sharper focus as a major character in the novel. The city is defined by its contrasts, a "city of horns and tight neckties" during the daytime but a "silent, idyllic small town" (37) after dark. It is a place where the optimism of the bicentennial celebration of 1976 has given way to hopelessness and despair. "The innocence of marijuana had ... become the horror of cocaine, and the economic and political emergence of minorities ... had been crushed by the moral bankruptcy of the Reagan years" (19). Stefanos notes the stark contrast as he walks down M Street:

Washington, D.C.

Underdressed homeless men shared the sidewalks with blue-blooded
attorneys in plain charcoal suits and with women dressed unimagina-
tively and mannishly in their pursuit of success. The West End balanced poverty and ambition, granite and spit, money as new as the
morning paper and glass-eyed hopelessness older than slavery [213].

(Before completing the Stefanos trilogy, Pelecanos, who had been
devouring the pulp novels of writers like Jim Thomson and David
Goodis — whose *The Burglar* Pelecanos ranks as his favorite crime novel —
wrote *Shoedog*, a tribute to the genre. Marked by elemental passions and
rough violence, *Shoedog* is a fast-faced but lightweight crime novel that
lacks the depth and intensity of the Stefanos books.)

Business is slow for Stefanos, so in *Down by the River Where the Dead
Men Go* he continues to tend bar at the Spot. And drink too much. Late
one night, nearly passed out in a drunken stupor in a deserted spot along
the Anacostia River, he witnesses the murder of a young black man.
Though he lacks a paying client, his investigative instincts draw him into
a case involving gay porn and drug running. Following a bloody shootout
in a warehouse in which several people are killed, Stefanos sets out to
secure his own brand of justice: he takes the businessman who is behind
the whole operation that was responsible for the young man's murder to
the location of the killing and executes him. At the end of the novel, he
heads back to the Spot for another drink.

A problem drinker who considers a bar his home is unquestionably
a man in trouble, and Pelecanos realized that in *Down by the River* he had
taken Stefanos (whom he describes as "a full-blown, fall-down drunk")
about as far as he could. He felt ready to move on to something else.

Having achieved little commercial success with his first four novels,
Pelecanos felt he had little to lose by going for broke with his next effort;
the impressive result, *The Big Blowdown*, signals an ambitious new direction in his work. The novel spans three decades in the lives of a trio of
boyhood friends who grew up together in a poor immigrant neighborhood
of Washington. Pete Karras, who survives the horrors of combat in the
Pacific in World War II, is later crippled in a mob beating. He ends up
working as a short order cook in a small lunch counter owned by Nick
Stefanos, grandfather of the private-eye hero of Pelecanos's earlier novels.
Joey Recevo becomes an enforcer for the mob boss who had ordered the
beating that crippled his old friend Pete Karras, Jimmy Boyle becomes a

67

Washington cop. Their intersecting stories comprise a saga of friendship, loyalty and betrayal which, with the inevitability of Greek tragedy, moves inexorably toward a tragic conclusion.

In *The Big Blowdown* Pelecanos tells the story not just of his three main characters but of immigrants like Nick Stefanos, whose hard work exemplifies the promise of the American Dream embraced by so many who came to these shores. Pelecanos also honored his own family, especially his father, much of whose story is mirrored in the experiences of Pete Karras. References to his real grandparents are also interspersed throughout the novel. Pelecanos also lovingly recreates the city of Washington in the forties and fifties, with its small family-owned businesses and lively nightlife.

Building upon *The Big Blowdown*, Pelecanos now saw an opportunity to compose a series of linked novels that could explore Washington in a more complex way than he had attempted heretofore. Based upon extensive research, the quartet of novels — *The Big Blowdown, King Suckerman, The Sweet Forever,* and *Shame the Devil* — have collectively become known as the D.C. Quartet (because of their surface similarity to James Ellroy's L.A. Quartet). Pelecanos himself, however, prefers to think of the series as his version of Sergio Leone's *Once Upon a Time in America*. Rather than building a series of novels with a single recurring character like Nick Stefanos, he instead began constructing a larger picture with interrelated characters and shifts in time. Though he wouldn't abandon Nick Stefanos altogether, he would relegate him to a minor role as other characters' stories demanded to be told.

King Suckerman introduces the first of two black-white pairs of characters who will figure prominently in Pelecanos's fiction: Marcus Clay, a black Vietnam veteran, and his lifelong white buddy, Dimitri Karras, son of the ill-fated Pete Karras from *The Big Blowdown*. Clay, owner of a small record shop, is determined to build a life for himself and his wife. Karras, who has an M.A. in English, and has taught part-time at the University of Maryland, lacks direction and ambition, though he picks up a few bucks selling marijuana to high schoolers. When his regular supplier goes on vacation and he is hooked up with a substitute, things quickly go very wrong for him and Clay, whom he had talked into coming along with him.

The events of the novel take place in the days leading up to the 4th of July bicentennial celebration in Washington in 1976. The final explosive showdown between Clay and Karras and their pursuers erupts just as the red, white, and blue fireworks are lighting up the nighttime sky over the nation's capital. But, as usual in Pelecanos's novels, the contrast between official Washington and real Washington is a wide one. A million people may have come to Washington's Mall to celebrate the nation's 200th birthday, but for many who live there, there is little reason to celebrate. As one black character replies when asked if he plans to celebrate, "Ain't *my* independence day" (253).

The Sweet Forever jumps ahead a decade to 1986. Washington has turned into a battleground between the forces of good and evil, i.e., between drugs and those who are trying their best to keep the deadly menace from further destroying their community and devouring their young. The novel opens with the horrifying death of a young drug runner who loses control of his speeding car, crashes and is decapitated. The accident occurs in front of Marcus Clay's record shop at 11th and U, once one of Black Washington's grand streets, now wracked by drugs and crime. A witness to the accident, Eddie Golden, rushes to the scene to offer assistance. It's too late to help the dead driver, so Golden instead helps himself to a pillowcase stuffed with $25,000 in cash he finds inside the wrecked car. The money belongs to Tyrell Cleveland, a powerful drug dealer who wants it back. Because Golden's girlfriend is a friend of Dimitri Karras, he and Marcus Clay again find themselves drawn into the ensuing deadly drama.

The Sweet Forever paints the bleakest picture yet in Pelecanos's expanding portrait of the city he loves. Once thriving local neighborhoods have been blighted by crime and indifference. The main culprit is drugs, specifically cocaine. But equally devastating has been the mismanagement and indifference of the district's leaders. Pelecanos's harshest complaints are leveled at Washington's unnamed mayor (unmistakably Marion Barry), a once-promising leader whom he characterizes as "an alcoholic, drug-addicted, pussy-addicted monster" (97). Like Nero, he fiddles (or more accurately toots) while his city burns. Widespread corruption also plagues his administration: an ex-wife was indicted on charges of skimming hundreds of thousands of dollars from an agency overseeing subsidized housing; his deputy mayor was accused of taking kickbacks; his longtime right-hand man pleaded guilty to stealing over $200,000 in city funds.

Sadly, help can't be expected from the nearby Reagan administration. As one character cynically observes:

> And you think that dried-up old husk of a man down on Pennsylvania Avenue cares? How about those horn-rimmed-glasses economic advisors of his, makin' the rich happy, pushin' the poor back further than they are? You think those Harvard boys care? Or the president's wife? "Just Say No," right? Easy to say no when you get born into alternatives and opportunities and a future [239].

Tragic casualties abound in *The Sweet Forever,* including two eleven-year-olds who think it's cool to play at being drug dealers but who are gunned down (one of them still clutching his favorite Spider-Man action figure in his fist) by an enforcer to ensure Tyrell Cleveland's drug monopoly. Pelecanos's picture of this urban nightmare isn't quite as forbidding as, say Dante's Inferno, where visitors are warned, "Abandon hope all ye who enter here." There is hope in *The Sweet Forever,* thanks largely to several individuals who try to Do The Right Thing. Kevin Murphy, a black cop who feels increasingly guilty for accepting a $4000 monthly payoff from Tyrell Cleveland, takes aimless eleven-year-old Anthony Taylor under his wing. He recovers the missing $25,000 stolen from Cleveland and uses it to help get Taylor out of town and rejoin his mother. After losing his arm in a bloody shootout, he spends time working with youths in a summer program. Clarence Tate is a caring single father who fights to keep his daughter from succumbing to the temptations of the street. Marcus Clay even persuades one youth to quit Cleveland's gang and gives him a job at one of his record shops.

The novel, however, ends on a sobering note. The action of *The Sweet Forever* takes place during the annual NCAA basketball tournament in March. All Washington is avidly following the exploits of local hero Len Bias, star of the University of Maryland team. At the end of the novel, Pelecanos describes a young boy watching a tape of Bias on TV, tears streaming down his cheeks. What goes unsaid but which everyone knows is that, two days after being selected second in the NBA draft by the Boston Celtics, Bias died of a heart attack while celebrating his new multimillion-dollar contract with cocaine. Though reportedly not a regular drug user, he becomes yet one more tragic victim of the evil infecting urban America.

Revenge is the driving force in *Shame the Devil,* the final installment in the D.C. Quartet. Four employees are gunned down in a local pizza parlor (an incident based upon a real-life massacre at a Starbuck's in Washington). What interests Pelecanos is the aftermath of the tragedy, including the effects on the families of the victims, especially on Dimitri Karras, whose young son was struck and killed by the assailants' car as they fled the crime scene. Devastated by grief, Karras lives only for revenge, as does Frank Farrow, one of the pizza parlor killers who vows retaliation against the policeman who killed his brother during their escape. Two and a half years after the murders, Karras, Farrow, and several others involved in the killings come together in another of those apocalyptic confrontations that routinely resolve the action in Pelecanos's books.

Pelecanos continues to hammer home the stark contrast between the two Washingtons, as in the following observation:

> The Capitol loomed dead ahead, crowning the street. On this particular winter day, the press and public were fixated on the alleged extramarital affairs of the sitting president and giving odds on his possible impeachment. It was the media event of the decade, the subject of sarcastic lunch conversations all across town. But few talked about the real crime of this city, not anymore: American children were undernourished, criminally undereducated, and living in a viper's nest of drugs, violence, and despair within a mile of the Capitol dome. It should have been a national disgrace. But hunger and poverty had never been tabloid sexy. Beyond the occasional obligatory lip service, the truth was that no one in a position of power cared [66].

In the final scene of the novel, Karras and Stefanos walk together in the park alongside the Washington channel, the very spot where Karras's father and Stefanos's grandfather used to gather some sixty years earlier. Having brought the saga of the two families full circle from 1938 to the present, Pelecanos was once again ready to move on to something new.

In his D.C. Quartet, Pelecanos celebrated Washington's past. In his next several novels, there is little to celebrate as Pelecanos continues to move farther away from traditional mysteries into what he calls "urban reportage" or "social crime novels," and which one reviewer aptly characterized as "reports from a war zone" (Jones). Urban blight permeates the books with Washington serving as a microcosm of pressing social issues — notably racism and drug abuse — that plague American cities big and small.

Right as Rain introduces yet another salt-and-pepper team, a pair of ex-cops named Derek Strange and Terry Quinn. As the action of

Pelecanos's novels moves closer to the heart of Washington's inner city, his characters increasingly become black. This is not surprising in a city whose population is 65 percent to 70 percent black. To write realistically about D.C. is to write about black people. This is, of course, a risky enterprise for a white writer: "If you are going to do it," Pelecanos cautions, "first of all you should do it right. Show people respect and make sure you get the voices right" (Birnbaum). Pelecanos has spent a lifetime listening to voices. As a youngster riding the bus, he was fascinated by the conversations he overheard: "I was always interested in not just what they were saying, but the rhythms of their speech, the slang. Just a love of the language" (Swilley). Thanks to an ear well tuned to the colorful dialogue of the streets, he manages to get all his characters, black and white, down on the page authentically and believably.

Strange and Quinn (twenty years his junior) are an unlikely duo. An ex-cop, Strange has owned his own detective agency in Washington for twenty-five years. He's hired by the mother of a black policeman, Chris Wilson, to clear his name in an incident where he was shot and killed by a young white cop named Terry Quinn. Unaware that Wilson was a fellow cop, Quinn shot him after spotting him holding a gun over a white man named Ricky Kane. Though exonerated by a police review committee, Quinn quits the police force after eight years on the job and takes a job in a used bookstore. Naturally, the first person Strange wants to question is Terry Quinn.

Strange instinctively assumes that Quinn's shooting of Wilson was a simple act of racism. As he tells Quinn:

> You saw a black man with a gun and you saw a criminal, and you
> *made up your mind*. Yeah, there was noise and confusion and lights, I
> know all about that. But would you have listened to him if he had
> been white? Would you have pulled that trigger if Wilson had been
> white? I don't think so, Terry. Cut through all the extra bullshit, and
> you're gonna have to just go ahead and admit it, man: You killed a
> man because he was black [223].

Despite his misgivings about Quinn, Strange recognizes some common ground between them (both are ex-cops and both share a love of western movies). He knows that the volatile Quinn is a mess of trouble, but he also knows he might be useful in his investigation business, so he offers him a job. Quinn, eager to prove his innocence, agrees to help Strange. Thus begins an uneasy alliance.

Washington, D.C.

As a white father of three adopted mixed-race children, Pelecanos has a strong personal interest in the subject of racism in America:

> Race is the defining issue in American life. That doesn't mean that I see everything through the prism of race, but it is an issue we need to confront if we are going to move forward. Race has been examined in literature, but it has rarely been examined with honesty. And frankly, when it *is* examined honestly, the author is committing commercial suicide.... People do not want to be told that they are "that way." In fact, readers are usually fed the notion that racism is some other guy's problem. I wanted to do something different. Terry Quinn is you and me. As for the milieu, D.C. is a city where the problem of the racial divide is inescapable and always in your face, so the setting could not have been more appropriate for the material [Cochran].

Strange and Quinn embody some of the contradictions and complexities of racial attitudes. Neither one is free of racist beliefs. However, despite his initial suspicions about Quinn's actions, Strange's investigation exonerates Quinn when he proves that Wilson was being set up by Quinn's partner, a cop on the take who was fearful that Wilson was on to him. Strange apologizes to Quinn for unfairly stereotyping him and his actions. But Quinn takes small comfort in being cleared of racist charges. Were his actions colored by racism, he wonders? Is his dating of a black woman simply an attempt to prove to himself that he's not a racist? His ultimate conclusion is unsettling: "For Quinn nothing had changed. Because Strange had been right all along: Quinn had killed a man because of the color of his skin" (358).

Chris Wilson's death came as a consequence of his attempts to find his sister Sonya, who had disappeared after succumbing to heroin addiction. Her rapid decline from promising college student to an emaciated wreck trading sex for drugs illustrates the devastating consequences of the drug epidemic in America. Her current residence, a rotted-out warehouse known locally as the Junkyard, symbolizes that decline. The rat-infested building, reeking of excrement and vomit, is the last refuge for junkies who have run out of places to go. Such locations are not unique to Washington; they are everywhere and Pelecanos suggests that Washington's problem is also America's problem. But once again, proximity to the nation's capitol only magnifies the continuing failure of the federal government to summon up the courage to address the problem in any realistic way. As Strange cynically puts it, "You put all those politicians down on the Hill in one room and you can't find one set of nuts swingin' between the legs of any of 'em" (290).

The Washington setting assumes a defining role as a social determinant in *Hell to Pay* with D.C.'s many public housing complexes taking center stage. Pelecanos captures the dilapidated atmosphere with telling details: "Rusted playground equipment stood silhouetted in a dirt courtyard dotted with Styrofoam containers, fast-food wrappers, and other bits of trash. The courtyard was lit residually by the lamps within the apartments. A faint veil of smoke roiled in the light" (59). But Pelecanos isn't content with simple description of place; he also explores the range of attitudes that living in such an environment inevitably produces: paranoia, hopelessness, fatalism. By chronicling the stories of several characters who live (or who grew up) in these projects, Pelecanos paints a haunting picture of some of Washington's true hellholes.

Above all else, *Hell to Pay* is a novel about child abuse. In this case, however, the source of the abuse is not an offending parent but the inevitable product of the twin evils of racism and poverty. Such conditions produce an almost endless supply of hard young men whom Pelecanos characterizes as "the malignant result of years of festering unchecked poverty and fatherless homes" (*Soul* 28).

But like Strange himself, Pelecanos refuses to surrender to a totally deterministic view of life in the ghetto. Maybe one person can't change the world, but a single individual can make a difference. "My heroes" Pelecanos has said, "are the mentors, teachers, big brothers and sisters, and coaches who help at-risk kids in the cities. They generally go unnamed and their deeds are unsung. In the absence of any true government assistance, these people step up to the plate" (Jordan). One such hero is Derek Strange. With the help of Terry Quinn and some other friends, Strange coaches Pee Wee and Midget football teams for young boys. His aim is not to teach the youths how to be better athletes, but to help them survive the world that threatens to devour them. Despite his best efforts, however, Joe Wilder, an eight-year-old player on his team, is killed by a trio of assailants who ambush his uncle and shoot him for failing to pay off a $100 debt. (*Hell to Pay* is dedicated to a seven-year-old boy shot to death by a criminal with a handgun in Washington in 1997.)

Sad as it is, Joe Wilder's story is but only one such example of a wasted life. For even when the young are not robbed of their lives, they are robbed of their youth. The struggle to survive can be exhausting in a place where you can be shot just for looking at someone the wrong way. "It was hard to keep doing right," one youth complains. "Hard to have to walk a certain way, talk a certain way, keep up that shell all the time out here, when sometimes all you wanted to do was be young and have fun. Relax" (126). For many, the struggle to stay straight isn't worth it. Why learn to read when you can pick up easy money selling drugs? Why worry about tomorrow when, as Lorenze Wilder defiantly tells Strange, "I ain't *got*ta do nothin' but be black and die" (50)? Sadly, his words prove to be prophetic, but his fatalistic attitude also costs the life of his eight-year-old nephew who by chance happens to be with him when his time runs out.

Ghetto justice ultimately prevails in *Hell to Pay*. Joe Wilder's killer is tracked down by drug lord Granville Oliver who, it turns out, is the young boy's father. But Oliver himself is eventually arrested on federal drug and racketeering charges. Now facing the death penalty, he asks Derek Strange for help. Although Oliver represents everything that Strange is fighting against, Strange has his own reason for agreeing to help. Racism and poverty are powerful forces that perhaps are beyond the power of any one individual to overcome. "But taking responsibility for your own," he argues, "this is something we have the power to do something about" (343). That's why he coaches youth football. And that's why he agrees to help Oliver, for he confesses that when he was a cop in 1968, he killed Oliver's father. He feels compelled to accept some responsibility for creating yet another fatherless child of the ghetto who ended up taking the wrong path.

Pelecanos can't resist taking another poke at politicians who fail to come to grips with the issue. The tragic death of Joe Wilder inspires national politicians to chime in with their usual denunciations of the culture of violence in the inner cities, singling out the twin villains of hip-hop and Hollywood. But Pelecanos adds that "at no time did these bought-and-sold politicians mention the conditions that created the culture, or the handguns, as easily available as a carton of milk, that had killed the boy" (194).

Soul Circus, the final installment in the Strange-Quinn trilogy, is mainly about guns. Guns have always figured prominently in Pelecanos's

novels, which often end in blazing shootouts. But in *Soul Circus,* he looks
beyond the shootouts to explore the addictive attraction of guns. He
describes the pivotal role they play in the inner city: "Long as there
was poverty, long as there wasn't no good education, long as kids down
here had no fathers and were looking to belong to something, then there
was gonna be gangs and a need for guns" (58). He also understands their
seductive allure: they are lovingly described and their owners are often
shown rubbing and fondling them in an almost masturbatory way. But
above all else, he understands how guns all too often lead to deadly consequences.

Pelecanos has earned the right to speak with authority on the subject of gun violence: at age 16 he accidentally shot a friend in the face while
playing with his father's .38 special. (Fortunately, his friend survived.)
Pelecanos doesn't want his readers to think the incident proves his tough-
ness: "I was just a stupid kid," he confesses. "Anybody can pull the trig-
ger of a gun. It doesn't take a tough guy" (Gross). While guns are a constant
presence in his books, the violence is never treated lightly. "I don't want
any teenager to pick up one of my books and think that the violence in
the books is cool," says Pelecanos. "I want people to get a little sickened
by it" (Connolly).

Mario Durham, nicknamed Twigs because of his extreme skinniness,
is a loser who has been the butt of jokes his entire life. But once he gets
a gun, things change: "He liked the way it made him feel. He was strong,
handsome, and tall, everything he had never been before" (106). He uses
the gun to threaten a woman who has made off with a pound of grass
belonging to his younger brother Dewayne, a major D.C. drug dealer. But
when he catches her laughing at his unstylish shoes, he savagely beats her
with the gun and shoots her dead. For the first time in his miserable life,
he feels like a man. Unfortunately for him, the feeling doesn't last long;
shortly afterwards, he's shot in the head by a disgruntled customer to whom
he sold a vial of fake crack cocaine.

It isn't only losers who feel transformed by holding a gun in their
hand. When Terry Quinn approaches a gang of black youths for information about the whereabouts of a missing girl, he is mocked and rebuffed.
Feeling humiliated by the experience, the hot-headed Quinn later returns
to confront them again, this time with his Colt .45. How easy things are,
Quinn concludes, when you have a gun. But his triumph is short lived.

As he drives away, two cars pull up alongside his and one of the youths he had earlier faced down pulls out his gun and kills Quinn.

Guns are also a political issue, especially in Washington. Though the residents of D.C. voted to ban handguns in the city, their effort to solve a critical problem is undermined by the fact that gun sales are legal in nearby Maryland and Virginia. Getting a gun remains as simple as buying a carton of milk. All an enterprising dealer like Ulysses Foreman (an ex-cop) has to do is pay residents of Maryland and Virginia to purchase guns legally for him, which he then sells or rents out. Consequently, guns continue to wreak havoc in D.C., with 60 percent of the handguns used to commit crimes in the city legally obtained in the neighboring states.

In *Hard Revolution,* Pelecanos once again turns back the clock, but while the year that opens the novel — 1959 — is portrayed with plenty of nostalgia, the other year the novel describes — 1968 — paints a much bleaker picture. Serving as a prequel, the novel provides important formative details about the young Derek Strange, first as a twelve year old, then as a rookie cop. But by recounting the violent eruptions in Washington in 1968 following the murder of Dr. Martin Luther King, Jr., Pelecanos also fills in the historical background that helps explain the current state of the city.

Pelecanos describes *Hard Revolution* as the book he's always wanted to write. He was only eleven years old when the riots occurred, much of the damage centered near his grandfather's lunch counter on 14th Street. "I have to say that it was all confusing to me," he admits, "and exciting as well, in the way that a boy gets jazzed behind rioting, war, street fights, etc. That confusion was one of the reasons I wanted to write this novel. I knew that in the research phase I would find the answers to some questions I had been looking for my entire life" (Cochran).

Pelecanos has done his research well, but the destruction in Washington he so vividly describes wasn't unique to the city. Sadly, it mirrored similar outbursts in Watts, Detroit, Newark and other large American cities. Also, youngsters in Washington were listening to the same music and watching the same television shows that everyone else in America was at the time. Getting the local details about long-gone factories and small shops may have an appeal to D.C. readers, but overall *Hard Revolution* doesn't evoke the specific sense of place as vividly as Pelecanos's other novels.

5. George P. Pelecanos

Having completed the saga of Derek Strange to his satisfaction, Pelecanos once again moved on to new territory in his next two novels. *Drama City* tells the story of Lorenzo Brown, a former drug dealer who spent eight years in prison. Now out on parole, he's struggling to stay straight while working as an enforcement officer for the D.C. Humane Society. *The Night Gardener* tells the tale of three cops (one active, one retired, and one who left the force under a cloud) who are brought together by a murder that resembles a case the trio had worked on some twenty years earlier. But while the characters are new, the city remains the same: the by-now familiar perilous streets of Washington, D.C.

Like many of his fellow residents, Lorenzo Brown hates to hear Washington called "Dodge City." "Drama City be more like it," he insists, "Like them two faces they got hangin' over the stage in those theatres. The smiling face and the sad" (259). His search for personal redemption takes place in a city which, like himself, is divided between the good and the bad, between the smiling face of possibility and the sad face of desperation. While there is little hope for a happy ending for most of the young men caught up in the drug trade, some lucky few like Brown, thanks to determination, strength of character, and the help of a 12-step program like Narcotics Anonymous, beat the odds. Vowing to put his criminal past behind him, he simply wants to be like those ordinary Washingtonians who "get up and go to work. Wash their cars out in the street, tend to their gardens. Watch their kids grow" (259). At the end of the novel, Brown observes the multifaceted face of the city as he walks up Georgia Avenue:

> He saw single mothers moving their children along the sidewalks, young girls showing off their bodies, church women, men who went to work each day, men who did nothing at all, studious kids who were going to make it, stoop kids on the edge, kids already in the life, a man smoking a cigarette in the doorway of his barbershop, and the private detective with the big shoulders [Derek Strange] talking to a white dude on the sidewalk in front of his place, had the sign with the magnifying glass out front. It was a city of masks, the kind Nigel had said hung in theatres. Smiling faces and sad, and all kinds of faces in between [283].

The picture of Washington that Pelecanos's fiction paints isn't always a pretty one, but it is balanced and honest. Pelecanos's affection for the city is mixed with anger over its decline thanks to overwhelming social, economic, and political forces beyond its control. One of his stated aims in writing — "I mean to leave a record of this town" ("Between" 88) — may be modest, but his success in carrying out such a task with artistry and uncompromising realism is nothing less than extraordinary. Thanks to his warts-and-all portrait of D.C., he has created the *real* Washington crime novel.

6

Sara Paretsky
Chicago

When Sara Paretsky first began toying with the idea of writing a novel about a female private detective who, like herself, lived in Chicago, she faced several obstacles. First of all, the very notion of a female private eye was a radical one. There were few models available. With the exception of P.D. James's *An Unsuitable Job for a Woman* in 1972 and Marcia Muller's *Edwin of the Iron Shoes* in 1977, no other serious attempt at creating a female private detective existed. Also, the prospect of a series set in Chicago didn't seem commercially viable; it was hard for New York publishers to imagine that anyone might want to read a private-eye novel set in the Midwest rather than on the East or West coast. Even more daunting a challenge was the perception Chicago had as a manly town, "City of the Big Shoulders" in Carl Sandburg's famous description, "a tall bold slugger set vivid against the little soft cities." (A book about Chicago's architecture and literature by Kenny J. Williams even bears the appropriate title *In the City of Men*.) Could Paretsky overcome the odds and create a believable female version of the male private eye and situate her in a setting that seemed so fundamentally inhospitable for a woman? A dozen or so books have answered a resounding yes to both questions.

A longtime reader of mystery fiction, Paretsky began writing about a female hard-boiled detective in the late 1970s while working as a middle manager in advertising and sales at CNA Insurance, a multi-national company in Chicago. (She continued to work there while writing her next two novels at night.) Insurance companies were traditionally conservative, male-dominated corporations and the rare women managers were always somewhat suspect. It was against this background that Paretsky made a

6. Sara Paretsky

New Year's resolution in 1979 to write a novel with a female character who's determined to succeed in a world that is predominantly male.

> A lot of men, including my first boss, were incredibly supportive and mentoring. Others, including my second boss, were not. He resented having women in the workplace. In October 1978 I was in a meeting listening to this guy and realized the detective I wanted was not Philip Marlowe in drag but rather a woman like my friends and me: holding jobs that hadn't existed when we were in high school and taking the crap we were taking. Instead of smiling at what the guy was saying, and inwardly gritting her teeth, my detective would say what was in the balloon above her head. She wouldn't care about getting fired or if anyone thought she was a nice girl [Locke].

She also saw an opportunity to portray women differently than had been the case in previous hard-boiled crime fiction. "As a reader of mysteries, I always had trouble with the way women are treated as either tramps or helpless victims who stand around weeping. I wanted to read about a woman who could solve her own problems ... someone who could operate successfully in a tough milieu and not lose her femininity" (Stasio "Lady" 39). It was also important to her that she be "very Chicagoan, which means very ethnic, so I gave her a Polish father," though as she later discovered Warshawski (inspired by the city of Warsaw, Poland) is not an authentically Polish name (Williams 54).

Paretsky was born in Ames, Iowa, in 1947 and grew up in rural Kansas outside of Lawrence, where her father, a microbiologist, was the first Jewish faculty member to get tenure at the University of Kansas. (As a child, Paretsky attended the same rural two-room schoolhouse famed mystery writer Rex Stout had many years earlier.) Though she wrote privately from an early age, she never seriously entertained dreams of becoming a writer. Growing up at a time and in a place when boys were expected to become professionals and girls mommies, she had few expectations. Her parents, for example, funded college education for her four brothers but not hers, for girls weren't considered worth educating.

Her first encounter with Chicago came at the age of nineteen when she moved to the city in the summer of 1966 to do community service work. (She helped run a summer day camp for kids on the South Side.) Following graduation from the University of Kansas with a degree in political science in 1967 (which she funded herself), Paretsky moved to Chicago. In 1976 she married University of Chicago physicist Courtney Wright (and became stepmother to his three sons). The following year she earned both a Ph.D. in history and an MBA from the University of Chicago and, given the scarcity of academic jobs for historians at the time, began working for CNA Insurance.

Her initial impression of Chicago was far from positive: "The vastness of the city at night was overwhelming. Red flares glowed against a yellow sky, followed by mile on mile of unbending lights: street lights, neon signs, traffic lights, flashing police blues — lights that didn't illuminate but threw shadows and made the city seem a monster, ready to devour the unwary" (*Windy* 2). But as she came to know and love the city, she saw it as far more inviting than the monster she first thought it was:

> This was a time of great intensity in America and in Chicago; it was the summer that Martin Luther King was organizing for open housing and equal pay, and the passions of the summer made the city seem like the realest, most vivid place on earth. When I finished my BA the following year, and was at loose ends for what to do next, I moved back to Chicago to find a job just because I kept hoping to recreate the intensity of that summer's experience [*Windy* 2].

Not being a native Chicagoan has not proven to be a hindrance to Paretsky in her portrayal of the city. Like her, many of the great Chicago writers (Theodore Dreiser, Carl Sandburg, Saul Bellow) were born elsewhere. But because Chicago was where she came of age, the city made such a powerful impact that it gave her a perspective she wouldn't have had otherwise. It made her aware of the city in ways that someone who grew up there might not be.

In "The Simple Art of Murder," his famous essay on the hard-boiled detective hero, Raymond Chandler proclaimed, "Down these mean streets a man must go who is not himself mean, who is neither tarnished nor afraid. The detective in this kind of story must be such a man" (20). But what if the hero happens to be a woman? For the female detective the mean streets are doubly dangerous. As David Schmid notes, "It is imperative to remember the simple and brutal fact that women's experience of public space is undeniably different from that of men, because of the ways in which women's mobility and behavior in that space is constantly regulated, or even prohibited, by violence and harassment" (260). Or to put it another way, as Hannah Wolfe, Sarah Dunant's private detective does in *Fatlands*, "Interesting how easily men own the space around them, while women just feel like visitors without a permit" (147).

6. Sara Paretsky

The traditional portrait of the big city in American crime fiction is, as David Lehman notes in *The Perfect Murder*, strongly influenced by Poe's vision of the city: "A vast metaphor for moral turbulence and social disorder, the modern city is conceived to be a barren place populated by phantoms, shadows, rootless hordes, and sundry agents of destruction: the city as envisioned in the most famous of all modern poetic nightmares, the city as 'The Waste Land'" (118). The picture of Chicago is no different, especially in the fiction of such noted Chicago novelists as Theodore Dreiser, James T. Farrell, Richard Wright and Nelson Algren. The city is routinely portrayed as a nightmarish and brutalizing place beyond individual control. Paretsky, on the other hand, offers something notably different, i.e., a woman's view of the city.

Feminist psychologists like Carol Gilligan, Nancy Chodorow, and others have identified important gender differences in the way men and women relate to the world. Men tend to value autonomy over connections with others. Women by contrast tend to define themselves "in relation to others, valuing interpersonal connections over autonomy, and perceiving relationships in terms of balancing needs" (Reddy 176). Unlike men, who tend to use images of hierarchy, women employ the imagery of networks and webs. Warshawski shows how the dangerous urban landscape can be managed by the construction of a supportive network. Paretsky's Chicago possesses neither the rootlessness of L.A. nor the anonymity of New York. It's a major metropolis but with a small-town feel — a city of neighborhoods, friends, and familiar places.

Indemnity Only, which introduced readers to V. (for Victoria) I. (for Iphegenia) Warshawski, more familiarly known as Vic, appeared in 1982, shortly before Sue Grafton introduced readers to another groundbreaking female private eye, Kinsey Millhone. A former public defender who became disillusioned with her job, Warshawski decides she wants to be her own boss; she goes into business as a private detective with hopes of being able to "do something that would make me feel that I was working on my concept of justice, not legal point-scoring" (141). Not surprisingly, she encounters opposition from many quarters. Before actually meeting her, for example, her client had assumed from her name that she was a man and is reluctant to hire her once he discovers she is a woman; "This really isn't a job for a girl to take on alone," he tells her. "I'm a woman," Vic retorts, "and I can look out for myself" (5). Bobby Mallory, her late father's closest friend on the police force, is another of those men who is convinced that she has no business doing a man's job: "Being a detective is not a job for a girl like you," he cautions (24). Her challenge is to prove to them (and to the reader) that she is up to the task.

Warshawski is a true Chicagoan, completely at home in the big city. Born on the South Side, she has an office in the Loop (until the run-down building is demolished and she moves uptown), and lives in an apartment on the North Side. "I never get lost driving in Chicago," (*Bitter* 30) she boasts, and as she ranges across Chicagoland from the blighted landscape of the South Side to the leafy Northern suburbs she navigates the clogged streets and expressways with impressive ease. Outside the city, she feels lost and out of place. Spotting the familiar Chicago skyline after a trip to the suburbs, she describes herself feeling like "Arthur seeing Avalon through the mists and eagerly returning" (*Hard* 69).

From her Polish father, Tony, she learned how to load and shoot a gun. From her mother, Gabriella, a half–Jewish immigrant from Italy, she inherited not only her olive skin and love of opera but also her fierce inde-pendence and drive to fight battles to the end. But her DNA was also formed by her South Side immigrant neighborhood, where she learned how to be tough: "I grew up on the South Side. Ninetieth and Commercial, if you know the area — lots of Polish steelworkers who didn't welcome racial and ethnic newcomers — and the feeling was mutual. The law of the jun-gle ruled in my high school — if you couldn't swing a mean toe or fist, you might as well forget it" (*Indemnity* 70).

As a detective, Vic is more like Philip Marlowe than Miss Marple. If she hopes to survive on the mean streets of Chicago, which Paretsky has called "the ultimate hard-boiled city" ("Writing" 59), she has to be able to take it as well as dish it out. Though she lacks the wisecracking tough-ness of Marlowe, she nevertheless proves her ability to survive in a rough-and-tumble world. She is beaten, shot at, slashed with a knife, felled by a stun gun, and has acid poured on her, yet like her male hard-boiled counterparts, she keeps on going. Though she can mix it up with tough guys and is willing to fire her Smith and Wesson when necessary, Paret-sky manages to make her toughness credible without undermining her believability as a woman.

One way she does this is to have Vic acknowledge her fears rather than hide them beneath tough-taking bluster. When an assailant pours acid on her outside her apartment in *Killing Orders*, she is shaken: "I was scared, and I didn't like it" (116). But she also knows that if she hopes to continue working as a private detective, she has to stand up for herself. "I just have to solve my own problems," she says. "I don't plan to turn into a clinging female who runs to a man every time something doesn't work out right" (*Killing 157*). And so, despite the acid attack and the subsequent arson which burns her apartment down, like all good private eyes she refuses to give up.

One major difference between Warshawski and male hard-boiled detectives like Sam Spade, Philip Marlowe, Lew Archer, and most of their brethren is that her private life isn't as lonely and solitary as theirs. The male private eye is traditionally defined by his isolation, both from society and from normal human relationships. He has no family and few if any friends. Though her parents are dead and she is unmarried (she is divorced after a brief marriage to a fellow attorney), Vic has created an extended surrogate family and a network of close friends that give her a strong sense of intimate connectedness that her male counterparts often (by choice) lack. Female values like solidarity and responsibility have greater prominence in Paretsky's novels than the alienation and isolation that traditionally characterize the male private eye.

Paretsky uses Warshawski's extended family as a way of domesticating, even feminizing the city. Her description of her investigative method — "My theory of detection resembles Julia Child's approach to cooking: Grab a lot of ingredients from the shelves, put them in a pot and stir, and see what happens"(*Killing 58*) — even employs a domestic image. While Chicago can be a dangerous place, Paretsky uses Vic's network of friends to emphasize its familiarity rather than its threat. Her main confidante is Dr. Lotty Herschel, a Jewish perinatologist who was forced to flee her native Vienna to escape the Nazis and who now operates a clinic for low-income families. Lotty is a combination surrogate mother and best friend who can both soothe Vic's worries and treat her wounds. Their friendship dates back to Vic's college days when both were involved in the abortion underground.

Vic's downstairs neighbor, a retired machinist and widower named Mr. Contreras, acts as a surrogate father, watching over Vic's safety and strictly monitoring her relationship with every man who visits her. He also helps her break into a lawyer's office and even takes a bullet in the shoulder for her in *Burn Marks*. Vic also shares custody of two dogs with her neighbor, a golden retriever named Peppy and her half–Lab son Mitch. Both dogs even get to play key roles in Vic's protective circle: Peppy saves her life when she leads Contreras to where Vic had been left bound and gagged in the middle of a swamp in *Blood Shot*; Mitch saves the life of Vic's friend by leading Vic to the landfill where the critically injured woman had been dumped in *Fire Sale*.

Chicago provides several other opportunities for Vic to create a sense of small-town community and connectiveness. Local establishments where she is known and warmly welcomed provide oases of comfort and familiarity. She regularly eats at the Belmont Diner in an old working-class neighborhood (where a helpful waitress foils a man shadowing Vic by deliberately dropping a pitcher of iced tea on him in *Guardian Angel*) and drinks at the Golden Glow, a South Loop saloon that dates back to the nineteenth century. And for many Chicagoans, there is no stronger community than that of the long-suffering Cubs fans, among whom Vic counts herself an avid member: she follows their games on radio, occasionally goes to Wrigley Field, and drops references to players that likely have meaning only to loyal Cubbies.

To the traditional male private eyes, the local police usually represent the enemy. For Warshawski, they too are just part of the family. For one thing, despite the size of the Chicago police department, the only cops she ever seems to have contact with are the same familiar faces: homicide detective Bobby Mallory, her father's old friend, and his fellow officers Terry Finchley, Conrad Rawlings, and Mary Louise Neely. Mallory is a second father figure, keeping an eye on Vic, but unlike the protective Contreras, he's a disapproving father. The animosity he exhibits towards her is more than the traditional dislike the police have for private eyes; his paternalistic attitude is, like so much else she faces, rooted in male prejudice. Mallory uses every opportunity he can to remind Vic that a woman has no business being a detective and that she should be home raising babies. His colleagues, however, are more supportive. Rawlings even becomes her lover for a while and Neely joins her as a part-time assistant after she resigns from the force.

"The one thing you must never forget in Chicago," Vic proclaims, "is to look out for your own" (*Burn* 336), which proves to be the guiding principle when it comes to her own work. Virtually all of her early cases begin with family or friends in need, then mushroom into complicated plots involving high-level financial chicanery of one kind or another. (Paretsky admits she plots too much. Sometimes she tries to pack too much in, as in *Tunnel Vision,* where the crimes range from abused wives and incest to the plight of illegal Romanian construction workers, violation of the Iraqi trade embargo, and laundered cash secretly flown into the U.S., all done with the complicity of a U.S. senator.)

In *Deadlock,* the death of her cousin, Boom-Boom Warshawski, an ex-pro hockey player who either jumped, slipped, or was pushed under a ship at the grain yard where he worked, brings Vic into a case that involves a scheme to control Great Lakes shipping. In *Killing Orders,* Vic's mother's Aunt Rosa, an angry, unpleasant woman, calls upon Vic for help. A bookkeeper for a Dominican priory in the suburbs, she has been suspended from her job when it is discovered that six million dollars worth of stock certificates in the priory's safe (to which she had access) are counterfeit. When a friend looking into the case is murdered and then she herself is attacked with acid and her apartment burned down, Vic knows there is more to the case than phony stock certificates. What she uncovers is a complex conspiracy involving some high-level members of the hierarchy of the Catholic Church and a supersecret organization called Corpus Christi.

In *Burn Marks,* it is Vic's father's sister Elena who comes seeking help when the fleabag hotel she lives in burns to the ground. Once again, helping out a relative in distress exposes a conspiracy, this one involving a powerful Cook County political boss, a Donald Trump–like land developer, a dummy construction company, and a cop who is a protégé of Bobby Mallory. Their scheme involves torching the last piece of property standing in the way of a planned stadium-retail housing complex. In the end, the conspiracy does more than simply inconvenience a few poor residents of the seedy hotel. Two innocent women are murdered because they have information that might lead to exposure of the crime. The evildoers, however, go free. As Vic's investigative reporter friend Murray Ryerson reminds her, "This is Chicago, sweetheart, not Minneapolis" (333). It's just business as usual.

Paretsky's focus on white-collar crime is deliberate and, in the crime novel, relatively rare. She has been singled out by Hans Bertens as "one of the few writers in any of crime writing's diverse traditions who consistently confronts the organizational crime — corporate, union, professional, or otherwise — that hides behind the glittering facade of the contemporary urban agglomeration" (32). By focusing on the often devastating effects of such crimes on individuals, especially the elderly, the poor, and the helpless, Paretsky effectively challenges the myth that because these crimes are committed by white, well-educated men, they're not as bad as other crimes. "If you have a hundred billion dollars at your disposal," she argues, "you can inflict so much more damage than someone who's shooting a Saturday night special on the street" (Lynn Miller).

In recent novels, Paretsky's themes have extended into areas far beyond white-collar crime. *Total Recall,* for example, incorporates Lotty Herschel's narrative of her flight from the Nazis as a way of addressing the issue of the Holocaust and the painful memories which haunt its survivors. In *Blacklist,* the murder of a black writer researching a figure from the past allows Paretsky to tackle the twin terrors of McCarthyism in the fifties and, because a witness to the crime was a young Egyptian dishwasher facing accusations he is a terrorist, the threat to civil liberties posed by the Patriot Act enacted in the wake of the 9/11 attacks. Because of the ambitious historical nature of the issues addressed, these two novels are the least rooted in the Chicago experience of all Paretsky's books.

While Vic no longer lives in an ethnic neighborhood, she is still very much a product of one. In fact, in many ways she can't escape her upbringing. An invitation to the twentieth-year reunion of her high school state championship basketball team brings Warshawski back to her South Chicago neighborhood for the first time in years in *Blood Shot.* An athletic scholarship to the University of Chicago provided a ticket out of South Chicago and she is not convinced you can (or should) ever go home again. Caroline Djiak, a childhood neighbor whom she always treated as a bratty little sister, uses the visit to try to convince Vic to help her find her father, whom she has never known. Her mother is dying of cancer and she now wants to know who her father was. Warshawski has little interest in getting involved in Caroline's family issues. But stung by her friend's accusation that she's "a la-di-da snot going off to the North Side and abandoning people to their fate" (6), she reluctantly agrees to take the case.

"I had forgotten the smell," Warshawski notes in the opening line of *Blood Shot* as she drives south to her old neighborhood. The swanky high rises and inviting beaches of Chicago, only twenty miles away, give way to smelly landfills and worn-out factories that dot the smoke-hung landscape of her youth. V.I.'s stomach turns at the thought of sticking her head in the Calumet River, where she and her friends used to swim. Rusted out mills and polluted waterways with names like Dead Stick Pond bear silent testimony to the days when towns like this were the backbone of industrial Chicago, indeed of America itself.

Warshawski eventually discovers the identity of Caroline's father, but in the process also brings to light the kind of collusion between powerful forces that characterizes the other books in the series. In this case, insurance companies, crooked politicians, and the head of a multi-national chemical company are all involved in an effort to cover up the extent to which toxic chemicals used in the plant have poisoned countless workers, including Caroline's mother. But the greater crime is the damage done to the land, which now looks like "earth after a nuclear decimation" (47).

Those responsible for the toxic damage manage to live in comfort far from the blight of South Chicago. Gustav Humboldt, chairman of the multi-million dollar chemical company that owns the solvent plant which has been poisoning its workers for decades, resides in an elegant high-rise apartment building overlooking Lake Michigan. Curtis Chigwell, the doctor who conspired with Humboldt to cover up evidence of sickness for decades, lives in the leafy town of Hinsdale, twenty miles west of the Loop, the kind of place that makes Warshawski feel that "after a day in South Chicago I felt I'd stepped into paradise"(68).

In the end, Warshawski has hopes that the truth about Humboldt and the toxic problems at his company will be brought to light. But seeing a newspaper photo of Humboldt throwing out the first pitch for the White Sox on opening day reminds her of how difficult it is to bring down the powerful, no matter how destructive their crimes.

Despite her vow never to return to her dying South Side neighborhood, a call from her old basketball coach begging her to take over the team while she undergoes cancer surgery drags Vic back again in *Fire Sale*. Conditions, if anything, have grown even worse since her last visit with unemployment rising and the crime rate soaring. Soon after her arrival, a case of arson and murder involving family members of her players requires Vic to do more than just coach basketball. As usual, she solves the crimes, but there is no fairy tale happy ending. Her team wins only five games and her former coach succumbs to cancer. But Vic takes some comfort from realizing that she has given a glimmer of hope to some of her players, encouraging them to use education as she did as a ticket out of the misery that surrounds them.

Paretsky's Chicago is a city in transition and the picture isn't a pretty one, especially on the South Side. Some changes are natural. For example, Catholic churches that once served Polish immigrants now minister to Mexicans. Other changes are more painful. The once mighty industrial city, like so many American cities, is dying. How, Vic wonders, could those massive steel mills of her childhood have become piles of rubble and weeds? Things are so bad in Vic's South Side neighborhood that seeing the house she grew up in vacant, the windows boarded up, weeds choking the yard where her mother lovingly tended her flowers, brings tears to her eyes. However, despite the decline, brave Chicagoans aren't giving up. Watching new townhouses being built on the rubble of her old neighborhood reminds Vic of the "gallant optimism ... splashes of hope against the general gray of the area" (*Fire* 119) that symbolizes her love for this tough old city and its people.

Chicago, for Paretsky, is a given. She doesn't explore its hidden mysteries as Donna Leon does with Venice, feel the need to correct the historical record by filling in the blanks as Walter Mosley does, or expose the real city behind the public monuments as George P. Pelecanos does. She presents the city as is and makes no effort to explain it. There are passing references to well-known Chicago landmarks like the Sears Tower, the Art Institute, the Hancock Building, and McCormick Place as well as to local political figures like Harold Washington and Eddie Vrdolyak without any clarifying information for outsiders. Even a comment like this — "Would Ron Kittle drop another routine fly ball?" — passes without any context that might be necessary for a non–Chicagoan who doesn't happen to be a long-suffering Cubs fan.

Paretsky doesn't devote much space to physical description of the city. While there are frequent references to streets in the Loop, the most extended description she ever provides is in *Tunnel Vision*, where she describes the extensive tunnel system that lies several levels below the streets. Her descriptions are mainly limited to brief telling snapshots of the city: one desolate neighborhood is likened to postwar Berlin; the Eisenhower Expressway resembles "a prison exercise yard for most of its length" (*Killing* 22); a handful of survivors of an urban renewal project stand forlornly "on the street like uneasy pins left after the efforts of a bush-league bowler" (*Bitter* 160). Other brief vignettes convey the changing face of the city's diverse population: "The decimation of Lebanon was showing up in Chicago as a series of restaurants and little shops, just as the destruction of Vietnam had been visible here a decade earlier" (*Killing* 46). Paretsky's goal is to capture the heart and soul of Chicago by narrowing in on those features that evoke the essence rather than the appearance of the city.

One defining feature of the Chicago landscape does figure prominently in Paretsky's work: Lake Michigan. Like her favorite restaurant and bar, the lake offers comfort and escape from the stresses of the city. In this respect, Paretsky resembles other Chicago women writers whose novels, according to Sidney H. Bremer, "usually embrace nature as a powerful, complex presence within the city, whereas the men's novels tend to idealize nature and to present it as apart from the city" (212). Vic often stops to take a swim in the lake's refreshing waters to enjoy the "sense of being rocked in the cradle of the deep, secure in the arms of Mother Nature" (*Bitter* 300). Even when she can't actually swim, just thinking of lying in Lake Michigan with the sun overhead proves comforting.

However, Vic is not blind to the lake's hidden dangers, the cold depths and sudden furies that "could kill you with merciless impersonality" (*Bitter* 50). But just like living in the city, the presence of danger doesn't preclude happiness. Through Warshawski, Paretsky shows how a strong and capable woman can negotiate what Margaret Kinsman in "A Quality of Visibility: Paretsky and Chicago" describes as "her share of both the risk and the excitement the city offers to women" (22).

Setting for Paretsky doesn't have quite the primacy it does in the works of some of the other authors included in this book. Nevertheless, it does provide a gritty foundation for the stories Paretsky tells. And while the white-collar crimes she describes could occur anywhere, Chicago effectively represents what Guy Szuberla characterizes as "a corporate megalopolis, and a vast theater for politicians on the take" (151), which makes it an ideal setting for Paretsky's themes. Paretsky makes no effort to construct an all-encompassing picture of Chicago. What she does do very effectively, however, is give a strong sense of the experience of living in the city as well as an example of how a strong, independent woman can successfully negotiate the urban landscape of a place like Chicago.

7

James Lee Burke

Southern Louisiana

The lush bayous of southern Louisiana and the Old World charm of New Orleans comprise a rich and exotic backdrop for James Lee Burke's novels about New Iberia deputy sheriff Dave Robicheaux. But for Burke sense of place is also vitally connected to a sense of the past; history is so indelibly inscribed in the Louisiana landscape that the past is never far from the present. Burke's novels reiterate the notion put forward by William Faulkner, another Southern writer for whom presence of the past is paramount, who declared in *Requiem for a Nun,* "The past is never dead. It's not even past" (80).

The history of New Orleans and its environs is unique in the United States. Discovered by the Spanish and settled by the French, New Orleans has more in common with the Latin and the Caribbean world than any other U.S. city. It is in many ways the least American of all American cities. And yet thanks to its historical role in the Confederacy and its legacy of slavery, Louisiana also typifies much of the American south. This exotic landscape, rich in mystery and romance, yet also haunted by ghosts of the past, gives Burke's novels both atmosphere and rich historical context.

Like Raymond Chandler, Burke came to crime fiction at a relatively late age. Chandler didn't begin writing mystery stories until his late forties; his first novel, *The Big Sleep,* wasn't published until he was fifty-one. Burke was forty-nine when his debut crime novel, *The Neon Rain,* was published. But unlike Chandler, who turned to writing after a career in the oil business, Burke had been a professional writer for thirty years, though his career had stalled after a promising start.

Burke was born in Houston, Texas, on 5 December 1936, but spent much of his childhood in southern Louisiana; his great-great-grandfather became a sugar farmer in New Iberia in 1836, and his family has been there ever since. Inspired by the success of his cousin Andre Dubus, who won first place in the Louisiana College Writer's Contest (and who went on to earn acclaim as one of America's best short-story writers), Burke began writing fiction. At the age of nineteen his first story was published in his college literary magazine. In 1965, his first novel, *Half of Paradise,* which weaves together a tale about a trio of men in Louisiana, appeared to positive reviews. He wrote three more novels in quick succession, the last of which, *To the Bright and Shining Sun,* about coal mining in Kentucky, was published in 1970. The following year saw the publication of *Lay Down My Sword and Shield,* a novel about migrant workers in Southwest Texas. At the age of thirty-four, with three published novels to his credit, Burke had seemingly established himself as a serious young writer with a promising career ahead of him.

Things did not work out that way. In 1973, he completed his next novel, *The Lost Get-Back Boogie,* about a country musician just released from prison in Louisiana after serving time for killing a man in a barroom brawl. In what may be a record in the American publishing world, the novel racked up over a hundred rejection notices during the next thirteen years. Aside from a few short stories and one paperback original, *Two for Texas* in 1982, Burke simply couldn't get anything published. (*The Lost Get-Back Boogie* would finally find a publisher, Louisiana State University Press, in 1986.) In 1985, at the urging of friend and fellow writer Rick DeMarinis, Burke decided to try his hand at a new genre, crime fiction. He felt that if he "tried to write a literary novel within a genre I'd really accomplish something" (Williams 60). Incorporating material from some of his unpublished work, Burke published his first crime novel, *The Neon Rain,* in 1987.

During most of these years, Burke, who attended Southwestern Louisiana Institute and later earned a B.A. and an M.A. from the University of Missouri, worked a variety of jobs (newspaper reporter, social worker, land surveyor, oil field worker) and taught at several colleges (University of Southern Illinois, University of Montana, Miami-Dade Community College, Wichita State University). But it wasn't until the success of the Dave Robicheaux books and the award of a Guggenheim grant in 1989 (the same year *Black Cherry Blues* won the Edgar Award as best mystery novel of the year) that he was able finally to become a full-time writer.

Despite his publication difficulties, the quality of his work remained consistently high. His novels were well-reviewed, his short stories appeared in prestigious publications (*Atlantic Monthly, Southern Review, Antioch Review, Kenyon Review*). *The Lost Get-Back Boogie* was even nominated for a Pulitzer Prize. So when Burke eventually turned to the crime novel, he brought with him the skills of an accomplished author of fiction.

Writing a crime novel did not, however, represent a dramatic departure. Burke didn't alter his style, his thematic concerns, or even his usual kind of protagonist. "*The Neon Rain* was different from earlier work only in one respect: the narrator," Burke insists. "The story, the locale, the themes, the people, are all the same. They are no different from the people, the themes, that we meet in the earlier work" (Coale 166). He simply made his protagonist a cop and proceeded from there.

The Neon Rain introduces New Orleans homicide detective Dave Robicheaux. The essential details of Robicheaux's life are these: a fourteen-year veteran of the New Orleans Police Department, he was an English major in college, served in combat in Vietnam, has been sober for four years after a battle with alcoholism, and is recently divorced. But the bare facts of his life fail to give a complete picture of the man whose past continues to haunt him; his painful memories of his Vietnam experiences coupled with a heavy load of guilt and regret over a variety of past sins often leave him feeling "like a leper who could not stop picking at his own crusted lesions" (254).

One day while fishing in a bayou, Robicheaux comes across the body of a young black woman floating in the water. The official police verdict of accidental death by drowning doesn't satisfy him, especially in light of the suspicious track marks on her arm. What begins as a simple enough investigation soon spirals into a complicated case involving the Mafia, secret conspiracies to ship arms to the contras in Nicaragua, and even events going as far back as the infamous My Lai massacre in Vietnam. Robicheaux's personal life also begins to spin out of control: he is suspended from the force when the body of a Treasury agent is found in his car; he resumes heavy drinking after a trio of bad guys force a mixture of beer and whiskey down his throat and he ends up in the drunk tank of his own police department; his brother is nearly killed in a shooting that likely was meant for him; and he kills two men which forces him to confront "that simian creature we descend from" who was "alive and well in my breast" (100).

Everything eventually is resolved, the bad guys get caught, and Robicheaux regains his sobriety. But serious damage has been done. At the end of the novel, he resigns from the New Orleans police force and with Annie, a social worker who will soon become his wife, escapes to the tranquility of his native New Iberia, a small town on Bayou Teche where he grew up, to open up a bait and boat-rental business with an old family friend, a black man named Batist.

The peaceful idyllic life Robicheaux had hoped for after leaving New Orleans for New Iberia is quickly shattered, however, in *Heaven's Prisoners*. While out on the Gulf trawling for shrimp with Annie, a twin-engine plane passes overhead and plunges into the water nearby. Robicheaux jumps in, but can't do anything for the four dead passengers in the submerged plane. However, a fifth passenger, a young girl trapped in an air bubble, is still alive. He rescues the girl, a six-year-old refugee from El Salvador, names her Alafair (the name of Burke's grandmother and also his daughter, now a mystery writer herself), and decides to keep her and raise her as his own. But his involvement in the case soon results in deadly consequences when Annie is shotgunned to death in their bedroom by a pair of killers looking to murder Robicheaux. He takes a job with the New Iberia Sheriff's Department and sets out to find Annie's killers.

Daily life continues to be a challenge for Robicheaux, as he struggles with his alcoholic urges and guilt over Annie's death. Burke is clearly interested in something far more ambitious than merely showcasing the heroic exploits of a Louisiana crime solver. It is the mystery of Dave Robicheaux that concerns Burke, not the mysteries he is faced with solving. Burke describes his hero this way:

> Dave is what I admire most in people.... He represents courage. He's
> ethical.... He understands the world of blue-collar people, people who
> are inarticulate but with profound feelings. And he's able to give voice
> to them. At the same time he's flawed, like the tragic hero — sometimes
> with pride, sometimes with anger. I guess he's my attempt at Every-
> man [Ringle D1].

Robicheaux is a thoughtful and moral man in a world where evil exists, a man of divided impulses, both drawn to violence yet wary of its allure. He acknowledges the attraction of violence — "you feel an adrenaline surge of pleasure at having usurped the province of God" — yet recognizes that "the unblemished place where God once grasped our souls becomes permanently stained" by that very same violent act (*Heaven's* 240). Burke is not reluctant to show Robicheaux in a bad light (lapsing into drunkenness, erupting into violence) as he launches his hero on a quest in search of answers to such questions as the nature of good and evil, right and wrong. The mystery Robicheaux is primarily interested in solving is the mystery of life itself.

Robicheaux maintains an on-again, off-again relationship with the Iberia Sheriff's Department throughout the rest of the series. He's frequently suspended for one infraction or another, usually related to his penchant for violent outbursts. Even when he's on duty, he's not much of a policeman; the only investigations that really interest him are those of a personal nature, which comprise most of the novels in the series. Characters from his past keep appearing, either seeking his help or representing unresolved issues that now demand to be addressed. His more personal cases include tracking down his wife's killers, rescuing his daughter from kidnappers, and even solving the decades-old mystery of the murder of his own mother.

Robicheaux is usually aided and abetted by the reckless efforts of his former Homicide partner Clete Percel, who now works tracking down bail skips after getting booted off the New Orleans police force. Although Robicheaux praises his old buddy as "the most intelligent and perceptive police officer I had ever known" (*Jolie* 326), we see scant evidence of either of these two qualities. Percel is a hard-drinking loose cannon, an irrepressible yet totally irresponsible thug with a penchant for head-bashing and over-the-top antics (like dumping the contents of a cement mixer into one gangster's vintage convertible and then later destroying his half-million-dollar home with a stolen earth grader). There's no question about his loyalty to his old friend, but his crime-solving techniques can more accurately be described as "periodic excursions into mayhem of epic proportions" (*Jolie* 326).

One of the most pronounced influences on Burke's writing is William Faulkner, whose *Sound and the Fury* he once lauded as "probably the greatest novel written in the English language" (Carter 42). Faulkner's fiction displays an almost obsessive fascination with the palpable weight of the past. In novel after novel, Faulkner dramatized what one might call the pastness of the present and the presentness of the past as he explored the various ways we are molded, shaped, and haunted by the historical and personal past and its continuing presence in our lives.

Burke shares Faulkner's interest in the same theme and has created a fictional setting, as Faulkner did, that embodies it. Because of its history, the south in general, and southern Louisiana in particular, have been left with a rich residue of the past. New Orleans and New Iberia are awash with mementos of the past, from the stately ante-bellum homes that line its storied streets to the Civil War minié balls, quartz arrowheads, and rusty Confederate revolvers that lie underfoot. As Robicheaux notes, "You cannot grow up in a place where the tractor's plow can crack minié balls and grapeshot loose from the soil, even rake across a cannon wheel, and remain impervious to the past" (*Stained* 265).

Robicheaux's relationship to the past is complicated. On the one hand, it offers escape from the troubled present. "I don't like the world the way it is, and I miss the past," he says, though he quickly adds, "It's a foolish way to be" (*Neon* 238). He seeks to create an Edenic idyll in New Iberia, living in the oak and cypress house his father built with his own hands during the Depression, marrying Bootsie Mouton, the first woman he ever fell in love with. His happy childhood memories of life with his father, a Cajun trapper and oil-field roughneck who raised him after his mother left, and the summer of 1957 when he first fell in love with Bootsie sustain his fantasies. That blissful summer remains for him "the cathedral I sometimes visit when everything else fails, when the heart seems poisoned, the earth stricken, and dead leaves blow across the soul's windows like bits of dried parchment" (*Black* 189).

But other memories of the past are less salutary: his ten-month ordeal in Vietnam, from which he returned with two Purple Hearts, a leg full of shrapnel, and a head inhabited by demons; his daily battle to "exorcise the alcoholic succubus that seemed to live within me, its claws hooked into my soul" (*Heaven's* 33); a steady parade of friends and lovers from the past who materialize with great regularity and cause his involvement in one bad situation after another. And so he faces a continuing struggle to come to terms with these reminders of the past and find a way to keep them from poisoning his present life.

The past assumes a mysterious and ominous presence in *In the Electric*

Mist with Confederate Dead. A Hollywood film company has come to New Iberia to shoot a movie about the Civil War; the producer, a New Orleans mobster named Baby Feet Balboni, is a boyhood friend of Robicheaux's. One day an actor in the film, Elrod T. Sykes, discovers the skeleton of a dead man wrapped in chains that Robicheaux believes may be that of a man he saw being murdered by two men some thirty-five years earlier. Sykes, who also claims to "see things," tells Robicheaux about a conversation he had with a dead Confederate general who accused Robicheaux's father of stealing his gun, the very same gun that Robicheaux's father once found and gave him when he was twelve, and which he now keeps in a box in his closet.

In a bold move, Burke brings Robicheaux face to face with the dead Confederate general and his men. A bolt of lightning explodes next to Robicheaux's truck while he's driving along a lonely dirt road late at night during a violent storm and sends him careening into the levee. Then, through the mist which was "as pink and thick as cotton candy and seemed to snap with electric currents, like a kaleidoscopic flickering of snakes' tongues" (159), he spots a company of wounded Confederate soldiers gathered around a campfire. Their leader, a one-legged man with a wounded arm, introduces himself as John Bell Hood (a famous Confederate general whom Burke once featured in an unpublished novel).

Are the dead soldiers real? Did Robicheaux slip through a hole in time and somehow end up back in 1865? Is this simply a delusion caused by a blow to the head he might have suffered when his truck crashed into the levee? Or, as a doctor speculates, did somebody slip some LSD into the Dr Pepper he drank earlier at the film director's birthday party? Whatever the explanation, Robicheaux's ongoing conversations with General Hood, who keeps popping up, play an important role in the novel.

Robicheaux has always enjoyed (and is often tormented by) a rich interior life. Memories assail him. During his heavy drinking days, he claims to have received phone calls from his dead comrades from Vietnam. He also experienced vivid dreams in which he had lengthy conversations with his dead father and Annie, his murdered wife. But the encounter with General Hood and his fellow dead Confederates is different. For one thing, others, including Robicheaux's daughter, also report seeing the general. His presence in the novel unquestionably heightens the gothic atmosphere that has lapped at the edge of the pages of the previous Robicheaux books. But it also vividly symbolizes the important role the past plays in Robicheaux's life.

The ghosts of the Civil War also serve to make a larger point. Robicheaux discovers that the killer of Dewitt Prejean, the black man whose bones were found, is a former deputy named Murphy Doucet, who is also the murderer of a nineteen-year-old prostitute, a murder that begins the action of the novel. Prejean was dragged from his jail cell and killed by Doucet because he was having an affair with a white friend's wife. The killing was prompted solely by racism which, as General Hood reminds Robicheaux in one of their many conversations, was the cause of the war they were fighting. "We were always honorable," he insists to Robicheaux, "but we served venal men and a vile enterprise. How many lives would have been spared had we not lent ourselves to the defense of a repellent cause like slavery" (317)? Doucet is gunned down when he trips over an old wooden crutch lying in a pile of rotting medical waste. The crutch bears an uncanny resemblance to the one Robicheaux saw being used by the one-legged General Hood. It is more than fitting that Doucet's demise might have been achieved thanks to the assistance of a Confederate general seeking to make amends for the past.

Robicheaux remembers hearing stories when he was a child about U.S. Navy destroyers sinking several Nazi submarines that were lying in wait off the Louisiana coast preparing to attack oil tankers. Reports of a sunken sub and its crew of drowned Nazi sailors gave the young Robicheaux nightmares for years. More than a simple historical curiosity, however, the sunken Nazi submarine in *Dixie City Jam* becomes, like the Confederate weapons that dot the landscape, a powerful physical emblem of evil from another time. And the young boy's nightmares become a present-day one when that evil from the past materializes to remind him how the past still exerts its power over the present.

In *The Neon Rain*, Robicheaux first mentioned seeing the barnacle-encrusted ruins of a Nazi sub while diving deep below the surface of the Gulf. Because of his knowledge of its general location, he's hired by Hippo Bimstine, a wealthy Jewish businessman, to find the submarine for him. Bimstine belongs to a Jewish organization that monitors the activities of "the guys who'd like to see more ovens and searchlights and guard towers in the world — the Klan, the American Nazi party, the Aryan Nation, skinheads out on the coast, a bunch of buttwipes called the Christian

Identity at Hayden Lake, Idaho" (82). There are rumors that the sub contains a large gold-plated swastika made from teeth pulled from the mouths of Polish Jews, a gift from Heinrich Himmler himself. Bimstine doesn't want it to get into the hands of someone like Will Buchalter, head of a neo–Nazi organization known as the Shield, who'd like to use it to promote his evil cause.

Evil is always a menacing presence in Burke's novels. In his Manichean view, "good and evil are very real elements in the world, and the forces which represent each are in constant struggle against one another" (Jeffrey 127). Both the personal and the political face of evil are represented in *Dixie City Jam* by Will Buchalter and his sister, Marie. Buchalter is one of Burke's creepiest villains. An insidious monster, he sneaks into Robicheaux's house to play his jazz records and to scrawl messages like, "I'll Love You In A Way That No Woman Can" on his bathroom wall; on one occasion, he arrives bearing candy and forces a deep kiss on Bootsie before leaving. She becomes so traumatized by the incident that, with the encouragement of Buchalter's sister, who poses as a friendly nun, she ends up with a serious drinking problem. Buchalter's smiling face can't disguise the evil in his eyes; during one close encounter with him, Robicheaux realizes he has "now seen the face that inmates at Bergen-Belsen and Treblinka and Dachau had looked into" (304).

Buchhalter doesn't represent the only evil in the novel. Several black drug dealers are murdered and their hearts ripped out of their chests by agents for the notorious Calucci brothers, who are trying to keep control of the drug traffic for themselves. But the overarching evil in the book is that represented by the sunken Nazi sub and which takes many forms in the novel, ranging from a videotape making the rounds composed of Nazi propaganda footage "that was almost like watching distilled evil" (14) to the bumper stickers supporting local neo–Nazi politician David Duke. In the end, Buchalter and his sister are dead, their bodies now lying with the dead Nazi soldiers beneath the water.

The novel closes with Robicheaux and his family enjoying a festive outing at the New Orleans Jazz and Heritage Festival. The picture Burke paints is a joyous one:

> The music rose into the sky until it seemed to fuse with the gentle and
> pervasive light spreading far beyond the racetrack, over oak-lined
> streets, paintless wood houses with galleries and green window shutters,

elevated highways, the Superdome, the streetcars and palm-dotted neutral ground of Canal, the scrolled iron balconies, colonnades, and brick chimneys in the Quarter, Jackson Square and the spires of St. Louis Cathedral, the Café du Monde, the wide, mud-churned sweep of the Mississippi, the shining vastness of the wetlands to the south, and eventually the Gulf of Mexico, where later the moon would rise like an enormous pearl that had been dipped in a glass of burgundy [494].

But one cannot forget such evil creatures as Buchalter and must remain vigilant to prevent those "protean creatures who rise from biblical seas or slouch toward Bethlehem to be born again" (490) from threatening the comfort and beauty of the warm spring night Robicheaux so lovingly describes.

Burning Angel contains no single dramatic symbol of the past like the ghost of a dead Confederate general or a sunken submarine full of Nazi sailors; the various physical relics of the past in this novel are widely dispersed throughout the landscape — bones from an ancient burial ground, an eighteenth-century silver spoon from Spain or France, coins that might be part of the loot buried by famous pirate Jean Lafitte, lengths of chain used in the slave trade growing out of the bark of an oak tree like "unacknowledged and unforgiven sins" (102). These scattered remnants of the past are fitting in a novel whose notions about the infiltration of the past into the present are less focused than in Burke's previous efforts.

Theme threatens to overpower character, plot and sometimes even plausibility in *Burning Angel* as Burke tries to integrate too many evils of the past — slavery, Vietnam, Central American politics — into one book. The theme is summarized in one of Robicheaux's mystical reveries:

> I've often subscribed to the notion that perhaps history is not sequential; that all people, from all of history, live out their lives simultaneously, in different dimensions perhaps, occupying the same pieces of geography, unseen by one another, as if we are all part of one spiritual conception.
>
> Attakapas Indians, Spanish colonists, slaves who dredged mud from the lake to make bricks for the homes of their masters, Louisiana's boys in butternut brown who refused to surrender after Appomattox, federal soldiers who blackened the sky with smoke from horizon to horizon — maybe they were all still out there, living just a breath away, like indistinct figures hiding inside an iridescent glare on the edge of our vision [49].

One of those mysterious beings out there is Robicheaux's old friend Sunny Boy Marsallus, who is gunned down before Robicheaux's eyes but who later seems to be making posthumous appearances everywhere. The red-headed Marsallus earned the nickname of "the red angel" in Guatemala for his miraculous ability to survive a gun battle. Now one of his friends claims to have seen him walking through the trunk of a tree into the water, "burning like hundreds of little tongues of flame under the water" (324). Even after Robicheaux has examined his decomposing body, he has a nocturnal conversation with him (or his ghost). Plausibility is seriously stretched when Robicheaux's wife Bootsie comes to her husband's rescue by shooting a woman who is about to kill him after she receives a phone call from the dead man warning her about the danger. (Another angel appears in *Jolie Blon's Bounce* in the character of the appropriately-named Sal Angelo, a homeless man who tells Robicheaux that he was the medic who saved his life in Vietnam. Angelo intervenes again at the end of the novel to help dispatch a demonic villain named Legion Guidry. When Robicheaux checks Angelo's military record, he discovers he was killed in Vietnam in 1965.)

Burning Angel ends with yet another of Robicheaux's mystical musings about the past:

> And if you should ever doubt the proximity of the past, I thought to myself, you only had to look over your shoulder at the rain slanting on the fields, like now, the smoke rising in wet plumes out of the stubble, the mist blowing off the lake, and you can see and hear with the clarity of a dream the columns marching four abreast out of the trees, barefoot, emaciated as scarecrows, their perforated, sun-faded colors popping above them in the wind, their officers cantering their horses in the field, everyone dressing it up now, the clatter of muskets shifting in unison to the right shoulder, yes, just a careless wink of the eye, just that quick, and you're among them, wending your way with liege lord and serf and angel, in step with the great armies of the dead [434].

The Southern landscape has often inspired similar thoughts about the enduring presence of the past in the minds of writers, but *Burning Angel* at times reads more like an episode from *The Twilight Zone* than the kind of realistic crime novel that Burke had heretofore been writing with great success.

Burke prides himself on the spontaneity of his plotting, insisting, "I never see more than two scenes away. Going into the last chapter, I do not know how the book is going to end" (Coale 166). The result of this method is less a tightly organized sequence of events and more a series of dramatic and often violent confrontations. But in *Sunset Limited*, for example, Burke keeps introducing so many new threads — the murder of two white brothers who raped a young black girl, the killing of the accountant on a film being shot on location in New Iberia, the murder of a pregnant black woman twenty years earlier, the killing of a man thrown out of a hotel room window in San Antonio, the death of a young woman in a Colorado avalanche in 1967, the unexpected arrival of a pair of hitmen, one an Argentine dwarf, the other a French-Canadian with an extensive record of international assassinations — that they never coalesce into a cohesive or plausible plot.

Burke, however, like Raymond Chandler, is an author one reads not for the plot but for the characters, the colorful dialogue, and the sheer brilliance of his language. Arguably the most descriptive and poetic of all contemporary crime writers, he has been called by more than one critic the poet laureate of American crime fiction. He composes such lush paragraphs of rich descriptive prose that readers can almost feel the humidity and taste the pungent air rising from the page, as the following eloquent passage illustrates:

> That night I dreamed of South Louisiana, of blue herons standing among flooded cypress trees, fields of sugarcane beaten with purple and gold light in the fall, the smell of smoldering hickory and pork dripping into the ash in our smokehouse, the way billows of fog rolled out of the swamp in the morning, so thick and white that sound — a bass flopping, a bullfrog falling off a log into the water — came to you inside a wet bubble, pelicans sailing out of the sun over the breakers out on the Gulf, the palm trees ragged and green and clacking in the salt breeze, and the crab and crawfish boils and fish fries that went on year-round, as though there were no end to a season and death had no sway in our lives [*Black* 174].

Burke generously draws from the broad spectrum of the artist's palette in describing all the subtle hues of the sky: lavender, bronze, magenta, burnt orange, lilac, mauve, pink, plum, vermilion, russet, gunmetal, pewter, bone, and ripe peach. The sound of rain is also a constant fact of life in South Louisiana, but in Burke's sensuous world, rain never merely falls, it clatters, pings, patters, tinkles, clicks, ticks, tumbles and drums. Waterfowl also contribute to the colorful tapestry as herons lift on extended wings "into the lavender sky like a whispered poem" (*Heaven's* 210) and egrets rise "like a scattering of rose petals" (*Cadillac* 259). Everything combines to produce a highly sensual portrait of a place which Burke has called both "an eternal song" (*Heaven's* 121) and "a goddam poem!" (Ringle D1).

Smells are also important to Burke. Whether he's evoking the char-acteristic fragrances of the French Quarter — "You could smell the river, the damp brick walls, a fountain dripping into a stagnant well, the sour odor of spilled wine, the ivy that rooted in the mortar like the claws of a lizard, the four-o'clocks blooming in the shade, and a green garden of spearmint erupting against a sunlit stucco wall" (*Heaven's* 20) — or the pungent odors of a biker bar redolent with the smell of "chewing tobacco, snuff, cigarette smoke rubbed like wet nicotine into the clothes, grease and motor oil, reefer, and a faint hint of testosterone and dried semen" (*Stained* 115), Burke's descriptions transport the reader solidly into the scene.

Although New Iberia is the primary setting for the Robicheaux nov-els, Burke also paints an equally vivid portrait of pre–Katrina New Orleans, some two hours away. He captures both the exotic beauty and wretched seediness of the city, a dual perspective befitting Robicheaux's largely Manichean world view. To Robicheaux, a stroll through the French Quar-ter in the morning is a genuine sensual delight:

> The streets were still deep in shadow, and the water from the previous night's rain leaked from the wood shutters down the pastel sides of the buildings, and you could smell coffee and fresh-baked bread in the small grocery stores and the dank, cool odor of wild spearmint and old brick in the passageways. Every scrolled-iron balcony along the street seemed overgrown with a tangle of potted roses, bougainvillea, azaleas, and flaming hibiscus, and the moment could be so perfect that you felt you had stepped inside an Utrillo painting [*Dixie* 19].

But then "the smell of urine in doorways, left nightly by the homeless and the psychotic," and the "broken fragments of tiny ten-dollar cocaine vials that glinted in the gutters like rats' teeth" remind Robicheaux that New Orleans "wasn't all a poem" (19).

Burke's descriptions do more than merely paint a picture. They often serve as markers or, to use T.S. Eliot's term, "objective correlatives" for Robicheaux's inner emotional state. For example, following a visit to Clete in the hospital, where he is being treated after being severely beaten, the atmosphere mirrors Robicheaux's sour mood: "The air tasted like brass, like it was full of ozone, and I could smell dead fish on the banks of the willow islands and the odor of brine off the Gulf" (*Stained* 108). After killing one of the men who murdered his wife Annie, Robicheaux's initial sense of satisfaction soon gives way to guilt. Burke describes him driving along the highway: "The sugarcane fields were green and thrashing in the wind, and the oak trees along the road trembled whitely in the explosions of lightning on the horizon.... I was left alone in the drumming of the rain against the cab, in the sulfurous smell of the air through the wind vane, in the sulfurous smell that was as acrid as cordite" (*Heaven's* 241). The repeated references to sulfur conjure up the hellfires of damnation, which underscores Robicheaux's sense of moral transgression.

Robicheaux's inner demons sometimes cause him to view the world as "a gray, desolate place without purpose, with no source of heat other than a perpetual winter sun" (*Purple* 332). But he struggles to keep from succumbing to such a bleak view, searching instead for signs of hope and redemption, as the following description suggests: "In the middle of the shower, shafts of sunlight cut through the clouds like the depictions of spiritual grace on a child's holy card" (*Heaven's* 43). On other occasions the life-affirming sunlight is likened to "gold needles," "hammered gold leaf" and "spun glass."

According to the old cliché, everybody complains about the weather but nobody does anything about it. That's certainly not true in the case of the novelist, as David Lodge reminds us in *The Art of Fiction*: "We all know that the weather affects our moods. The novelist is in the happy position of being able to invent whatever weather is appropriate to the mood he or she wants to evoke" (85). Burke artfully employs ordinary meteorological phenomena not only to mirror Robicheaux's inner emotions, but also to evoke a sense of purity and innocence, a note of affirmation his tortured soul senses behind the evil he so often contends with. In his lush sensory descriptions of the land, sky and atmosphere of Southern Louisiana, Burke produces what Samuel Coale describes as "a lyrical prose, a pastoral vision, filled with affirmation and awe, that pointedly contrasts his naturalistic dialogue and savage contests"(147).

The persistent intrusion of the past into Robicheaux's world serves as a potent reminder of time's cyclical pattern, and Burke also finds in nature an appropriate symbol of this phenomenon. In *Pegasus Descending*, Hurricane Katrina bears down on Southern Louisiana, bringing apocalyptic devastation to Robicheaux's beloved New Orleans. Time appears to be repeating itself as the approach of Katrina forces Robicheaux to re-live the terrifying memory of the havoc he witnessed being unleashed on the Louisiana coastline by another deadly hurricane, Audrey, in 1957. Robicheaux has always borne a profound awareness of loss — of youth, of innocence, of departed friends, even a pair of deceased wives. Now, with the destruction of New Orleans, something equally vital in his world has been taken away that reminds him of nature's power to replay the past.

When asked to identify the strongest influences on his use of language, Burke named F. Scott Fitzgerald and Gerard Manley Hopkins. From Fitzgerald he obviously learned about the effectiveness of vivid visual description. From Hopkins he learned something more, i.e., about the power of language to evoke a spiritual realm. Hopkins was a late Victorian religious poet whose works illustrated his belief in the existence of the palpable presence of God in nature. "The world is charged with the grandeur of God," he wrote in one of his most famous poems, "God's Grandeur." Nature to Hopkins was a book written by God which could lead the viewer to a contemplation of the divine. Hopkins's spiritual longing eventually led him on a path first to Catholicism and then later to the Jesuit priesthood. Burke shares with Hopkins not only his Catholic beliefs but also his rare ability to evoke the natural world in strikingly original language whose beauty reminds the reader of the presence of a transcendent power.

The Southern tradition in American writing — represented by William Faulkner, Flannery O'Connor, and Tennessee Williams, among many others — has produced some of this country's greatest literary achievements. Burke's novels, with their focus on the past and its historical, political, familial, and personal legacy, have earned a rightful place in that noble tradition. Gifted with a prose style as lyrical and as descriptive as that of any other author who has written in the genre, Burke has produced some of the most literate and original of all contemporary crime novels.

8

Carl Hiaasen
South Florida

Setting sometimes serves as more than a colorful backdrop, more than a mood enhancer; it is instead the primary inspiration for the work itself, the engine that drives the creation. Such is the case with Carl Hiaasen. Just as a field of golden daffodils could inspire a Romantic poet like William Wordsworth to sit down and dash off a poem, South Florida has been Hiaasen's muse, both for a regular newspaper column as well as a series of comic crime novels. But in Hiaasen's writing, it isn't the beauty of nature that inspires; it is the destruction of that beauty that fuels his creativity.

Florida, especially South Florida, has proven to be a fertile setting for crime and mystery writers. Miami, which Hiaasen describes as "one of the weirdest, most-screwed up places on the planet" (Shea), is a great place to be a writer, he argues, because "it is the best place in America to be a criminal. It is to hard-core felons what Disneyland is to Michael Jackson" (*Kick* 198).

In his book *The Naked City: Urban Crime Fiction in the USA*, Ralph Willett notes that by the early 1980s, Miami had largely replaced Los Angeles in the American consciousness as lotus land, "the main centre for opportunity and easy living" (76). But that dream tropical locale was also rapidly turning into a hotbed of crime:

> Miami, a clearing house for immigrants and refugees was becoming an entrepôt for illicit goods, a city of touts and pimps and middlemen, importing or distributing whatever prospective buyers wished to acquire. Its internationalism would embrace not only cafe society Europeans and, more recently, fashion models but Colombian cocaine cowboys, French-speaking Haitians and the "marielitos" tossed out from Mariel by Castro and described as the most ruthless criminals ever seen in the USA. Many of those involuntary immigrants were

addicts, prostitutes and homosexuals; among the rest were large numbers of petty crooks, usually vicious, and about two thousand hard
core villains who would send Miami's crime figures through the roof
[76–77].

Add to the mix the greedy and corrupt bankers, developers, and politicians who have turned South Florida into "an unbroken panorama of
greed" (*Kick* 360) and the result is a heady brew irresistible to writers of
crime fiction. Among the many authors who have capitalized on the South
Florida setting are John D. MacDonald, Elmore Leonard, Charles Wille-
ford, Edna Buchanan, James Hall, and Laurence Shames. But no one has
used the setting to greater effect than Carl Hiaasen.

Hiaasen loves his native South Florida as much as Tony Hillerman
loves the Desert Southwest, but where Hillerman celebrates the land's
noble grandeur, Hiaasen can only bemoan its despoliation. What permeates his novels is not joy in the depiction of paradise but sadness and anger
over a paradise lost or, better yet, to borrow the title of a recent collection of his newspaper columns, *Paradise Screwed*. "Why," Hiaasen asks,
"did the destruction have to be such complete obliteration of the natural
world without the slightest regard for the land and the water?" (Silet
11). Instead of portraying the natural beauty of a place he calls "one of
the prettiest states in the union" (Silet 16), he paints a graphic picture
of its destruction by capturing the ugliness that has supplanted the beauty.
One of his protagonists' nighttime musings about Miami spotlights the
issue:

> On nights such as this, Stranahan regarded the city as a malignancy
> and its sickly orange aura as a vast misty bubble of pustular gas. The
> downtown skyline, which had seemed to sprout overnight in a burst of
> civic priapism, struck Stranahan as a crass but impressive prop, an
> elaborate movie set.... He wondered what it would be like to wake up
> and find the city vaporized, the skies clear and silent, the shoreline
> lush and virginal! He would have loved to live here at the turn of the
> century, when nature owned the upper hand [*Skin* 310].

A rarity among his fellow Sunshine State residents, Hiaasen is a third-
generation Floridian. His grandfather moved to Florida in 1922 and opened
the first law office in Ft. Lauderdale. Hiaasen was born in 1953 in Plantation, a tiny suburb of Ft. Lauderdale. His world view was influenced by
the dramatic changes he witnessed to the landscape he knew as a child.
The dirt-bike path he and his friends rode on at the edge of the Everglades

became a highway lined with nine shopping malls. To some, this is progress. To Hiaasen, this transformation only inspires outrage and moral indignation:

> I think that Florida's attraction when I grew up is that it's such an overwhelming place to be that it becomes a character in my novels, and when that character is violated by somebody — whether it's a developer or a lobbyist or a tourist throwing a carton of hamburgers out the window they all become a target to me because I just see no greater sin than to come to a place that's so beautiful and trash it out, you know, and so bad things happen to those people in my books [Byrne].

Hiaasen has been writing about Florida ever since his father gave him a typewriter at age six. While in high school he published an underground newspaper. Following graduation from the University of Florida in 1974, he became a reporter for *Cocoa Today.* Two years later he joined the *Miami Herald* as a general assignment reporter. He eventually became a member of their investigative team and in 1985 began writing a regular column. In the early 1980s, he also co-authored three conventional thrillers (*Powder Burn, Trap Line, A Death in China*) with friend and *Miami Herald* editor William D. Montalbano before publishing his first solo effort as a novelist, *Tourist Season,* in 1986.

The most popular and most successful of all Florida writers was John D. MacDonald. In a career that began with his first novel in 1950 and continued until his death in 1986, MacDonald published sixty-nine novels, almost all set in Florida. As early as 1962, in *A Flash of Green,* MacDonald began voicing dire warnings about the dangers of overdevelopment in Florida. He also created one of the most popular of all mystery characters, Travis McGee, who appeared in twenty-one novels between 1964 and 1985. McGee often served as a mouthpiece for MacDonald's ecological complaints. In *The Turquoise Lament,* for example, McGee becomes so angered at the sight of chemical pollutants being belched into the air by a Borden phosphate plant near Bradenton that he invites his readers to write to members of the company's board of directors. His most pointed barbs are aimed at what he sees as the consequences of the short-sighted quest for the tourist dollar which, in his view, has destroyed the very qualities that attracted newcomers to the state in the first place. Overdevelopment has become so widespread in some coastal areas that, McGee complains, "Had I not seen a boat for sale every few hundred yards, I would never have known I was within five hundred miles of salt water" (*Turquoise* 167).

Hiaasen discovered MacDonald's Travis McGee books at an early age; he was especially thrilled to read about a character who lived in the same town, Fort Lauderdale, that he did. In an introduction to a 1995 reissue of *The Deep Blue Good-By*, the first of the McGee books, Hiaasen wrote about his affection for MacDonald's novels: "His [McGee's] bittersweet view of South Florida was the same as my own. For me and many natives, some of McGee's finest moments were when he paused, mid-adventure, to inveigh against the runaway exploitation of this rare and dying paradise" (vi). He also admired MacDonald's crusading spirit: "MacDonald wanted his readers to do much more than see Florida. He seemed to want them to care about it as deeply as he did; celebrate it, marvel at it, laugh about it, grieve for it, and even fight for it" (viii).

Beginning with *Tourist Season*, which appeared in 1986, the year of MacDonald's death, Hiaasen has taken up MacDonald's environmental cause. The novel features a popular newspaper columnist named Skip Wiley who, like his creator, has become increasingly agitated about the "shameless, witless boosterism" (29) that has resulted in excessive growth in South Florida. But Wiley does more than simply complain; he and some like-minded friends form a terrorist group dedicated to bringing the tourist industry to its knees.

They start by killing the head of the Chamber of Commerce and stuffing a toy rubber alligator into his mouth. Wiley described his victim as "the Sultan of Shills, the perfect mouthpiece for the hungry-eyed developers, hoteliers, bankers, and lawyers who have made South Florida what it is today: Newark with palm trees" (24). Then they kidnap and kill tourists, feed an elderly retiree to a hungry crocodile, bomb a golf course, and drop hundreds of snakes on a cruise ship filled with travel writers. They intend to cap things off by kidnapping the Orange Bowl queen during the annual parade. This subversive comic nightmare (later celebrated in a song by Jimmy Buffett entitled "The Ballad of Skip Wiley") represents a kind of apocalyptic wish fantasy for those who dream of restoring Florida to its pre-development past. Wiley's campaign ultimately fails, though not before Hiaasen scores several direct hits aimed at deserving targets of his scorn.

Double Whammy begins like a conventional mystery novel. R.J.

Decker, an ex-newspaper photographer who now works as a private eye, is hired by a professional bass fisherman to investigate his suspicions that a fellow competitor (host of a popular TV fishing show on the Outdoor Christian Network) is cheating by salting the lakes with pre-caught fish. When another pro fisherman is murdered, Decker finds himself with a murder case on his hands. But as usual, Hiaasen is less interested in the mystery than in its potential for satiric exploitation.

The novel also introduces a backwoods hermit named Skink, a 6'6" giant who wears a flowered shower cap over his unruly gray hair and who subsists largely on roadkill. His scary appearance is only magnified when he loses an eye and replaces it with a glass one removed from a stuffed owl. Hiaasen's novels don't really comprise a series. What links them, in addition to the Florida setting, is the recurring presence of Skink, who we learn is really Clinton Tyree, a former governor of Florida. Tyree was a genuine rarity, an honest politician. But when his fellow officeholders banded together with greedy developers to continue working "to surrender every inch of Florida's beachfront to pinky-ringed condominium moguls" (94), he knew he was doomed.

After one particularly painful political defeat, he abruptly walked away from his job and headed for the wilderness. Now he lives in the backwoods, emerging from time to time to perform outlandish acts of environmental terrorism, like shooting at jetliners bringing more tourists to Florida or tossing a dead manatee on stage during the Miss Florida pageant to protest the tragic consequences of waterfront development. (He also takes special satisfaction in using a buzzard's beak to carve the word SHAME into the bare buttocks of one of his successors as governor of Florida.) Skink isn't the murdering terrorist that Skip Wiley was in *Tourist Season*, but like Wiley his outrageous actions, driven by anger and frustration, reflect the helplessness of the outraged idealist.

Skin Tight is a tale of murder and its coverup, but infused as it is with Hiaasen's customary taste for the outlandish, it too is no conventional thriller. The cover-up of the death of a young woman who died during a botched nose job starts to unravel four years later when the guilty surgeon's nurse offers to sell her story to a tabloid TV show. More murders follow, but Hiaasen's main targets here are the plastic surgery industry and tabloid TV shows, as well as shyster lawyers, quack doctors, crooked cops and greedy politicians. Though none of these targets are exclusive to Florida, the setting once again proves to be a fertile environment for their illegal shenanigans.

The colorful cast includes Reynaldo Flemm, the vain host of a tabloid TV show with a reputation for getting beat up on camera (Flemm bears more than a passing similarity to Geraldo Rivera) and Chemo, a 6'9" hitman. Chemo's first murder victim was the dermatologist who botched an electrolysis procedure on his face, leaving it looking like someone had pasted Rice Krispies on every square inch. His efforts to cover up the blemishes with Wite-Out only make matters worse. When he loses his arm to a hungry barracuda, instead of a normal prosthesis, he attaches a working model of a Weed Wacker to the arm, which he puts to inventive uses. The satire may be heavy-handed and the targets pretty obvious, but the madcap results are nonetheless hilarious.

There is also nothing specifically Floridian about the setting Hiaasen employs in *Strip Tease,* a Ft. Lauderdale strip bar called the Eager Beaver. Using such an exotic setting, however, gives Hiaasen ample opportunity to exploit various kinds of sleaze; one of the club's most popular attractions, for example, is topless wrestling in ninety gallons of creamed corn, an activity, Hiaasen assures his readers in a note, that is based on reality. But the real sleaze occurs not on the stage of the strip bar but in the corridors of power. One of the Eager Beaver's faithful customers is David Dilbeck, a U.S. congressman from South Florida. Dilbeck tends to lose control around naked women, and it is the job of his key aide, "Moldy" Moldowsky, to keep him out of trouble. Moldowsky will stop at nothing (including the murder of a potential blackmailer) to keep Dilbeck in office so he can continue to vote in support of important special interests, chief among them the Florida sugar industry. Among Dilbeck's biggest supporters (and the major beneficiaries of his vote) are the Rojo brothers, whose family owns a huge Florida sugar farm (and whose ninety-foot luxury yacht, *Sweetheart Deal,* sums up the happy arrangement they have with Congressman Dilbeck).

The whole corrupt system of influence peddling is exposed under the harsh light of Hiaasen's satire. What interests him above all is not simply the existence of influence peddling, which is rampant among politicians, but how that activity adversely affects South Florida.

> The congressman saw no injustice in the price supports that had made multimillionaires of the Rojos. The grain, dairy, and tobacco interests

had soaked taxpayers for years by melodramatically invoking the plight of the "family farmer." Why not sugar, too? Similarly, Dilbeck lost no sleep over the damage done to the agricultural economies of impoverished Caribbean nations, virtually shut out of the rigged U.S. sugar market. Nor did the congressman agonize over the far-reaching impact of cane growers flushing billions of gallons of waste into the Everglades. Dilbeck didn't understand what the fuss was about. In truth, he didn't much care for the Everglades; it was torpid, swampy, crawling with bugs [320].

In the absurdly ridiculous figure of Dilbeck, Hiaasen has created an ideal vehicle for satirizing all the self-serving, venal politicians who have contributed to the problems facing South Florida rather than devoting any effort to remedying them.

Hiaasen's genius for combining moral outrage with wildly comic invention is fully on display in *Native Tongue*. The crime that triggers the action of the novel is the murder of Dr. Will Koocher, a biologist employed by the Amazing Kingdom of Thrills, a theme park on North Key Largo, to monitor a pair of rare blue-tongued mango voles, an endangered species. The voles turn out to be fakes (their distinctive blue tongues are created by food coloring), and Dr. Koocher's body ends up in the belly of Orky the Killer Whale, a popular park attraction. But the real crime, as is usually the case in Hiaasen's novels, is environmental and cultural devastation.

The main target of the satire in *Native Tongue* is the Amazing Kingdom of Thrills, which aims to compete with Disney World for the Florida tourist dollar. Hiaasen's animosity toward Disney World is well known, his numerous complaints against the Magic Kingdom itemized in his book *Team Rodent: How Disney Devours the World*. Chief among his charges is that "Disney had dignified blind greed in a state pioneered by undignified greedheads" (*Team* 5). Along with the money, amusement parks also produce "traffic, garbage, litter, air pollution and effluent" (*Tongue* 83), all of which are damaging to the environment.

Like its more famous Orlando counterpart, the Amazing Kingdom of Thrills is shameless in its pitch for the tourist dollar. The whole enterprise is a model of deceit, from the fake blue-tongued voles to the tacky nightly panorama of Florida history, where even the most shameful episodes are given a positive commercial spin. (One popular act features breakdancing migrant workers.) The Amazing Kingdom's founder and owner,

Francis X. Kingsbury, honored by the Rotarians as "Citizen of the Year," is likewise a fraud: he's really a mob snitch named Freddie King. "Miami was the prime relocation site for scores of scuzzy federal snitches," Hiaasen wryly notes, "on the theory that South Florida was a place where just about any dirtbag would blend in smoothly with the existing riffraff" (39). In one of Hiaasen's many ironic touches, the winner of the Amazing Kingdom's "Five Millionth Special Guest Award" (itself a fraud, since park attendance is nowhere near that number) is a hitman dispatched by the mob to kill Kingsbury.

The hero of the novel is Joe Wilder, a public relations writer for the park. After learning about the fraud with the voles and the subsequent murder of Dr. Koocher (who had threatened to expose the deception), Wilder sets out to destroy the park and its adjoining golf course, which is under construction (and which will usurp the remaining waterfront acreage on North Key Largo). As he tells Kingsbury, "I'm just sick of asshole carpetbaggers coming down here and fucking up the place" (296). Wilder begins sending out fake news releases announcing hepatitis outbreaks and poisonous snake infestations at the park. In an apocalyptic ending reminiscent of Nathanael West's *The Day of the Locust*, the park erupts in flames and construction is halted on the golf course. At least in Hiaasen's comic fantasies, the good guys win.

And though Skink makes a return appearance in *Native Tongue,* lending a subversive hand to the efforts to stop the development, he is far from the oddest character in the novel. That distinction goes to Pedro Luz, head of security for the park. Luz is a bodybuilder who sucks a steady diet of steroids through an IV tube, the effects of which are dramatic: his body is covered in acne; his genitals are dramatically shrinking; and he is an inferno of mood swings and unbridled confidence. He bench presses mobile homes and when a car parks on his foot, trapping it under a tire, he simply chews the foot off. It was his murder of Dr. Koocher that begins the downfall of the park; in an absurd bit of poetic justice, he himself is killed in an attack by an overly amorous bottle-nosed dolphin.

Hiaasen once declared that "there's nothing wrong with South Florida that a good Force Five hurricane couldn't fix" (Rosenbaum 128). He gets his wish in *Stormy Weather* (dedicated to "Donna, Camille, Hugo and Andrew," all major hurricanes). But he isn't so much interested in wreaking havoc on his fellow Floridians as in using the storm and its aftermath to expose yet more evidence of the environmental consequences of human greed and stupidity.

The devastation left by the hurricane is enormous thanks largely to the destruction of shoddily-constructed homes (150,000 houses need new roofs). Many of these houses were allowed to be built this way thanks to the careless efforts of a building inspector named Avila, who managed to inspect upwards of eighty houses a day without ever bothering to leave his car. He drives past home sites so quickly that contractors have to jog after his car in order to deliver their bribes. After a police videotape exposes his scam, he is demoted to inspecting mobile homes which, thanks to his customary negligent efforts, all get blown away in the storm.

The hurricane damage draws an army of con artists who descend upon South Florida; the destruction is so bad, boasts Avila, that "only a damn fool couldn't make money off these poor bastards" (96). But the horde of swindlers who show up are only the latest in a long line of "low-life hustlers, slick-talking scammers and cold-blooded opportunists" (170) who have been coming for decades. "Every shitwad in America turned up here sooner or later," Hiaasen complains in *Skinny Dip*, "such were the opportunities for predation" (37). Edie Marsh is a typical example: she moved to Florida in hopes of finding a young Kennedy to seduce so she could try to extort a small fortune from his family in return for her silence about the sordid tale of rape and torture she would invent.

Sick Puppy introduces Twilly Spree, another of Hiaasen's avenging angels. The story behind Spree's activist crusade mirrors Hiaasen's own experience: as a young boy, Spree lived on Marco Island, where he fondly remembers collecting ornate tropical seashells along the white sandy beaches. Returning to the place several years later, he is shocked to see the waterfront gone, replaced by a "concrete picket of towering hotels and high-rise condominiums" which cast "tombstone shadows across the sand" (24). In his opinion, "somebody ought to have their nuts shot off for what they did" (228). To make matters worse, one of the main culprits in the remaking of Marco Island is his very own father, who made a fortune selling waterfront property. The whole experience pushes him over the edge. Using a hefty inheritance from his grandfather to finance his efforts, he launches a one-man crusade to right environmental wrongs wherever he finds them.

One object of his enmity is litterers. Spotting a man tossing trash out the window of his Range Rover, he follows him home and later dumps the contents of a garbage truck into his BMW convertible hoping to teach him a lesson. The man, a big-time Florida lobbyist named Palmer Stoat, turns out to be a slow learner. After spotting Stoat littering again, Spree this time dumps thousands of dung beetles into his Range Rover. Witnessing a third littering incident, Spree kidnaps Stoat's wife and his dog, Boodle. When he learns that Stoat is a major player in arranging the construction of a new bridge that will allow tiny undeveloped Toad Island to be turned into a championship golf resort, he decides to use the dog as a hostage to try to stop the destruction of the island.

There is no shortage of villains in *Sick Puppy*: Palmer Stoat, "the boss hog of them all" (125), who will support any cause, no matter how abhorrent, provided the price is right; Karl Krimmler, the project supervisor of the golf resort who sees in nature "neither art nor mystery, only bureaucratic obstacles" (29); Governor Dick Artemus, a former Toyota salesman whom even Stoat dismisses as "an obsequious glad-handing maggot" (122). Separately, each is a ridiculous figure; together they comprise a powerful chain of influence dedicated to preserving not the environment but "the swamp of teeming greed known as Florida" (263). It will take an almost superhuman effort to stop the juggernaut determined to see that Toad Island is dredged, drained, graded, and transformed into the island resort of Shearwater. But once Spree is joined by Hiaasen's other avenging angel, Skink (now wearing a kilt made from a checkered racing flag and sporting a pair of vulture beaks tied to the end of his silver beard), victory is possible. In the end, the bad guys are defeated (in one absurd twist, Stoat is gored to death by an aged rhino), the development goes bankrupt, and the island is saved. In Hiaasen's madcap world, justice triumphs.

Hiaasen tones down the satire somewhat and sets his sights on a smaller target than usual in *Nature Girl*. Here his avenging angel is a protective single mother named Honey Santana whose "tolerance of cretins, liars, and lowlifes had dwindled to zero" (207). Her target isn't the usual greedy waterfront developer or sleazy politician on the take; this one is an irritating telemarketer from Fort Worth, Texas, named Boyd Shreave, a lowly-paid salesman trying to peddle whatever is left of undeveloped Florida to gullible buyers. Shreave interrupts Holly's dinner one night and ends up insulting her when she rebuffs his sales pitch. Vowing to "fix the entire human race, one flaming asshole at a time" (207), she tracks Shreave down and cons him into thinking he has won a free eco-tour trip to Florida. She takes him to an isolated island in the Ten Thousand Islands area of the Everglades named Dismal Key to show him the real Florida and try to awaken his shriveled soul.

At the same time, the isolated island is also host to a colorful cast of other visitors: Sammy Tigertail, a half-breed Seminole looking to escape the corruption of the white world; Louis Piejack, a horny fish seller with lecherous designs on Santana; Gillian St. Croix, a randy Florida State coed searching for excitement; and Lester Dealey, a private eye hired to video-tape in explicit detail Shreave's sexual encounters with his tongue-stud-ded girlfriend, Eugenie Fonda. The motley crew soon becomes embroiled in a series of outlandish misadventures that would shame the inhabitants of Gilligan's Island.

Dismal Key gives Hiaasen an opportunity to sing the praises of the real Florida, the unspoiled land as it existed before man came to exploit and ruin it. Here is a reminder of the paradise that once was Florida: "The vista from atop the poinciana was timeless and serene — a long string of egrets crossing the distant 'glades; a squadron of white pelicans circling a nearby bay; a pair of ospreys hovering kite-like above a tidal creek. It was a perfect picture and a perfect silence" (225). This was the place where the Calusa and the Seminoles once lived in harmony with nature before being killed off or driven away. But the Seminoles get even by cashing in on the casino craze and selling cut-rate cigarettes to the white man. Even Mother Nature exacts a small measure of revenge when a bald eagle drops a load on the hapless Shreave.

Hiaasen's novels offer an ideal illustration of Philip Roth's definition of satire as "moral rage transformed into comic art" (53). Hiaasen's opin-ions about the sorry state of affairs in Florida are well known thanks to his career as a columnist for the *Miami Herald*. And he has always pos-sessed a satiric bent: "Writing satire is quite natural for me, in terms of my outlook on things, which is pointed and confrontational," he confesses (Silet 11). Switching from journalism to fiction freed him up and gave him a new vehicle for expressing his message. He could now transform his anger and frustration into wildly inventive comic novels that satirize the worst of the excesses he had been writing about in his newspaper columns. (He has recently found another popular vehicle for his views in a pair of critically-acclaimed children's books, *Hoot* and *Flush*.) Sarcasm and satire are incredibly effective weapons, especially against politicians: "Politicians don't mind if you get up on a soap box and scream and yell at them. They can take that — but if you're making fun of them that drives them nuts," Hiaasen notes (Byrne). And so his mission is to mock and lampoon as much as possible.

Catholic novelist and short-story writer Flannery O'Connor, describing the challenge of writing for an audience that did not share her religious beliefs, explained her strategy for grabbing the reader's attention: "To the hard of hearing you shout and to the almost blind you draw large and startling figures," she proclaimed (113). The same can be said of Hiaasen, who has populated his satiric novels with large, oversized characters and devised for them outlandish activities. Wild exaggeration and comic distortion are highly entertaining and attention-grabbing techniques. But Hiaasen's gift for depicting the absurd in human behavior in no way detracts from the seriousness of his efforts. The crimes in his books are real; people die, and so does the environment.

That many of Hiaasen's characters and escapades are cartoonish is certainly appropriate in a state ruled by Disney. However, the line between the fictionally outlandish and the merely bizarre is often difficult to determine in a place like South Florida: "It's very hard to beat the fountain of weird news that's South Florida," Hiaasen complains "It's very hard to surpass that craziness in fiction" (Silet 12). Are the phony religious tourist attractions depicted in *Lucky Me* — the fiberglass madonna that weeps expensive perfume, the road stain in the shape of the face of Jesus Christ, the turtles adorned with the faces of the apostles on their backs — real or invented? When Hiaasen insists in an author's note that events like the aberrant sexual behavior of bottle-nosed dolphins in *Native Tongue* and the topless creamed-corn wrestling in *Strip Tease* are based on fact, his readers need to be prepared to accept almost anything as real. Hiaasen is simply fortunate to be blessed with a setting that doggedly defies exaggeration.

The weapons of satire range from the delicate sharpness of a scalpel to the blunt edge of a cudgel. Literary historians usually divide satirists into two main types, Horatian and Juvenalian, named after the two early Roman satirists whose works illustrated the subtle and gentle (Horace) versus the blunt and angry (Juvenal). Hiaasen's fiction definitely falls into the Juvenalian category. Juvenal was a first-century A.D. satirist known for his angry diatribes against the follies and values (or lack of them) of his fellow Romans. He became so angered at what he witnessed around him that he confessed, "It is difficult NOT to write satire. What human being /Has such iron control of himself in this city of evil/As to hold his tongue" (Juvenal 18). His most famous satire, "Against the City of Rome," is a prime example of a work whose setting itself served to inspire the writing. All around him, Juvenal saw examples of human greed, hypocrisy, and folly. He also bemoaned the physical condition of the city where grassy areas were replaced by marble monuments, shoddy construction was rampant, and the streets were crowded with traffic. Juvenal piled example upon example in painting a devastatingly critical portrait of his city.

Hiaasen shares with Juvenal that all-consuming sense of outrage that makes it difficult to remain silent in the face of such pervasive evil. "I need to be mad to write," he confesses (Howard 135). His attitude is summed up in the advice Skink gives Tilly in *Sick Puppy*: "There's probably no peace for people like you and me in this world. Somebody's got to be angry or nothing gets fixed. That's what we were put here for, to stay pissed off" (304). Just as Juvenal found inspiration in the ancient city of Rome, Hiaasen has been creatively stimulated by his Florida setting. South Florida may not be a modern-day Babylon, but it is a place steadily being destroyed by human folly, greed, and downright stupidity. But like all good satire, Hiaasen's novels ultimately serve a constructive purpose; they can be seen, as Donald Westlake has aptly put it, as "God's way of telling Florida it's gone too far" ("Mess").

9

Ian Rankin

Edinburgh

A persuasive argument can be made that the grittiest contemporary hard-boiled crime fiction is currently being written in, of all places, Scotland. Ian Rankin, Val McDermid, Denise Mina, Peter Turnbull, Christopher Brookmyre and others are turning out a steady stream of edgy crime novels dubbed "tartan noir" by writer James Ellroy. Most of the above writers make Glasgow their turf. Ian Rankin, on the other hand, has made Edinburgh, Scotland's picture-postcard city, all his. (Though Rankin shares the Edinburgh setting with another local crime writer, Quintin Jardine, artistically and commercially his novels far outshine Jardine's.)

Edinburgh has been home to many literary giants over the years: Robert Burns, Robert Louis Stevenson, Sir Walter Scott, J.M. Barrie, and Arthur Conan Doyle are all former residents of the city. But few places can boast the concentration of writers living today in Scotland's capitol city. Ian Rankin, for example, lives only two doors away from Alexander McCall Smith, author of the popular No. 1 Ladies' Detective Agency series. They both live within shouting distance of Harry Potter's creator, J.K. Rowling, arguably the most popular writer on the planet at the moment. This unusual confluence of writers living in Edinburgh is one reason the city was selected by UNESCO as its very first City of Literature in 2004.

In *The Edinburgh Literary Companion*, Andrew Lownie identifies over five hundred novels that have featured Edinburgh as setting. However, when Rankin began writing, it seemed to him that the most recent novel to have employed Edinburgh was Muriel Spark's *The Prime of Miss Jean Brodie*, published in 1961 but set in the 1930s. Edinburgh was more than ripe for fictionalizing, and few writers have employed place in fiction more effectively than Rankin. Fewer still have written so extensively about the meaning of place to them as Rankin, who in 2005 devoted an entire book, *Rebus's Scotland*, to the subject of Edinburgh and the Scottish character. For Rankin, setting is every bit as much the subject of his novels as the crimes they describe.

Rankin was born in Cardenden, Fife, some thirty miles north of Edinburgh, on 28 April 1960. Cardenden was a small mining town under-going a slow death as the mines began to shut down and unemployment rose. As a youngster, Rankin's initial literary efforts consisted of writing and drawing his own comic books and composing song lyrics for a non-existent band. In high school he moved on to poetry and short stories. In 1978 he left Fife to attend the University of Edinburgh, where he majored in English with a specialization in American literature. Between 1983 and 1986, Rankin studied for his Ph.D. in Scottish literature, focusing on the novels of Edinburgh-born writer Muriel Spark. While a student, he wrote three novels: a comic novel set in a Scottish Highlands hotel (never published); *The Flood*, a semi-autobiographical story about a young man from Fife who moves to Edinburgh, published by a student cooperative in 1986; and *Knots and Crosses*, which featured as its protagonist a police detective named John Rebus.

Some writers plan well in advance before launching a mystery series. John D. MacDonald, for example, wanted to be certain he could sustain a series, so he wrote five complete Travis McGee novels before allowing the first to be published. And any writer who titles her first novel "*A*" *is for Alibi*, as Sue Grafton did with her first Kinsey Millhone book, has at least a rough plan in mind for additional books. Ian Rankin, on the other hand, not only had no plans to write a mystery series, he was even surprised to discover that *Knots and Crosses* was being shelved with the mystery books. "I was appalled!" he confessed. "I thought, here I am doing a Ph.D., and I'm going to be a professor of English ... and *I've written a whodunit*" (Pierce). Strongly influenced by two famous Scottish novels that both deal with man's hidden dark side, James Hogg's *The Private Memoirs and Confessions of a Justified Sinner* (1824) and Robert Louis Stevenson's *The Strange Case of Dr. Jekyll and Mr. Hyde* (1886), Rankin thought he had written a psychological thriller with gothic overtones. But when the Crime Writer's Association invited him to join, he concluded that it was he who had made the mistake.

The idea of writing a second Rebus novel didn't even occur to Rankin until after he and his wife had moved to London and he had written a pair of thrillers (*Watchman* and *Westwind*). People continued to ask him about Rebus. He began to see that a police detective like Rebus would make an effective vehicle for what he has described as a series of "commentaries on Scotland's present, its foibles and psychoses, the flaws in its character. I'm dissecting a nation" ("Exile").

Rankin lists Anthony Powell's *A Dance to the Music of Time*, a multi-novel series which paints a panorama of English society, as his favorite novel. In twelve volumes published over a twenty-five-year period, Powell chronicled the changing fortunes of Britain's upper class from 1914 to the 1960s. Rankin began to see how he could explore not just a single character in depth, but also a place and, like Powell did, an entire society. "Everything I wanted to say about Scotland," he realized, "I could say in a crime novel" (McCrum). From an inauspicious beginning has emerged in less than a decade the biggest selling series in the United Kingdom (in 1999, eight of the ten best-selling novels in Scotland were written by Rankin) and a rapidly growing international reputation.

Rankin chose the name Rebus for his protagonist because a rebus is a kind of picture puzzle, and as a student of modern literary theory who was "reading a lot of semiotic and deconstructionist nonsense at the time" (*Rebus's* 19) he liked the idea of a book that played games with the reader. (Naming Rebus's boss Watson and one of his trusted colleagues Holmes is another example of Rankin's game-playing sense of fun.) However, the notion of a puzzle, especially a jigsaw puzzle, also explains Rankin's approach to his use of setting in the series. Each book focuses on a different aspect of the city. Taken together, they combine to create a portrait that conveys much more than any single entry can. (Fittingly, a character in *The Falls* is putting together a jigsaw puzzle of an aerial view of Edinburgh. One piece is missing, suggesting that the picture of the city can never be a complete one.)

Rebus is a maverick, never comfortable with the authorities above him. In many ways, he resembles the classic American private eye who follows his own dictates and has his own sense of justice. Rebus is devoted to his job; to a loner like him, it's all he has: "Police routine gave his daily life its only shape and substance; it gave him a schedule to work to, a reason to get up in the morning. He loathed his free time, dreaded Sundays off. He lived to work" (*Let* 97). But his sense of justice is not dictated by his job; justice is for the victims to whom he feels allegiance.

While many readers will agree with Peter B. King's assessment that Rebus's "mixture of doggedness and pigheadedness is endearing," even his friends find the moody and cynical Rebus a hard man to like at times. An obsession with his own personal principles of justice coupled with his independence and contempt for proper police procedure frequently get him into trouble with his superiors. His go-it-alone attitude also exacts a steep price in terms of failed personal and professional relationships. And his failures don't sit easily on his conscience as he occasionally finds himself in tears at thoughts of "all the victims he couldn't help and would never be able to help" (*Black and Blue* 256). All these ghosts "yelling at him ... begging him ... shrieking" (301) produce unsettling guilty dreams which he tries to quiet by heavy drinking, which only leads to other problems. Rankin admits that there is much about the complicated Rebus he himself doesn't fully understand, which is one of the reasons he enjoys writing about him and a key reason why he is such an interesting character for the reader.

The relationship between a writer and his series hero is often a complicated one. This is certainly true in the case of Rankin and Rebus. When he first created Rebus and had no plans for ever using him again in a series, Rankin made him much older — Rankin was only 25 and Rebus 41— and much more cynical than he himself was. "I may share some of my memories with Rebus," Rankin admits, but adds "we are far from being the same person, and we do not inhabit the same Scotland" (*Rebus's* 24). He also confesses that he doesn't entirely like the figure he describes as "this curmudgeonly, old, chain-smoking bugger" (Shields). Nevertheless, he soon became fascinated by his creation, especially as he realized that there was so much that he didn't know about him. Discovering Rebus's hidden layers keeps Rankin (and the reader) interested in this most complicated hero and keeps the books fresh, especially as Rebus continues to age from book to book. (Rankin admits that if he had it to do all over again, he would have made Rebus younger. He is now only a few years away from mandatory retirement, which will soon present Rankin with a real dilemma.)

The tension between surface and what lies beneath it makes Edinburgh, a city Rankin variously describes as "schizophrenic," "invisible," and "hidden," a fascinating place to write about. And Rebus offers an especially illuminating perspective on that city, even though it is often a dark and gloomy place seen through his eyes. Rankin has made it clear, however, that Rebus's attitude toward Edinburgh differs from his own: "His Edinburgh is not mine," he insists (*Rebus's* 24). Rankin considers Edinburgh "one of the best and most beautiful places in the whole world" (29). Rebus, on the other hand, seldom sees its beauty. His experiences with crime and with criminals have given him a more cynical view:

> So that now when he saw beauty, he could do little but respond to it
> with the realisation that it would fade or be brutalised. He saw lovers
> in Princes Street Gardens and imagined them further down the road,
> at the crossroads where betrayal and conflict met. He saw valentines in
> the shops and imagined puncture wounds, real hearts bleeding [*Hang-
> ing* 51].

Occasionally, however, even he is forced to acknowledge Edinburgh's beauty: "Jesus, it's a beautiful city, isn't it?" he is almost surprised to hear himself say in *The Falls* (203). But such tributes are rare and given Rebus's dark view, Rankin knows he "can't put the nicey-nicey stuff about Edin-burgh in the novels because Rebus wouldn't see it" (Kean). Instead he uses Rebus's seasoned eyes to explore the darker side of the city.

Rebus also allows Rankin to explore his own dark side: "Lots of dark stuff comes out through him," he confesses (Kean). For example, during the writing of *Black and Blue*, Rankin learned that his son Kit had Angel-man syndrome, a rare genetic disorder that left him blind and unable to walk or talk. Rankin found himself writing his own despair into Rebus's life. In *The Hanging Garden,* for example, Rebus's daughter, Samantha, is crippled in a hit-and-run accident, which sends him into the same unset-tled emotional terrain as his creator.

Rebus's black moods might become unbearable if they weren't light-ened by his refreshingly sardonic wit. Whether self-deprecatingly admit-ting his mistakes — "He'd had wrong hunches before, enough for a convention of the Quasimodo fan club" (*Mortal* 199) — bemoaning his pro-fessional status — "Another black mark against me. I've got so many, I could play Al Jolson on stage (*Black and Blue* 212) — or accounting for his rep-utation as a hard-drinker — "Teetotal is my middle name.... Trouble is ... my first name's Not-at-all" (*Black and Blue* 165), his suffering is made palatable by turning it into a joke. His jokes offer a glimpse into the Scottish tactic of employing humor as a self-protective device.

Rankin's stated project of using crime fiction to explore the Scottish character coincided with a period of unprecedented Scottish self-consciousness. After three hundred years of English rule, Scotland in the 1970s first began debating devolution, which culminated in 1999 with the establishment of the Scottish Parliament in Edinburgh. Along with Scotland's new autonomy came a rethinking of what being Scottish meant. The Scots were now forced to stop thinking of what they were not — English — and began seriously to face up to what they were, both good and bad. As Peter Kravitz noted in his introduction to a recent collection of Scottish short fiction, Scottish writers were now becoming "more comfortable criticizing their own country than ever before" thanks to "a degree of cultural security moving beyond the see-saw of self-love (in the form of blind patriotism) and self-loathing" (xxxii). Like many of his countrymen during this period of reflection, Rankin began to take a good hard look at the strengths and weaknesses of his country and of his adopted city.

A fifteen-year-veteran of the Lothian and Borders Police in Edinburgh, John Rebus carries a full measure of regret, emotional pain and self-pity. His marriage has gone bust and he's the absent father of a twelve-year-old daughter. He has a strained relationship with his brother, who will later end up in prison for drug-dealing. His main burden, however, is a direct result of his Army experiences some fifteen years earlier. During training for an elite Special Assignments group, he underwent an intense and emotionally punishing ordeal (described in harrowing detail during a session under hypnosis) that pushed him to the breaking point. He resigned from the Army and shortly thereafter suffered a nervous breakdown, which still plagues him with unexpected bouts of weeping. Both that traumatic training experience and the fellow soldier he shared it with come back to haunt him in new ways in *Knots and Crosses*.

Rebus is assigned the case of a serial killer who is kidnapping and murdering young girls in Edinburgh. The story takes an unexpected turn when Rebus's life and work suddenly become entangled. A phone call from an Edinburgh University professor whose specialty is acrostics and word games alerts Rebus to the unusual fact that the first letters of the names of the four victims spell out the word "Samantha," which happens to be Rebus's own daughter's name. Before he can get her to safety, however, she is seized by the killer. Suddenly, a series of crank letters Rebus had been receiving in the mail containing enigmatic messages and small pieces of knotted string and tiny crosses makes sense: the kidnapper is Gordon Reeve, Rebus's fellow Army trainee with whom he used to play noughts and crosses (tic-tac-toe) on the wall of their cell. Reeve is now seeking revenge against Rebus, whom he blames for abandoning and betraying him fifteen years earlier.

The brutal murders by the man dubbed "The Edinburgh Strangler" send shock waves through the city. Such crimes happen elsewhere, the locals insist, not in lovely Edinburgh, a world-renowned tourist destination that is home to the Festival and the Castle. Rebus and his creator, however, know otherwise. "Edinburgh is the perfect setting for crime writing," says Rankin. "It has a split personality — on the one hand it is the city of history and museums and royalty, but at the same time there is this feeling that behind the thick walls of those Georgian townhouses there are all sorts of terrible things happening" ("Tartan").

Dr. Jekyll and Mr. Hyde, which exerted such a powerful influence on *Knots and Crosses,* plays an even larger role in Rebus's second outing, *Hide and Seek.* The novel is filled with references to Stevenson's text, including the pun in its title, quotes used to introduce each chapter, even characters (e.g., Lanyon) who share the same name with Stevenson's characters. But *Hide and Seek* is more than a parody or a tribute to a Scottish classic; it embodies Rankin's attitude toward the present state of Edinburgh.

The discovery of the dead body of a junkie killed by an overdose of tainted heroin is the crime that launches Rebus's investigation. The trail eventually leads him far from the seedy squat where the man's body was found to an upscale men's club located on a fashionable street of immaculate Georgian mansions. Hidden within the club is a subterranean club, named Hyde's Club after Stevenson's villain, a character Stevenson modeled on a local figure, Deacon Brodie, businessman by day, robber by night. Here Edinburgh's elite — its lawyers, judges, politicians, businessmen — can satisfy their hidden base desires in secret. Like Stevenson's respectable Dr. Jekyll and his evil alter ego, the two clubs symbolize the close bond between proper appearance and hidden evil that in Rankin's view characterizes his own city, a duality that Marilyn Stasio describes as "the stern public face of Calvinist probity trying to avert its eyes from the wild thing grinning from the mirror" ("Wonderful").

Thanks to his new reputation as "some kind of serial killer guru" (53), in *Tooth and Nail,* his next outing, Rebus is dispatched some four hundred miles south to assist the London police in capturing a serial killer known as the Wolfman. Though Rebus leaves Edinburgh temporarily behind (as did Rankin, who had moved to London with his wife and family), he can't escape a confrontation with yet another Jekyll-Hyde figure, this time a well-respected prosecuting counsel whose alter ego is a violent killer of young women. Setting the book in London gives Rankin an opportunity to capitalize on some famous locations (Rebus eventually apprehends the Wolfman in a room at the National Gallery; the Wolfman had fled there after crashing his car into the building after circling nearby Trafalgar Square). But setting is largely window dressing in *Tooth and Nail,* not the vital element Edinburgh is in the rest of the series.

Rankin brings Rebus back to Edinburgh in *Strip Jack,* though he and his family wouldn't return for ten years, four of them spent in London, six in rural France. "I loved getting away from Edinburgh," Rankin says, "as it meant that it did become fiction. I wanted to recreate the city as a kind of fictional construct, so getting away was the best thing that I could possibly have done" (Macdonald). When a member of Parliament is among those arrested during a police raid on a local brothel, and then shortly afterwards his wife is found murdered, Rebus becomes involved in an investigation marked by scandal, infidelity, and assorted other crimes. Rankin is still getting accustomed to the genre he had stumbled onto almost accidentally, and *Strip Jack* only hints at the depth and complexity that will soon begin to characterize the Rebus books.

Rankin employs one of Edinburgh's physical curiosities to great effect in *Mortal Causes.* The body of a young man who had been six-packed (shot in the ankles, knees and elbows, a favorite punishment of the IRA) and then shot fatally in the head is discovered in an alley located several levels beneath the floor of the City Chambers building. St. Mary's Close was abandoned in the 1600s because of the plague and eventually built over. The Poe-like setting offers an appropriate gothic location for the grisly killing. (To further emphasize the Poe parallel, the victim hears the phrase "Nemo me impune lacessit," the motto of the killer's family in Poe's "Cask of Amontillado," spoken just before he's shot to death.) But the location also serves as a powerful metaphor for Rankin's recurring theme of Edinburgh's buried past and hidden secrets: "They'd covered the street up and built on it anew: that was the Edinburgh way, to bury and forget" (*Let* 128).

It's no accident that the body is discovered during the annual Edinburgh Festival, the city's showcase event. The contrast between the picturesque celebration and the grisly horror is yet another reminder of Edinburgh's dual personality. Early in the novel, a priest friend points out to Rebus that the beauty of Edinburgh is that "you're never far from a peaceful spot." To which Rebus replies, "and never far from a hellish one either" (*Mortal* 18).

Throughout the series, Rankin often returns to another favorite theme: the connection between Edinburgh's blood-soaked past and its glittery present. In *Set in Darkness*, for example, a body that had been hidden for decades behind a fireplace is exposed during the renovation of Queensberry House, the site of the new Scottish Parliament. The find reminds Rebus of the infamous story of the demented son of the Duke of Queensberry who, on the day in 1707 when the Act of Union between England and Scotland was signed in the house, roasted a servant in the fireplace, possibly the same one where the body was found.

In *The Falls*, the discovery of a small wooden coffin with a doll inside following the disappearance of a young woman leads to the discovery of a series of similar incidents stretching back almost three decades. Past and present intersect when it appears that the coffins were modeled on a group of seventeen miniature wooden coffins found on Arthur's Seat in 1836 and now on display in the Scottish Museum. The connection between past and present is further strengthened when the missing woman's body also turns up on Arthur's Seat. Speculation suggests that the Arthur's Seat coffins are connected to Edinburgh's most famous serial killers, William Burke and William Hare, who in the 1820s killed as many as sixteen people and sold their bodies to an anatomist for medical research. (Present-day Edinburgh has a curiously perverse way of honoring its notorious evildoers from the past: a local lap-dancing bar bears the names of Burke and Hare; another tavern in the city is named in honor of Deacon Brodie, the model for Stevenson's Dr. Jekyll.)

Not all of the buried bones found in Edinburgh connect with the past; some relate more to the present. A pair of skeletons buried under concrete in the basement of a pub are dug up in *Fleshmarket Alley*, though they turn out not to be real but plastic skeletons used in medical-school classes.

Rebus learns that they were being used to scare illegal immigrant slave laborers into toeing the line by showing what would happen to them if they didn't. But the buried skeletons also resonate with symbolic meaning as the murder of a Turkish Kurd immigrant in the novel exposes yet another of Scotland's little secrets, this time its underlying racism and animosity towards unwanted immigrants and asylum seekers.

The crime at the heart of *Let It Bleed* calls to mind the kind of white-collar crime regularly exposed in Sara Paretsky's books. The novel opens with a pair of dramatic suicides: two buddies whose car is being chased by Rebus get out and suddenly leap together off a bridge to their deaths; a recently released convict, dying of cancer, blows his head off in front of a member of the City Council whom he had never met. As in Paretsky's fiction these seemingly unrelated incidents soon mushroom into a complex conspiracy involving some of Scotland's most powerful political figures and prominent businessmen. But things are even more complicated in Rebus's world than in V.I. Warshawski's. The conspirators in *Let It Bleed* have profited from fraudulent business practices, but some of those profits are now being used to build factories crucial to furthering the burgeoning Scottish computer industry. "If bad money is used to good purpose," one culprit challenges Rebus, "can it really be called bad money?" (260).

Rebus is left with a major dilemma: if he makes public the damaging information he has gathered, hundreds, maybe thousands, will be put out of work. And so, like so much else in Scotland, the truth remains buried. In the end, Rebus keeps his silence about the corruption in return for the resignation of Sir Ian Hunter, one of the most powerful figures in Scotland, and a promise that Rebus's police superior will never receive the promotion to chief constable he expected to get.

Ghosts of the past — Scotland's, Edinburgh's and Rebus's — play a key role in *Black and Blue*, a critical and commercial milestone in Rankin's career. The novel quadrupled the sales of the previous Rebus books, bringing Rankin an army of new readers that enabled him for the first time to make a living solely from his writing. The novel garnered enthusiastic critical response and was also the subject of a critical monograph published in 2002 by the Scottish literary critic Gill Plain. *Black and Blue* also signals an ambitious new direction in Rankin's work: "Suddenly I felt more confident that the crime novel could do more than I was doing with it, that I wasn't stretching myself and it was time to do that" (Plain 15).

Henceforth, the Rebus novels would become longer, denser, and more emotionally complex, often with multiple plot lines. Sometimes, as in *The Hanging Garden,* the various strands — a Bosnian woman forced into prostitution, the search for a Nazi war criminal, and the hit-and-run accident that cripples Rebus's daughter — fail to coalesce successfully. But at their best (*The Falls, Set in Darkness, A Question of Blood, Fleshmarket Alley*) the various subplots dovetail effectively to a final satisfying conclusion.

The primary ghost from the past who resurfaces in *Black and Blue* is the infamous real-life serial killer nicknamed Bible John, who terrorized Scotland in the late 1960s. Now almost three decades later, he has apparently spawned a copycat killer dubbed Johnny Bible, who is killing young women in a manner similar to his infamous predecessor. Rebus becomes obsessed with the case, but an incident from his own past also resurfaces to haunt him. In 1976 he was involved in a case in which Lawson Geddes, his mentor on the police force, may have planted evidence to convict a man named Len Spavin of murdering a young woman. Spavin became something of a celebrity after writing a book in prison staunchly maintaining his innocence. After he later commits suicide, the case draws renewed attention with reporters preparing a television show about the case now actively pursuing Rebus with questions about his role in the episode. He also faces tough questions from his own superiors about his involvement. These two cases swirl round yet another crime in the novel, the death of a North Sea oil worker who was tied to a chair and about to be tortured to death. Rather than submit to his killers, he crashed through a window and plunged to his death on the spiked railing several floors below.

Rankin deftly combines these multiple plot lines with Rebus's journeys to various geographical settings — Edinburgh, Glasgow, Aberdeen, and even some remote North Sea oil platforms — to paint his most complex portrait yet of Rebus and of modern Scotland.

Rankin is fond of open endings, and he leaves much unresolved at the end of *Black and Blue.* Bible John himself suddenly resurfaces after all these years to track down and murder Johnny Bible, the copycat killer he resents and calls the Upstart. In the end, he slips away undetected, still out there perhaps to kill again some day. Lawson Geddes commits suicide after sending Rebus a note which seems to exonerate him of blame in the Spavin case. Rebus, however, doesn't himself know what the truth is. His own memory isn't clear enough to allow himself to know for sure whether the evidence used to convict Spavin was illegally planted. The only thing he is certain of is that the voices of the victims — Spavin's, Bible John's, Johnny Bible's — won't let him rest: "As a detective, he lived in people's pasts: crimes committed before he arrived on the scene; witnesses' memories ransacked. He had become a historian, and the role had bled into his personal life. Ghosts, bad dreams, echoes" (368).

Rankin's decision to have Rebus exist in real time as the series progressed has allowed him to make significant changes in his hero's life. His daughter grows from a rebellious teenager into a mature young woman; he has on-again, off-again affairs, first with a doctor, Prudence Aitken, and later with Jean Brutal, a museum curator. Colleagues come and go, notably his young protégé Brian Holmes, who decides he can no longer handle the demands of his job and quits the force; he is replaced by Siobhan Clarke, who assumes an increasingly important role in the series (and comes to resemble Rebus more and more as the series develops). Old friends die, like Father Conor Leary and Jack Morton, who is killed on the job. And though Rebus never fully escapes his inner torments, their nature changes. Early in the series, it was his SAS training trauma and a restless spiritual questioning that troubled him. As the series progresses, however, his torments become more personal as he becomes haunted by his failures as a father, a husband, a lover, and most importantly, as a policeman.

Like other writers discussed in this book, Rankin creates an authentic sense of place. The Rebus novels contain frequent references to Edinburgh's many monuments, historical sites, tourist attractions, and real streets, shops, and businesses, especially its many pubs where, given Rebus's love for drink (and the prominent role they play in Scottish life), much of the action is set. Rankin is deliberately following the example of James Joyce, who said of *Ulysses* that if Dublin ever disappeared, it could be rebuilt again just by reading his novel: "I feel like that about the Rebus series," Rankin notes. "If Edinburgh were to disappear in a puff of smoke, you could bring it back to life using my books as a template" (More). The novels are so place specific that a Rebus walking tour has become a very popular Edinburgh tourist attraction. (Not surprisingly, it ends up at the Oxford Bar, the favorite drinking establishment of both Rebus and Rankin.)

Rankin also creates a vivid sense of physical atmosphere, ranging from Edinburgh's gloomy weather — "Nearest we get to the sun here is when the toaster's on" (*Black Book* 257)—to the yeasty smell in the air from the nearby breweries. We are also never far from vivid reminders of the leaden sky, chilling rains and the relentless north wind: "Ah, the Edinburgh wind, that joke of a wind, that black farce of a wind. Making everyone walk like mime artists, making eyes water and then drying the tears to a crust on red-nipped cheeks" (*Strip* 54).

But Rankin is interested in far more than landscape and weather. He seeks to peel away surface layers to get at the essence of the Scottish character. Rebus himself, very much a product of an environment and culture that privileges guilt and values repression over any display of emotion, comes to embody many of those essential traits. As Rebus notes, Scots are "not very good at going public. We store up our true feelings like fuel for long winter nights of whiskey and recrimination. So little of us ever reaches the surface, it's a wonder we exist at all" (*Mortal* 168). Or, as a friend puts it when Rebus notes that Scots are famous for their sweet tooth and alcohol consumption: "Two more things we're famous for.... Avoiding the issue and feeling guilty all the time" (*Black and Blue* 67).

Over the past two decades, Rankin has systematically constructed a large-scale portrait of his native Scotland. In addition to regularly exposing vital connections between past and present, he has also addressed important contemporary issues related to religious sectarianism (*Mortal Causes*), the economics of oil (*Black and Blue*), politics (*Set in Darkness*), illegal gun trafficking (*A Question of Blood*), and immigration (*Fleshmarket Alley*). In the process, he has achieved his aim of showing outsiders that there is more to his native land than "shortbread and tartan, golf and whisky and castles" (*Rebus's* 165). The glue that holds everything together, however, is Edinburgh, and Rankin's detailed portrait of this complex city remains one of the most effective ever painted in crime fiction.

10

Alexander McCall Smith

Botswana

Although Scotland, as noted in the previous chapter, is home to authors of some of the most hard-boiled contemporary crime fiction, Edinburgh is also home to Alexander McCall Smith, known for some of the gentlest, most humane and life-affirming mysteries currently being written. McCall Smith's journey to international fame as a popular mystery writer is far from ordinary. For one thing, even though he didn't write his first mystery until he was in his fifties, he had already published some fifty books prior to that. What is surprising about this impressive output is that writing for McCall Smith was an avocation, not a profession. For decades he was a professor of medical law at the University of Edinburgh; he also served as vice chairman of the Human Genetics Commission of the United Kingdom and as a member of the International Bioethics Commission of UNESCO. His many publications range from learned tomes on legal subjects (e.g. *The Forensic Aspects of Sleep*) to a collection of African stories and over thirty children's books (e.g., *The Bursting Balloon Mystery*). But it wasn't until he began writing about an overweight African woman detective that he became a household name.

Writers are often drawn to exotic locales and few places on earth are more exotic than Africa. Africa has fascinated authors since classical times. The Africa that is usually represented, however, bears scant resemblance to the real Africa. Too often for Western writers, Africa is reduced to little more than a mysterious region of primitive savages, teeming wildlife and steaming jungles. The place known as "the Dark Continent" is often depicted as a repository of European fantasies and fears with the African landscape serving largely as an exotic canvas for exploration of the

European psyche. The Africans themselves in such works are marginalized or, even worse, dehumanized. In classic works ranging from Joseph Conrad's *Heart of Darkness* to Isak Dinesen's *Out of Africa* to Edgar Rice Burroughs's Tarzan novels, the misrepresentation of Africa persisted.

Given this history, one might ask whether it is even possible today for a white European writer to portray Africa in a positive and non-exploitive manner. Can writers, wonders Brenda Cooper, "avoid the pitfalls, conventions, distortions and stereotypes, the exploitation, objectification and oppression all of which have historically characterised European representations of Africa?" (1). One writer who has clearly demonstrated he can is Alexander McCall Smith.

One problem with much of the popular writing about Africa is that it has been produced by authors who have had very little firsthand experience of the place. Edgar Rice Burroughs, one of the most widely-read writers about Africa, never even set foot there. Others, like Joseph Conrad and Graham Greene, were only visitors for a brief time. McCall Smith has a distinct advantage over most white writers when it comes to depicting Africa: he is a native-born African. Born in Southern Rhodesia (now Zimbabwe) in 1948, the son of a Scottish public prosecutor, he lived there until he left at age eighteen to study law in Edinburgh. He later returned to Africa to teach at the University of Swaziland and while there visited nearby Botswana and fell in love with the country. In 1981 he helped create that country's first law school. He later taught law at the University of Botswana and assisted in writing the criminal code for the country. But his greatest contribution has been the attention brought by a series of best-selling mysteries about Botswana's first female private detective, Precious Ramotswe.

Botswana is one of postcolonial Africa's major success stories. A former British territory known as the Bechuanaland Protectorate, Botswana gained its independence in 1966. Under the wise leadership of Sir Sereste Khama, its first president, Botswana grew from a poor country with only three secondary schools and eight miles of tarred roads into a thriving modern state. Thanks to the discovery of diamonds, it experienced one of the fastest growths in per capita income in the world. In addition to economic prosperity, Botswana has also managed to avoid many of the problems faced by its poorer and politically unstable neighbors and today enjoys a reputation as Africa's least corrupt country.

Botswana gives McCall Smith an opportunity to offer an alternative view of Africa, a corrective to the prevailing images that have been so powerful. Like Walter Mosley in his Easy Rawlins novels, McCall Smith repositions the Africans from the margin to the center of the action. Also like Mosley, he self-consciously echoes some of his predecessors. For example, the opening line of *The No. 1 Ladies' Detective Agency*—"Mma Ramotswe had a detective agency in Africa, at the foot of Kgale Hill"—calls to mind the opening line of *Out of Africa*, Isak Dinesen's memoir of life in Kenya—"I had a farm in Africa, at the foot of the Ngong Hills" (3). The phrase "heart of darkness" (the title of Conrad's famous novella) also frequently recurs in the book. But in McCall Smith's novels, Africa is a place of decency rather than depravity, of civility rather than savagery, of morality rather than mystery; his Botswana is the heart of goodness rather than the heart of darkness.

The gentle and unassuming Precious Ramotswe, a large woman "blessed with generous girth" and the most famous (and only) female detective in Botswana, made her characteristically modest debut in a short story. She was inspired by a large woman in Botswana McCall Smith witnessed one day chasing a chicken and then wringing its neck so it could be cooked for his lunch. "The chicken looked miserable" he remembers. "She looked very cheerful. At that moment I thought that I might write a book about a cheerful woman of traditional build" ("Author Talk"). Fifteen years later he did, but the character of Precious Ramotswe became so interesting to him that he expanded the short story he initially wrote into a novel entitled *The No. 1 Ladies' Detective Agency.* Thus was launched what soon became one of the most internationally popular of all contemporary mystery series. (The novels are now available in upwards of thirty foreign languages).

Shortly before his death, Mma (an honorific term like "Madam") Ramotswe's beloved father sold his large cattle herd in order to provide the money for his daughter to open a business. He was surprised when that business turned out to be a detective agency, but he would undoubtedly be proud of his thirty-five-year-old daughter's success. Though lacking any formal training (aside from reading a manual on private detection she ordered by mail), Mma Ramotswe felt she already had what it took to be a successful detective. First of all, she was a woman and "women are the ones who know what's going on.... They are the ones with eyes" (61). She also felt she possessed the intuitive ability to read people's faces:

"Everything you wanted to know about a person was written in the face, she believed" (7). Soon clients come calling and in her first outing she solves a variety of cases, most of them ordinary problems: a wife wants to find out if her husband is cheating on her; an overly protective father wants to learn if his sixteen-year-old daughter is seeing boys against his wishes; a woman wants to know if the car her husband is driving has been stolen and if so wants it returned to its rightful owner.

A more serious case involves insurance fraud. Hired to investigate a man's claim that he lost his finger in an industrial accident, she uncovers evidence of two earlier successful efforts by the man to sue for damages for the loss of the same finger. But Mma Ramotswe differs from the ordinary crime solver in that justice for her is always trumped by compassion and understanding. When the man with the missing finger confesses that his scam was motivated by a need to support his aging parents and a sick sister, she forgives him as long as he promises not to do it again. Such forgiveness rarely figures in mystery novels, yet it is a fundamental principle of Mme Ramotswe and a key reason for her widespread appeal. Unlike most of her crime-solving colleagues, she looks for the best in people and justice always takes a backseat to compassion.

The most important mystery she solves in *The No. 1 Ladies' Detective Agency* isn't one she gets paid to solve. A young boy, the son of a teacher, has gone missing. Though his father seeks Mma Ramotswe's help, he admits he cannot offer to pay her. She worries that the boy might have been kidnapped and killed by a witch doctor for *muti* or medicine, the continuing presence of which in modern-day Botswana is one of the country's dirty little secrets, what McCall Smith describes as "this heart of darkness" which "thumped out like a drum" (91). When by chance some witchcraft material is found in a car being repaired by her good friend and soon-to-be husband Mr. J.L.B. Matekoni, proprietor of Tlokweng Road Speedy Motors, she pressures the car's owner to tell her where he got it. She tracks down the address and locates the boy who is being held captive in the bush by some shepherds. Her reward for rescuing him is purely personal. The only child of her own unhappy marriage to an abusive jazz musician died just five days after birth. Saving another mother's child gives her pleasure. More importantly, "there was so much suffering in Africa that it was tempting just to shrug your shoulders and walk away. But you can't do that, she thought. You just can't" (230).

Mma Ramotswe is often described as a Botswanan Miss Marple, but there are important differences between the two. Agatha Christie's elderly spinster is a purely amateur detective whose nosiness enables her to solve murders that crop up in the quintessentially cozy English village of St. Mary Mead. Mma Ramotswe, on the other hand, is a professional detective and proud of it. Though she can barely afford the cost, she hires the skillful Mma Makutsi (proud recipient of an unprecedented 97 percent grade on her final examinations at Botswana Secretarial College) as secretary because she believes that if a business wishes to be taken seriously it has to have someone present at all times to take calls and greet visitors. Mma Ramotswe herself reports to her office every day promptly at 9:00 A.M. even though clients seldom arrive until much later in the day because that's what the sign outside her office promises.

Her office, however, bears little resemblance to those of conventional private detectives who, for one thing, don't have to contend with stray chickens wandering in as she does. And bush tea, not bourbon, is the drink of choice in her office. Though Mma Ramotswe feels very much at home in Gaborone, Botswana's largest city, she would be woefully out of place on the mean streets of any other major metropolis. Nevertheless, she enjoys an enviable record of success and as long as she can continue to help others with the problems in their lives, she will be happy.

Mma Ramotswe has only one case to solve in *Tears of the Giraffe*. She is hired by an American woman to find out what she can about the disappearance ten years earlier of her son, Michael Curtin, an idealistic youth who had fallen in love with Africa when his father moved the family to Botswana to take a temporary job. Michael had remained behind when the family left to work on an experimental agricultural project, and then one day mysteriously disappeared without a trace. Because Mma Ramotswe feels a special connection with mothers of lost children, she agrees to take the case. Her first piece of business is to visit the remote settlement where the young American was last seen.

Mma Ramotswe may lack the impressive analytical skills of a Sherlock Holmes, but her intuitive insights would be the envy of any detective. Spotting an old photograph on the wall of the hut where the boy lived, she immediately concludes that one person in the photo, Dr. Oswald Ranta, an economist at the University of Botswana, is evil. She searches him out and questioning him confirms her suspicion that he is lying. "It

141

was so easy to tell," she says. "Mma Ramotswe could not understand why everybody could not tell when another person was lying. In her eyes, it was so obvious, and Dr. Ranta might as well have had an illuminated liar sign about his neck" (190). Who needs a manual of private detection when intuition can so easily sniff out evildoers?

It turns out that Ranta's crime was not murder but rather silence about the circumstances of Michael Curtin's death. The young American had discovered that Ranta was having an affair with his girlfriend. After angrily confronting him, Michael accidentally tripped and fell into a ravine, breaking his neck. Fearful of damage to his reputation, Ranta buried the body and kept silent about the incident.

Mma Ramotswe is far more than a crime solver, however; she is also a healer. During her conversation with Dr. Ranta, she learns that Michael Curtin's girlfriend was pregnant with the American's baby at the time of his death. She locates the woman, now living in neighboring Zimbabwe, and asks her to introduce Michael's mother to her ten-year-old grandson, thus bringing the case to a happy conclusion.

McCall Smith has described himself as a "utopian writer" and his Precious Ramotswe novels as "fables" (Guttman). The books, however, aren't fables of good versus evil; the evil characters are usually not all that bad. For example, there isn't a single murderer in the series. Instead, the books are fables of goodness and as is often the case in fables, the good characters are often almost too good to be true. McCall Smith's description of Mma Ramotswe in *The No. 1 Ladies' Detective Agency* as "a good detective, and a good woman. A good woman in a good country, one might say" (4) sets the stage for the parade of kind and decent characters to follow. For example, in *Tears of the Giraffe*, Mr. J.L.B. Matekoni visits a local orphanage to fix some of their equipment. While there he succumbs to pressure by the pushy Mma Potokwane, matron of the place, to adopt two children, a twelve-year-old girl in a wheelchair and her younger brother, without even consulting his future bride about the wisdom of his action. But when Mma Ramotswe learns what he has done, she tells him that he is the kindest man in Botswana and is as accepting of his decision as if he had simply invited an extra guest to dinner. These people could shame Mother Teresa as far as goodness of the heart is concerned.

In *Morality for Beautiful Girls*, the cases range from the serious (who is trying to poison a member of an important government official's family?)

to the practical (how can the best candidate be identified from among the finalists in the Miss Beauty and Integrity contest in order to insure that the winner brings no discredit to the competition or to her country?) to the personal (how can Mma Ramotswe put an end to the depression which has befallen her fiancé, J.L.B. Matekoni?). As usual, Mma Ramotswe and her assistant come up with solutions to all the problems, using common sense and a certain amount of guile. No one gets poisoned, the most deserving candidate becomes Miss Beauty and Integrity, and J.L.B Matekoni, thanks to the medication Mma Ramotswe secures for him, begins to come out of his depression.

Serious crime seldom figures in the No. 1 Ladies' Detective series, but in *The Kalahari Typing School for Men* crime itself has become all but non-existent. Business is so slow that Cephas Buthelezi, proprietor of the rival Satisfaction Guaranteed Detective Agency (whose ads implore customers to "Entrust your enquiries to a MAN!"), closes his business because things are so boring. Mma Makutsi has so much free time on her hands (even given her additional duties as assistant manager of J.L.B. Matekoni's Tlokweng Road Speedy Motors) that she opens a typing school for men.

Mma Ramotswe has only two clients. One is a man who stole a typewriter from his landlady to pay for his girlfriend's abortion twenty years earlier. Now he seeks Mma Ramotswe's help in tracking down the injured parties so he can make amends for his past. Her other client wishes to learn whether her husband is being unfaithful. When Mma Ramotswe learns that the man is one of Mma Makutsi's typing students who has expressed a romantic interest in her, she has to figure out a way of putting an end to the relationship without hurting her devoted secretary. Not to worry. Nothing ever goes wrong in these books and Mma Ramotswe as usual arranges matters so deftly that no one is hurt, all is forgiven and everyone lives happily ever after.

Crime is also notably absent from *The Full Cupboard of Life*. Mma Ramotswe has but one client, a rich woman who wants to learn which of her many suitors are more interested in her money than in her. But the real problem in the novel is how to extricate J.L.B. Matekoni from a promise he was pressured into making (by the same woman who convinced him to adopt the two orphans) to make a parachute jump from an airplane to raise money for the orphan farm. Fortunately for him, one of his bumbling apprentices is convinced to take his place. In his relief, he finally stops dragging his feet about getting married and the novel ends happily with his long-promised wedding to Mma Ramotswe.

Mma Ramotswe's personal troubles mount in *In the Company of Cheerful Ladies*. Her abusive ex-husband returns after many years and attempts to extort money from her by threatening to reveal that she was still married to him when she wed J.L.B. Matekoni. And then her beloved little white van is stolen. But thanks to her own snooping and the able assistance of a new associate, her ex-husband's threat is ended (she learns that he was already married to someone else when he wed her, which means that her marriage to him was illegal and therefore her marriage to J.L.B. Matekoni is legal after all) and the little white van is located and safely returned to her. The smiling African sun sets on a happy scene once again.

The mystery writer McCall Smith most resembles is Tony Hillerman. Both are outsiders writing from the point of view of characters largely unfamiliar to their readers. Both celebrate a remote landscape of stark beauty, a dry and dusty place rich in emptiness under a vast sky "so wide and so free that the spirit could rise and soar and not feel in the least constrained" (*Full* 4). Both find beauty amidst all of this harshness. The sun may shine mercilessly on Botswana, but when it rises "the trees and the hills and the very earth were golden. It was a beautiful place to be" (*Morality* 202). Rainfall may be rare but its annual arrival is cause for celebration as it magically turns the brown earth green and allows colorful flowers to suddenly grace the earth with their beauty. And finally, both believe that restoring harmony is as important as solving crimes.

Though he lacks the poetic touch of a writer like James Lee Burke, McCall Smith's simple and unadorned prose manages to capture with convincing concreteness the rough beauty of the land. Telling details like the fine dust from the Kalahari that coats everything with a red-brown blanket and the omnipresent smell of dust, grass and wood smoke in the air combine with frequent mention of native trees — acacia, jacaranda, pawpaw, mopipi, mopani, wagenbikkie — and wildlife — hornbills, molopes, hoopoes, louries — to evoke a convincing sense of place.

McCall Smith's description of the traditional culture of Botswana serves a dual purpose: to educate his mainly Western readers about an unfamiliar and often misunderstood land while at the same time using that information as a commentary on the West. By including many simple lessons in civility, proper manners and responsibility, he offers a primer in good behavior aimed at his non–African readership. This led one critic to conclude that Mma Ramotswe often "acts as much like Miss Manners as Miss Marple" (Becker). Indeed, the more we learn about the Botswanan values of respect and responsibility, the more we may begin to regret the lack of such virtues in Western society. Like the satirist, McCall Smith holds a mirror up to Western society that raises questions about behavior that is often simply taken for granted.

Though Mma Ramotswe's comments are aimed specifically at her countrymen, people living far away from Botswana might also benefit from her wisdom:

> It was all very well being a modern society, but the advent of prosperity and the growth of the towns was a poisoned cup from which one should drink with the greatest caution. One might have all the things which the modern world offered, but what was the use of these if they destroyed all that which gave you strength and courage and pride in yourself and your country? Mma Ramotswe was horrified when she read of people being described in the newspapers as consumers. That was a horrible, horrible word, which sounded rather too like cucumber, a vegetable for which she had little time [*Company* 163].

Elsewhere, Mma Ramotswe dreams that in her retirement she will return to the village where she was born to grow melons, sniff at the familiar wood-smoke, and spend the day talking with her friends. "How sorry she felt for white people, who couldn't do any of this, and who were always dashing around and worrying themselves over things that were going to happen anyway. What use was it having all that money if you could never sit still or just watch your cattle eating grass? None, in her view; none at all" (*No. 1* 162).

Although outsiders seldom figure in the action of his books, McCall Smith does employ an American visitor, a woman who once lived in Africa, to sing the praises of her adopted land: "We had found a country where the people treated one another well, with respect, and where there were values other than the grab, grab, grab which prevails back home. I felt humbled, in a way. Everything about my own country seemed so shoddy and superficial when held up against what I saw in Africa" (*Tears* 29).

Though Botswana comes close to embodying McCall Smith's utopian ideal, not everything is perfect in this African Eden. For one thing, mambas, cobras, and other deadly snakes inhabit the landscape, and the wise

Botswanans exercise caution to avoid any lethal encounters. And even Mma Ramotswe has to concede that though Botswana may just well be the perfect place, "it would be even more perfect if the three hottest months could be cooled down" (*Morality* 47). But the country also faces problems far more serious than snakes and heat. Botswana remains a very patriarchal society. When one client expresses concern about whether Mma Ramotswe can be trusted to keep information confidential because he knows that women like to talk, she retorts that "there is a lot of talking that goes on in this country, and most of it, in my opinion is done by men. The women are usually too busy to talk" (*Morality* 52). And for all its relative prosperity, even in Botswana "it seemed as if the reservoirs of suffering were never empty, and no matter what progress was made there would always be people for whom there was no job, or no place to live, and not enough food" (*Company* 135).

The single greatest problem facing Botswana, however, is one that is barely acknowledged: Botswana suffers from one of the highest rates of AIDS in the world. McCall Smith never mentions the dread disease by name, referring to it only as "this cruel disease that stalks Africa" (*Company* 31). Nevertheless its presence is unmistakable. Mma Ramotswe knows one elderly grandmother raising twelve grandchildren orphaned by the disease. Even Mma Makutsi's brother is a victim of the epidemic. McCall Smith doesn't emphasize AIDS more strongly because, as he explains, "The Botswanans themselves don't dwell on it…. They don't talk about it all the time — they're obviously sensitive about it — so there's no reason why I should" (Berlins).

Times are also inevitably changing in Botswana and the old ways are gradually being undermined by selfishness and other assaults on human decency. Mma Ramotswe bemoans the erosion of tradition and vows to do all she can to preserve them:

> There were many good things about the old ways, and it made Mma
> Ramotswe sad to think that some of these ways were dying out.
> Botswana had been a special country, and still was, but it had been
> more special in the days when everybody — or almost everybody —
> observed the old Botswana ways. The modern world was selfish, and
> full of cold and rude people. Botswana had never been like that, and
> Mma Ramotswe was determined that her small corner of Botswana …
> would always remain part of the old Botswana, where people greeted
> one another politely and listened to what others had to say, and did
> not shout or think just of themselves [*Full* 8].

This nostalgia for a lost innocence helps to explain the widespread appeal of McCall Smith's books to an audience seeking refuge from the problems and indignities of the modern world. As Christine Matzke puts it, in a world where "seemingly stable categories are increasingly eroded in this transcultural, transnational day and age, Mma Ramotswe promises readerly respite from postmodern fragmentation and insecurities by offering wholeness for body, spirit and nation" (66). Precious Ramotswe inhabits an uncomplicated world where human dignity and common decency triumph. His books, McCall Smith admits, are about the world "as we'd like it to be; we want to believe that there are people who are kind and decent — and are happy to see such a world exist" (Nayar). It is beside the point to question the realism of his depiction of Botswana or of people like Mma Ramotswe and her circle of friends and family. As with all such exercises in nostalgia, it is simply refreshing to be reminded of the best rather than the worst in human nature.

Because Mma Ramotswe prefers to think of herself as a people helper rather than a crime solver, her adventures end up containing very little in the way of mystery, suspense, or even action. The novels move at the same unhurried pace she does. The minor mysteries that do exist simply allow McCall Smith to celebrate Botswana by spinning warmhearted tales about a charming cast of characters. Readers looking for pure mystery need to look elsewhere. On the other hand, those who are open to sharing simple pleasures with Mma Ramotswe — who, when the rest of the world might work itself into a frenzy of activity, can still enjoy sitting quietly, a mug of bush tea in hand, talking about very small things — will be amply rewarded. It is these readers who have made McCall Smith's quiet and warmhearted novels about a simple woman in Africa an international phenomenon.

11

James McClure

South Africa

Like Alexander McCall Smith, James McClure was also born in Africa. However, the Africa he describes in his crime fiction bears little resemblance to McCall Smith's. Where McCall Smith celebrates the decency and the goodness of heart of the people of Botswana, McClure exposes the human cruelties and injustices of the system of racial segregation known as apartheid that was imposed upon the citizens, both black and white, of his homeland, South Africa.

McClure is a prime example of a writer whose interest in setting extends far beyond landscape and culture. His main focus is on the political aspects of setting, e.g., how life is affected not by physical environment (life lived in a teeming metropolis, say, or in a remote desert landscape) but dictated by laws and rules of conduct imposed by a repressive political system. Whether that authoritarian system be communism or apartheid, the result is that human behavior becomes regulated, constricted and profoundly altered. Apartheid controlled the lives of South Africans every bit as much as the canals of Venice or the wide-open spaces of the desert southwest shape the lives of those who live there.

Apartheid (the Afrikaans word for "apartness") was the law in South Africa between 1948 and 1990, when world pressure finally forced its end. Under this system, all residents were legally classified into one of four racial groups: White, Black, Asian (mostly Indian) and Colored (mixed race). Segregationist laws, enacted to ensure white supremacy, restricted nonwhites in every way, including where and how they were allowed to live, work, and play. Blacks were even prohibited from working in white areas unless they possessed a pass; such workers had to leave their families behind in restricted non-white areas. Consequently, interaction between citizens of different races was strictly limited. Because of its all-encompassing role in daily life, no one in South Africa, white or non-white, could escape its effects.

James Howe McClure was born in Johannesburg, South Africa on 9 October 1939 to British parents and grew up in Pietermaritzburg (the model for Trekkersburg, the setting for his novels), where he attended local schools. Upon graduation from Maritzburg College in 1958, he worked first as a commercial photographer and then as an English and art teacher at a boys' prep school in Pietermaritzburg. In 1963 he began working as a crime reporter for the first of several local newspapers, where he began to cover the police and their activities in the local townships. By 1965, however, he concluded it was time for him and his family, which included his American-born wife, Lorly, and a young son, to leave South Africa and its policy of apartheid behind. He cited two reasons for his decision:

> One, I had a son, James, and I was convinced that anybody who grew up in that environment grew up neurotic because his feelings were legislated and divided. It was a curious world, and I couldn't justify it to a child because children don't accept the answer that it's a curious world. If the son of my parents' servant played with my children in the garden, that was one thing; but if we went to the beach, that black child couldn't come on the same beach. Now how can you explain that to a child? [Carr 28].

Secondly, he felt that South Africa was a place where you could live only if you took sides on the issue of apartheid. So, with only eighty pounds in his pocket, he moved his family to Scotland. Six days after arriving he landed a job on the Edinburgh *Daily Mail*. He later moved to Oxford, England (where his family now included three children), and began working as an editor, first for the *Oxford Mail* and later for the *Oxford Times*. Until his retirement in 2003, he combined fiction writing with his newspaper duties. He died in 2006.

Influenced by the crime fiction of Chester Himes (whose novels he claimed taught him more about Harlem than he ever knew before) and the 87th Precinct procedurals of Ed McBain, he began to see how crime fiction could be an excellent vehicle for exploring the consequences of apartheid in an indirect way: "I have always felt that if a truth exists, you don't have to argue it. You just put it down — people aren't so dumb they can't make up their own minds about it" (Wall 117). A straight novel about apartheid, in his view, almost of necessity becomes an overtly political one. By focusing on a criminal investigation set in a place where apartheid is a way of life, he felt he could convey the experience of apartheid without having to confront it directly. Thus while McClure's detectives go about solving their crimes, Richard Peck notes, "South Africa's recent history passes by in our peripheral vision (often clearer than central vision, as mariners searching for stars have long known). That the history lesson is never intrusive makes it more effective" (45).

It might be useful to compare McClure's work with Walter Mosley's. Both authors aim at exposing the human suffering resulting from what can best be described as institutional racism. Mosley, however, adopts a historical approach, artfully re-creating the past in order to shed light on the present. McClure's novels are more like actual historical documents bearing witness to a way of life in a specific time and place. Apartheid no longer exists. But read today as eye-witness accounts, McClure's crime novels can reveal as much about that dark period in South African history as anything else written during the same time.

In his first crime novel, *The Steam Pig*, McClure introduces a pair of South African policemen, Afrikaans Lieutenant Tromp Kramer of the Trekkersburg Murder and Robbery Squad and his assistant, Bantu Detective Sergeant Mickey Zondi. The mere fact that the two policemen are of different races introduces a complication that exposes some of the contradictions of apartheid. The crime they are called upon to investigate — the murder of a young white woman who was killed by a Bantu method of using a piece of metal to pierce the heart — allows McClure to explore some of the tragic complications of the system within the context of a criminal investigation.

The Steam Pig opens, as many of McClure's novels do, with a scene of characteristically grisly humor. An undertaker, distracted by the beauty of the young woman's body he is examining, absentmindedly sends another body off to be cremated instead of hers. This mistake enables him to make a startling discovery: a small wound under the armpit where a bicycle spoke had been inserted into her heart. Now that it is clear that the woman, identified as Theresa le Roux, is a murder victim, the police are called in. Kramer and Zondi establish that the young woman was a music teacher who had turned to part-time prostitution servicing a quartet of prominent local businessmen. But the case takes on a different complexion (pun intended) when they discover that the woman is not white but colored, or mixed race. This fact casts a whole new light on her death and on her relationship with the businessmen.

The Steam Pig, like a Faulknerian tragedy of race, reveals Teresa le Roux to be a victim of a corrosive system that arbitrarily classifies people by the amount of non-white blood in their veins. Teresa grew up enjoying the privileges of being white in a mixed-race society. However, one day after being hospitalized for tuberculosis, her father was reclassified under South Africa's often bewildering race laws as colored and moved to a native hospital. The consequences are devastating: the father commits suicide, and Teresa and her family now must face the hardships associated with not being white, including being forced to move into a non-white neighborhood. Because of her light skin, Teresa moves away and is able to continue living as a white woman, but her brother's dreams of becoming a pilot are dashed (such jobs are not open to non-whites). He becomes increasingly bitter and eventually it is he who has his sister killed when she threatens to expose his role in turning her to prostitution.

Teresa's life as a prostitute also illuminates another side of apartheid. The four men who use her services are shown to be sexually frustrated by a puritanical system that attempts to regulate sexual behavior, such as by banning magazines like *Playboy* and dictating that sunbathers must keep eighteen inches apart from one another. Things take a bad turn for the men when they learn that the woman they think they are safe having sex with is colored, which is forbidden under apartheid. The gangster who had arranged their private little sex club uses their transgression to blackmail them into awarding political favors to his cronies. Even whites can be victimized by a system set up to ensure their favored status.

The Gooseberry Fool illustrates McClure's skill in combining a complex and satisfying mystery with political elements that elevate the novel to a level beyond mere entertainment. The murder of Hugo Swart, a pious bachelor and devout Catholic churchgoer, brings Kramer to the scene of the crime. However, he is unaccountably reassigned to the scene of a single-car traffic accident in which a man died. Suspicious about his transfer, Kramer doggedly continues investigating both cases until he uncovers a startling connection between the two. In so doing, he also exposes secrets that turn the case into yet another indictment of apartheid.

Kramer learns that Swart was actually an informer hired by the Bureau of State Security (BOSS), a secret South African government agency, to spy on a liberal priest whose political activities are seen as a threat to the regime. Swart pretended to be hard of hearing so he could wear a hearing aid that was actually a listening device that allowed him to eavesdrop on private conversations in the priest's confessional. He gathers no useful information for the government. However, he uses personal revelations he learned from some of these confessions for the purpose of blackmail. Pushed to the breaking point, one of his victims ultimately kills him and then himself by deliberately crashing his car.

The real crime here, however, is the government's: its secret plan to spy on its citizens directly led to a crime that left two men dead, one of them an innocent victim of a questionable government scheme gone bad. Earlier in the novel, a black doctor quoted to Kramer the Roman writer Juvenal's famous warning about the abuses arising from lack of proper oversight — *Quis custodiet ipsos custodes?* or "Who shall guard the guard?" (135). Though Kramer later mangles the Latin when he quotes it to Zondi (*quis pus custard et*), there is no mistaking its dire implications in this case.

Sadly, there is another innocent victim. The prime suspect in Swart's murder is his Bantu houseboy, Thomas Shabalala, who has suddenly gone missing. Even Kramer concedes he is a likely candidate, reasoning that "inside every wog was this big sense of outrage and all you needed to do was add a touch more and the whole lot went up" (17). Assigned to investigate Shabalala's whereabouts, Zondi learns that the man fled not because of guilt but out of concern for his family, who under apartheid laws were arbitrarily being relocated. He is hiding not to escape a murder charge but to avoid the authorities who have total control over the movement of black Africans in and out of white areas: "Zondi knew that at the stroke of a clerk's pen, a man could be endorsed out of a city in which he was born to a homeland hundreds of miles away" (75).

While searching for Shabalala, Zondi witnesses what is called a Black Spot eviction, a scene of utter horror as an entire community is bulldozed and the residents shipped elsewhere, usually to a less desirable area. This community tragedy is compounded when the innocent Shabalala is killed while riding in Zondi's car, which crashes as he attempts to elude a car driven by government secret agents following him. Sadly, this is yet one more fatal chain of events set into motion by the climate of fear and suspicion engendered by apartheid.

The Sunday Hangman focuses on a single consequence of South Africa's political system rather than on its deleterious effect on the daily lives of its citizens. A body is found hanging from a tree in an isolated picnic area, an apparent suicide. But dogged investigation by Kramer and Zondi determines that the man was murdered; it also uncovers a series of similar incidents in which victims were killed by hanging. However, *The Sunday Hangman* is more than a conventional serial killer novel. The murderer is revealed to be an Afrikaner farmer whose son was hanged by the government. Becoming increasingly obsessed with his son's death, he sought revenge by hanging the man who testified against his son; he later selected other victims to hang in order to determine for himself whether his son's execution was the quick and painless death the government authorities claimed.

McClure uses this individual's campaign of revenge and his obsession with hanging as a commentary on the South African government's own practice. Kramer learns, for example, that the number of hangings in South Africa increased by 600 percent between 1947 and 1970 (225), making the country a world leader in executions. However, due to the rigidly restrictive nature of apartheid, the government also became increasingly obsessed with censorship, secrecy, and subterfuge, refusing to allow any information about hanging to be made public. This policy only fueled the killer's obsession to learn more, which he did, in the process deluding himself into thinking he was no more a murderer than the state executioner. Oddly enough, given their highly critical portrayals of apartheid, the only one of McClure's novels to be officially banned in South Africa was *The Sunday Hangman*, which ran afoul of the government's restrictions against disclosing anything related to the subject of prisons and hanging.

Like many of McClure's novels, *Snake* opens in dramatic fashion. An exotic dancer known as Eve is killed, although it is unclear whether by the pet python she uses in her act which is wrapped around her or by the unidentified man for whom she was giving an after-hours private performance in her dressing room. Kramer and Zondi also have a second crime to solve, a series of robberies and murders of small-time shopkeepers in Peacevale, a black township. It turns out that the two crimes are not related and neither has the kind of connection to apartheid that characterized the crimes in the earlier books in the series.

Nevertheless, McClure still manages to include some pointed reminders of the daily injustices and indignities of life under apartheid. When a colleague notes that the murders in the black township haven't been reported in the newspapers, Kramer explodes: "What's news to them? You tell me. Another coon killed in Peacevale? Hell, no. That happens all the time — that's not news. But let a Monday Clubber lift a bottle of sherry in a supermarket, and they bloody crucify her on headlines so wide" (21). And when a teacher politely asks if his class of black schoolchildren can view a wildlife film being shown in the theater at the Trekkersburg Natural History Museum, he is turned down by an official who reminds him that the film is "For Whites Only." Even though the theater is only a quarter full and the teacher offers to have the children stand in the back, rules are rules in South Africa.

Like *Snake, The Blood of an Englishman* doesn't feature a crime that has anything specifically to do with apartheid: the crime in question here is the murder of one Englishman visiting South Africa by another, a long-time resident of the country who killed his former RAF colleague to prevent him from exposing his complicity with the Nazis during World War II. Nevertheless the novel still adds to our understanding of the daily experience of life under apartheid. For example, even the simple matter of buying an atlas as a reward for his children's success in school is complicated for Zondi by racism. The store clerk, lacking any understanding of why a black man like Zondi might want such an expensive book, tries to steer him to another purchase. Only Zondi's fabrication that he's buying the book for his white boss satisfies the clerk: "It wasn't a very honest way of going about things, " Zondi concedes, "but often it was much simpler" (206).

A visit to Zondi's home also highlights the dramatic gap in the standard of living between blacks and whites in South Africa. Zondi, his wife, Miriam, and their five children live in a cramped two-room concrete-block home in Kwela Village, a black township surrounded by a high security fence. The thousands of homes there are identical; the only feature that distinguishes Zondi's residence from the others is the path in front carefully edged with condensed milk tins. The homes have no electricity; only a few street lamps and the residence and office of the white superintendent have power. Against the odds, Zondi's resourceful wife has made a determined effort to beautify the house as best she can: she has carefully drawn lines in the dirt to give the effect of a plank floor and has taken pains to fashion a lacy tablecloth of cleverly scissored newspaper. McClure never comments on the stark living conditions Zondi is forced to live under; as with so much else in his novels, he trusts his readers to conclude for themselves how the demeaning restrictions of apartheid penetrate into every aspect of life.

The murder of a Naomi Stride, a prominent South African writer, brings apartheid back to the center of the action in *The Artful Egg*. Though her novels (like McClure's) enjoy an international reputation for penetrating "to the very heart of the tragedy of apartheid" (39), they have been banned as subversive in South Africa because of their sympathetic portrayal of blacks. Even though it eventually turns out that she was murdered more for her money than her politics, her killer is revealed to be a veteran of a militia group who gunned down terrorist blacks in neighboring Rhodesia and who hates Stride as a "terr-loving bitch."

A second death, which turns out to have no connection to Naomi Stride's murder, also serves as an oblique commentary on the system. The wife of retired Major Willem Zuidmeyer of the South African Police Security Bureau has died as result of a fall in her bathtub. But since Zuidmeyer had earned a reputation as "Many a Slip" thanks to a history of bad luck with political prisoners who died "accidentally" while in his custody (including three who succumbed after slipping on soap in the shower), Kramer and Zondi have their suspicions. It turns out that Zuidmeyer's wife was inadvertently killed by their son, who intended to kill his father but whose plan was foiled when his mother unexpectedly stepped into the tub before her husband. The son had become so angered by his father's brutal treatment of his mother (he routinely took out his frustration on her after being reprimanded after yet another of his accidents) that he set out to kill him. Rather than face prosecution, the son jumps to his death from a tenth-story window with his father looking on just as a pair of political detainees in his father's custody had done years earlier. The political becomes personal as the brutality aimed at the powerless that is engendered by the political system comes back to destroy the perpetrator's own family.

One of McClure's complaints about much South African fiction written about apartheid, including novels by such luminaries as Alan Paton and Nadine Gordimer, is that it is humorless. Humor is an essential part of life, McClure argues; when he recalls life in South Africa, he says, "I always hear laughter as well as sobbing" (Wall 116). For McClure, humor helps rather than hinders treatment of a serious subject like apartheid. And so his novels are filled with humor, ranging from comic situations to one-liners, most of them from the irreverent mouth of Kramer.

His most inspired comic creation is Ramjut Pillay, the lecherous Indian postman who longs to emulate Mahatma Gandhi's *brahmacharya* experiments in self-control, if only he could find a woman willing to lie naked beside him. It is he who discovers the naked body of the dead Naomi Stride. He flees the scene only to realize later that he has taken her mail with him. When he reads one letter that appears to contain a threatening message, rather than bring it to the police, he grabs his pipe and magnifying glass and sets off like Sherlock Holmes to solve the crime. His bumbling efforts eventually land him in a mental hospital where he is suspected of suffering from delusions. His comic misadventures add little to the plot, though they add immeasurably to the overall entertainment of the story. Equally important, his character contributes its own share of indirect commentary on apartheid. A visit to the corrugated lean-to he lives in in the shanty town reserved for Asians gives us an insight into the living conditions non-whites are forced into. And when a cashier places his change on the counter so as to avoid any contact with his fingers, we also learn how much apartheid diminishes the humanity of its victims.

The final entry in the series, *The Song Dog,* appeared in 1991, two decades after the first, *The Steam Pig.* Set in 1962, it is a prequel which lays out the roots of the relationship between Kramer and Zondi. Kramer has been sent to a remote province in Northern Zululand some two hundred miles from Trekkersburg to assist in the investigation into the death of a popular local police officer killed in a bomb attack. He is assigned the case because the officer who normally would have been in charge is busy with another matter, tracking down a troublemaker named Nelson Mandela. Kramer doesn't recognize the name and Zondi dismisses him as only "some Xhosa." However, even this fleeting reference to the man who would become the face of resistance to apartheid serves as a powerful reminder of its presence. It is also ironic that it is because of Mandela that Kramer meets his future partner.

Early on, Kramer spots a "cheeky-looking Zulu" sauntering in jauntily "like a bloody Chicago gangster" (19), even though apartheid laws forbid blacks from watching gangster films for fear they will get ideas. He dubs the man "Short Arse" and decides to keep a close eye on him. One night, he narrowly escapes being killed by a man he is following thanks to the fortuitous intervention of "Short Arse," who identifies himself as Mickey Zondi. He explains that he too is a Trekkersburg policeman who has been working undercover in an attempt to locate his cousin, Matthew Mslope, who is wanted for raping and killing three nuns and burning their mission school down. Zondi is also a product of that same school where the white nuns taught the black children that they were the equal of any man and could achieve anything they wanted. But apartheid turned Mslope into an embittered killer who took out his rage on "those stupid, kind women, who believed all men were brothers" (180). Now Zondi must track down and kill his cousin.

Even though Kramer is a loner who won't even work with white officers unless he's forced to, he partners up with Zondi in a relationship that will last for the next two decades. *The Song Dog* fills in a great deal of background information about both characters. We learn how Kramer first meets his longtime lover, the Widow Fourie, and in a wonderfully comic scene how Zondi meets his wife, Miriam. We also witness how the two men quickly develop both a close personal and a working relationship that will prove to be an ongoing rebuke to apartheid.

Kramer and Zondi's friendship calls into question the basic premise of racial separation and white supremacy underlying apartheid by demonstrating that a black man and a white man can work together as equals. Kramer is not out to demonstrate his openmindedness about race. He has no use for liberals and employs demeaning racial epithets as freely as any of his countrymen; he routinely refers to blacks as coons, wogs, and kaffirs. But his racist words don't blind him to a recognition that blacks are neither better nor worse than whites. Kramer isn't introspective or reflective enough to stop and analyze his feelings on the subject of race or his attitude toward apartheid. But his actions are revealing. In *The Artful Egg*, for instance, he spots a man drive off without paying for the newspaper he has taken from a poor Indian newsboy. He goes out of his way to follow the man's car, stop him and handcuff his hands to the steering wheel before driving off. As with his attitude toward Zondi, McClure lets Kramer's actions speak for him.

One reason Kramer and Zondi work together so effectively professionally is that they both bring individual strengths to the partnership. Kramer is doggedly persistent when it comes to pursuing answers. For his part, Zondi is able to go places and talk to people that Kramer can't. He knows how to talk to the black cooks, maids, houseboys, and the like who often prove to be valuable sources of important information. Having himself worked as a houseboy before becoming a policeman, he also has a perspective on whites that is valuable. He is fluent in several languages, including Afrikaans, English, Zulu, Xhosa and Sesuto. Finally, as a product of South Africa's segregated school system, where textbooks were scarce in black schools, Zondi has of necessity been forced to develop a computer-like memory, which frequently comes in very handy.

In public, the two play the roles dictated by their racist society. Zondi shuffles a few steps behind Kramer in a show of deference to his "superior." Kramer has to be careful about publicly praising Zondi and lets others assume he's just his driver or, worse, his "pet monkey" (*Snake* 192). When Kramer sends Zondi on an important solo mission and tells him to take their car, Zondi would like to thank him. But because another white officer is present, "instead he gave a sulky shrug and shuffled off back to the garage," prompting the white officer to mistakenly conclude, "like bloody children they are, always wanting you to help them" (*Gooseberry* 21).

But in private, it's an entirely different matter. Here, genuine affection colors their relationship. They are often shown grinning or laughing together as if they were enjoying a private joke, which of course they are. Only individuals comfortable enough with their racial differences could joke as Kramer does when he asks Zondi to give him the chocolate ice lollipop he's carrying: "I'll have the chocolate one," he says. "Can't have you turning into a bloody cannibal or something," he explains (*Gooseberry* 8). When Zondi is seriously injured in *The Gooseberry Fool*, Kramer's concern for his partner exposes the depth of his genuine affection for his friend. He even gives money to Zondi's wife, though he disguises his generosity by claiming that the money is a Christmas bonus her husband hadn't picked up.

McClure includes no speeches about brotherhood and he never lets either of his characters reflect too much about what the other means to him. Their affection for each other is largely instinctual. When Zondi's injured leg threatens to cost him his job, Kramer does all he can to cover for him: "Kramer knew where it mattered most — in his gut — that Zondi needed his backing all the way" (*Sunday* 52). When on another occasion Zondi fears that Kramer might go through with his threat to resign from the force, McClure writes: "If the Lieutenant left the force, life would be — Zondi stopped thinking, lit a cigarette, and started to pace again" (*Blood* 153). The message is clear yet unspoken.

It is certainly no accident that McClure chose to set the action of *Song Dog* in 1962, the year Nelson Mandela was arrested and sent to prison for the next twenty-seven years. His release in 1990 followed by his election four years later as South Africa's first black president brought an end to apartheid. Instead of dealing with its demise, McClure returns to its early days. Having lived in exile for so long, he admittedly hadn't kept up with developments in his native country and consequently went back to a period he was more confident about. But the end of apartheid would also bring termination to the Kramer and Zondi books. In a very real sense, McClure had no reason to continue the series; the novels had served their purpose in shedding light on a cruel and unjust system that was now being dismantled. Also, the conditions that had inspired the creation of the novels no longer existed, and the Kramer and Zondi novels are unimaginable without apartheid.

South Africa as a geographical place still of course exists unaltered. But with the political system changed, life is dramatically different than it was during the decades of apartheid. However, a contemporary reader wishing to go back in time and understand something about the nature of life under that system might well begin with McClure's artfully subversive novels about a pair of South African police detectives.

12

Maj Sjöwall and Per Wahlöö

Stockholm

Urban settings are common in crime fiction, where the city is often depicted as a center of corruption and decay, a place where crime, pollution, and general degradation of life are concentrated. What is unusual about the urban setting employed in a series of ten crime novels by the Swedish husband-and-wife team of Maj Sjöwall and Per Wahlöö is how they portray it as a construct of a political system they vigorously denounce.

Sjöwall and Wahlöö were each working as journalists in Sweden when they first met. Finding themselves both politically and romantically aligned, they soon entered into two fruitful partnerships: they married and then began collaborating on a groundbreaking series of police procedurals with an overtly ideological purpose. For them, setting was far from incidental; it was the center of their political agenda. They were drawn to crime fiction as a way of critiquing what they viewed as fundamental flaws in Swedish society beginning in the mid–1960s. As avowed Marxists, their stated intention was to "use the crime novel as a scalpel cutting open the belly of an ideological pauperized and morally debatable so-called welfare state of the bourgeois type" (Lundin 1014).

Sjöwall and Wahlöö envisioned their project not as a series of ten separate books but as a single epic novel numbering exactly three hundred chapters. (Either through oversight or for some other unexplained reason, only eight of the novels have thirty chapters; *The Locked Room* contains only twenty-eight, *The Terrorists* twenty-nine.) There would be no more than ten books, a prescient decision as Wahlöö died in 1975 after completion of the final volume. Before beginning, they carefully plotted each of the novels. Then they wrote the books together, penning alternate chapters. The result is a well-organized series of seamlessly written novels that rank among the finest police procedurals ever produced. But what distinguishes their work above all is the skillful way they use the crime novel to both mirror and critique the society where the action takes place.

Unlike most series, which are usually open ended and often static in terms of character development, the Beck series (named after the main character, Martin Beck) incorporates the notion of change from the very beginning. Characters age, suffer expanding waistlines and receding hairlines, develop new friendships and face life-changing experiences, including divorce, serious injury, and even resignation from the force. Events are carefully dated as the series moves forward chronologically from the summer of 1964 to January 1975. Each novel also builds upon an awareness of earlier cases; in *Cop Killer,* for example, two murderers from previous cases are among the prime suspects in the unsolved killing of a woman. All of this lays the effective groundwork for a gradually unfolding exposé of the changes that in the authors' acid view were destroying Sweden.

Like Ed McBain's 87th Precinct novels (which were introduced to Swedish readers in translations done by the Wahlöös), Sjöwall and Wahlöö's series focuses on a group protagonist, members of Sweden's National Homicide Squad. The center of the group is Chief Inspector Martin Beck, a melancholy man whose disintegrating marriage is one of many ongoing personal stories in the series. (Beck's dour demeanor was effectively captured by Walter Matthau in the 1974 film version of *The Laughing Policeman.*) Other members of the squad include Lennart Kollberg, a thoughtful and sensitive man who emerges as the conscience of the group; Fredrik Melander, who never forgets any detail he has seen or heard or read and whose stoical demeanor "in no way challenged the hypothesis that the worst bores often made the best policemen" (*Laughing* 55); and Gunvald Larsson, an ill-tempered individual whom even his colleagues consider a thug. Comic relief is provided by radio patrolmen Karl Kristiansson and Kurt Kvant, a pair of clumsy Keystone Cops whose bungling antics often inadvertently thwart their colleagues' best efforts.

The first several books in the series are fairly conventional in their approach to the genre. Beck and his colleagues solve the murder of a female

American tourist whose body is discovered in a channel (*Roseanna*), appre-
hend the sex-murderer of several young girls (*The Man on the Balcony*) and
in the Edgar Award–winning *The Laughing Policeman* solve the puzzling
murder of nine passengers gunned down on a bus. In each case, the police
are portrayed as dedicated and hardworking professionals who methodi-
cally join together in pursuit of a solution to the crime.

As the series develops, a key issue that emerges is a dramatic change
in the police force and its role in society. The authors focus on what they
view as (a) a serious decline in the quality of the police as a result of the
nationalization of the force in 1965 (applicants to the police academy now
need only a D average and the average IQ of patrolmen in Stockholm
drops to 93), and (b) a dramatic rise in violent tactics. Situations that formerly could be settled by a single man "equipped with a lead pencil and
a pinch of common sense" now require a busload of policemen equipped
with automatics and bulletproof vests (*Locked* 56).

The decline is viewed mainly through the eyes of Lennart Kollberg,
the conscience of the group. As he witnesses police tactics and philosophy
change and begins to hear "the rats of fascism pattering behind the wain-
scoting" (*Locked* 57), he concludes that he can no longer remain a policeman. After twenty-seven years on the force, he submits a letter of
resignation announcing that he has become so ashamed of his profession
his conscience would no longer permit him to practice it.

Kollberg's malaise and growing sense of alienation from his profession parallels the police's increasing alienation from the rest of society and
mirrors conditions that in the authors' view are afflicting the country at
large. Unhappiness and discontent have resulted in an epidemic of drug
addiction, on the one hand, and a shocking rise in the suicide rate on the
other. Things are falling apart and the fabric of Swedish society is being
destroyed.

Urban ills are familiar to readers of crime fiction, where the city is
regularly portrayed as a place of darkness and evil. Stockholm is no exception. Gunvald Larsson calls Stockholm "an insane city in a country that's
mentally deranged" (*Abominable* 208). To Për Mansson, his colleague from
Malmö (where the Wahlöös lived, some 360 miles from Stockholm), "the
Venice of the North was more or less equivalent to the Gates of Hell" (*Fire*
152). However, where in most novels the city's crime and deprivation can
be attributed to economic conditions, in Sjöwall and Wahlöö's view the

causes are political, the result of Sweden's misguided and mismanaged welfare state. For them, Stockholm is a symbol of the negative changes wrought by what they denounce as a "catastrophic philosophy" (*Balcony* 122).

One of the most dramatic of all changes is physical, as the city's landscape is transformed under the new government. Irreplaceable old apartment buildings give way to sterile office monstrosities; lively neighborhoods are reduced to rubble. "Behind its spectacular topographical facade and under its polished semi-fashionable surface" the authors complain, "Stockholm had become an asphalt jungle" (*Murder* 82). The many ill-advised changes result in a nightmarish picture in which the inner city is reborn as "a clamorous, all but impassable construction site from which the new city slowly and relentlessly arose with its broad, noisy traffic arteries, its shining facades of glass and light metal, its dead surfaces of flat concrete, its bleakness and its desolation" (*Abominable* 45).

The physical changes also result in devastating human consequences, with the city's hard naked surfaces of metal, glass, and concrete embodying the dehumanization that inevitably accompanies the changes. As Robert P. Winston and Nancy C. Mellerski note in a chapter devoted to the Beck series (aptly titled "Brave New Sweden") in their book, *The Public Eye: Ideology and the Police Procedural,* Sjöwall and Wahlöö combine the use of landscape with their ideological aims in order to create "a moral ecology of Sweden" (21). Crime increases; drug trafficking flourishes; the suicide rate rises; homelessness abounds. The main culprit, as the authors see it, is "the so-called Welfare State" which "wore down the weak-willed and the maladjusted and drove them to senseless actions" (*Murder* 121).

Another measure of the deteriorating conditions is reflected in the changing nature of the crimes in the series. Whereas the crimes in the early books are committed by individuals for the usual pathological reasons, by the time of *Murder at the Savoy* things begin to take on a different hue. Prominent Swedish businessman Viktor Palmgren is gunned down while having lunch in one of Sweden's most fashionable restaurants. Beck's investigation turns up damaging information about Palmgren, which exposes the complicity of the government in his profitable trade in international arms sales. That Palmgren's killer turns out only to be a disgruntled former employee in no way blunts the authors' point about the uneasy alliance between the government and big business, which will continue uninterrupted under the direction of Palmgren's business associate.

Things become even worse in *The Abominable Man,* where the killer turns out to be an angry ex-policeman who blames the police for the death of his wife, who died of diabetic shock while being held in police custody by mistake. He begins by exacting revenge against the man he holds most responsible, a chief inspector known as the "abominable man" for his brutal tactics. During a bloody shootout at the end of the novel, he kills several more policemen, including the clumsy Kvant, and seriously wounds Beck. The disorder that is sweeping Sweden now has poisoned even its sworn defenders.

The Locked Room opens with a bank robbery during which the robber, a woman, shoots and kills a man who tries to stop her. We later learn that the woman, a single mother struggling to get by, was driven to crime by economic conditions. The relationship between poverty and crime is well known. But Sjöwall and Wahlöö make it clear that the cause of the woman's dire economic situation can ultimately be traced to the social and political system they despise. She desires to get herself and her daughter out of Sweden, for she "had begun to hate this society, which boasted of a prosperity actually reserved for a small privileged minority while the great majority's only privilege was to keep moving on the treadmill that turned the machinery" (199). In her view, robbing a bank provided the quickest solution to her problem.

Another example of a crime being attributed to the failures of the welfare state rather than to the individual can be found in *The Terrorists.* Eighteen-year-old Rebecka Lind is a naive flower child frustrated by the harsh demands of life in the new city. When the welfare system fails her in numerous ways, in desperation she shoots and kills the prime minister as he walks up the stairs to a church. (A prophetic act: in 1986, Swedish prime minister Olaf Palme was shot and killed by a single gunman as he and his wife strolled along the street after leaving a Stockholm theater.) In a passionate defense of the young woman, her defense attorney castigates the system and its exploitation of the powerless: "On not one single occasion has society, or the philosophy that created it, given her any help or offered her its understanding" (285). Arguing that hers was a political act, he indicts those "who from a lust for power and financial gain have led their peoples into an abyss of egoism, self-indulgence and a view of life based entirely on materialism and ruthlessness toward their fellow human beings" (286). In the end the young woman is sent to a mental institution, where she later commits suicide by banging her head against a wall.

The early books in the series contain only isolated instances of the kind of political commentary that would become more and more insistent as the series develops. For example, in the second novel in the series, *The Man on the Balcony,* the narrator makes a passing comment about a police roundup and notes wryly that it succeeded only in gathering up "the homeless, the alcoholics, the drug addicts, those who had lost all hope, those who could not even crawl away when the welfare state turned the stone over" (*Balcony* 117). By *The Laughing Policeman,* we begin getting more detailed evidence of the authors' attitude toward the evils of the consumer society that was being bred:

> The consumer society and its harassed citizens had other things to think of. Although it was over a month to Christmas, the advertising orgy had begun and the buying hysteria spread as swiftly and ruthlessly as the Black Death along the festooned shopping streets. The epidemic swept all before it and there was no escape. It ate its way into houses and apartments, poisoning and breaking down everything and everyone in its path. Children were already howling from exhaustion and fathers of families were plunged into debt until their next vacation. The gigantic legalized confidence trick claimed victims everywhere. The hospitals had a boom in cardiac infarctions, nervous breakdowns and burst stomach ulcers [*Laughing* 103].

Gradually the authors' criticisms about Sweden's political state become more overt and their tone turns increasingly bitter and sarcastic. For example, bemoaning the status of Sweden's dispirited citizens, they observe that there is no escape for most; "after all," they note, "they couldn't all emigrate or commit suicide" (*Locked* 142). Noting the dramatically higher cost of living needed to finance the new system, they describe a man struggling to live on a pension as belonging "to that category for whom the chain stores maintain overstocked counters of dog and cat food" (*Locked* 159). Even the constant repetition of the phrase "the so-called welfare state" takes on sarcastic overtones, similar to the way in which Shakespeare's Marc Antony's repeated description of Julius Caesar's assassins as "honorable men" alters the meaning of the words from a compliment to outright ridicule.

Sjöwall and Wahlöö insisted that the modern crime novel should serve as "a social alarm clock" (Scott 298). If alarm clock is understood to mean a simple device for objectively measuring the passing of time, the statement would not apply to their novels. There is nothing objective about the way the authors portray Swedish society. But if, on the other hand, the emphasis is on the clock as an instrument of alarm, then the term is apt, for their books clearly serve as a loud wake-up call about the inherent flaws in a system that in their view produces far more problems than solutions.

13

Paco Ignacio Taibo II
Mexico City

Like James McClure, Maj Sjöwall, and Per Wahlöö, Mexican author Paco Ignacio Taibo II employs a setting that is primarily political in nature. In his portrayal of Mexico City, the location for a series of novels featuring a private detective with the unusual name of Héctor Belascoarán Shayne, Taibo also challenges the notion of realism in his use of setting. He infuses the hard-boiled detective genre with a Kafka-like surrealism that positions Mexico City, "the most marvelously absurd city in the world" (*Uncomfortable* 30), as both a physical space and a symbol of the evils perpetuated by the Mexican state.

One of the oldest cities in North America, Mexico City, with twenty million residents, is also one of the world's most populated urban centers. Located 7,000 feet above sea level, the city stretches over 540 square miles. Its immense size and population produce unimaginable levels of stress, congestion, pollution, crime, and corruption. The toxic air, filled with industrial pollutants and automobile exhaust that get trapped in a bowl formed by the surrounding mountains, threatens to choke the city to death.

Yet for all its many problems, Mexico City is a vibrant place with a rich culture and history, filled with museums and monuments. It is a city, Taibo freely admits, that he loves: "This city produces more stories in one day than Balzac would have been able to tell in numerous lifetimes. There's in this a perverse condensation of schizophrenia and horror, adorned in a mountain of myths, an incredible fountain of inspiration" (Stavans 205).

Paco Ignacio Taibo II was born 11 January 1949 in Gijon, Asturias, Spain. His father, a journalist and novelist, moved the family to Mexico in 1958. At an early age Taibo dreamed of being a writer: "At age eleven,

13. Paco Ignacio Taibo II

I was making steps toward printing a magazine, and at thirteen, I wrote my first short story. I have been a journalist since age fifteen, an obsessive reader since five, and I managed to finish my first novel, which fortunately was never published, at twenty" (Stavans 202). As a college student in 1968, Taibo joined the ill-fated student protest movement, which soon turned into a mass populist uprising demanding democratic reform and increased civil liberties. On October 2, a peaceful demonstration at the Plaza de las Tres Culturas was crushed by the Mexican army in a bloody attack that left over three hundred dead, though the government claimed there were only thirty casualties. Reports of the massacre and the government's involvement in it were suppressed so as not to interfere with the upcoming Olympic Games scheduled to open just ten days later in Mexico City. The bodies of the dead were reportedly collected by the army and dumped into the ocean so evidence of the killings could not be found.

The actions exposed the government's willingness to exercise its might against its own people and its ability to manipulate the truth, which led Taibo to conclude, "The only health that counts is mental health. The only way to preserve yours is never to believe the Mexican government" ("Help" 55). Since his first publications in the 1970s, he has turned out everything from fiction and history to journalism and comic books, all of it an expression of his strong political views. Of all his many works, it is his highly original mystery novels about Mexico City private detective Héctor Belascoarán Shayne that are most familiar to English-speaking readers.

Early on, Taibo concluded that detective fiction could provide an effective vehicle for expressing his political concerns: "In the mid–1970s, I realized that crime fiction was the most important literature being produced in the world at that time, the most interesting space for ideas, perceptions of society, reflections about relations between crime and structures of power, racial issues" (Baker). He was strongly influenced both by what he calls "the ugly-dirty-fucking realism of Chester Himes and Jim Thompson" (Stavans 204) as well as the American hard-boiled fiction of Dashiell Hammett and especially Raymond Chandler. He remembers reading Chandler's *The Long Goodbye* three times when it was first published in Spanish. (In 1988 he also contributed a Philip Marlowe story to a centenary collection of Marlowe tributes written by fellow mystery writers indebted to Chandler.)

Taibo saw in the works of the American hard-boiled writers attitudes toward crime and corruption that matched his own. Their fiction portrays a vision of society in chaos, where crime is rampant and often reaches into the upper classes, and where logic is powerless to restore a sense of order. Taibo takes it a step further, suggesting that the state is often the force behind the crime. He used the term *neopoliciaco* to describe his crime novels which he says have the defining characteristics of an "obsession with cities" and "a recurring thematic incidence of problems with the State as a generator of crime, corruption, political arbitrariness" (Close 145). Juan Hernández Luna, a fellow Mexican mystery writer, describes the *neopoliciaco* this way: "It is a genre in which an initial crime or a crooked situation allows for narration of an entire social context, a city, regardless of whether you resolve the crime or not. To hell with detectives and investigation. Crime is only a pretext for narrating cities" (Close 148).

There has always been something slightly absurd about Hammett's Continental Op and Chandler's Philip Marlowe, men who go about risking their lives only to see the corruption remain. Like Albert Camus's Sisyphus, they push the rock to the top of the hill, only to watch it roll back down again. At the end of Hammett's *Red Harvest,* for example, his detective hero, the Continental Op, succeeds in cleaning up the corruption-ridden town of Poisonville. However, he knows that the victory is only temporary, that it won't be long before the town goes to the dogs all over again.

In Mexico, the detective's quest for justice is even more openly absurd. As Mexican social critic Carlos Monsiváis observed, "We don't have any detective literature because we don't have any faith in justice" (Paul 180). If what Belascoarán reports is true — "the police are behind something like seventy-six percent of the serious crime in Mexico City" (*Some* 101) — then a Mexican detective is "by definition a laughable solitary accident" (*Frontera* 8). His quixotic pursuit of justice in a society where, as Taibo says, Kafka is "the patron saint of the Mexican judicial system" ("So" 46), is madness. Taibo exploits the absurdity that is only hinted at by his predecessors: "Raymond Chandler's character moves within rational boundaries," Taibo explains, "whereas mine is surrounded by a chaotic atmosphere, Kafkaesque and corrupt: Mexico City" (Stavans 203).

Héctor Belascoarán Shayne (whose name reflects his Basque father and Irish mother) made his debut in *Días de combate* in 1976, but *An Easy Thing*, published a year later, was the first to be translated into English.

It is widely assumed that the name Shayne is a tribute to the 1940s American private eye Michael Shayne, created by Brett Halliday, the pseudonym of Davis Dresser, who claimed to have based his hero on a redheaded American he saw in Tampico, Mexico. However, in an interview with John F. Baker, where the name is unaccountably spelled Shane, Taibo says he based it on the name of the title character played by Alan Ladd in the classic Western film *Shane*.

Belascoarán is thirty-one years old, divorced, and a fan of private-eye novels. He has been a private detective for two years, ever since he ditched his comfortable middle-class life as an engineer (he has an M.A. in industrial engineering from an American university) and obtained his investigator's license from a Mexican correspondence school for three hundred pesos. His reasons for this are unclear. In *An Easy Thing* Taibo writes, "He wished someone conducting an opinion poll would get in the car and ask him a few questions. He'd tell them he didn't have the slightest idea why he'd become a detective" (108). But elsewhere Taibo suggests that as one formerly guilty of a "willing submission to the status quo" (99), Belascoarán is now seeking to make amends for his previous "disdain for the workers, all the times he'd driven through the working-class neighborhoods like a man traveling through a disaster zone" (99). He shares a messy one-room office with a sewer expert, a carpenter, and a plumber, and the space is cluttered with pipes, broken faucets, maps, and pieces of furniture in various stages of disrepair.

The three cases he investigates in *An Easy Thing* have nothing in common. He is hired by a former movie star who fears her seventeen-year-old daughter intends to kill herself and she wants him to prevent it; a factory owner wants him to find out who killed an engineer in one of his plants that is in the midst of labor unrest; and he is asked to find out if a ninety-seven-year-old man hiding out in a cave could actually be the legendary hero of the Mexican Revolution, Emiliano Zapata, who the history books say was gunned down in 1919. The oddity of the cases is a tip off to the reader that *An Easy Thing* is anything but an ordinary private-eye novel. And what Belascoarán finds out confirms the suspicion: the young girl's troubles began when she stole photographs of her mother having sex with ex-government ministers which a man was planning to use for blackmail; the engineer was killed by a commander of the Judicial Police to keep him from exposing the company's illegal activities so he could continue blackmailing the company; and Zapata lives, at least in the dreams he had for his country.

For his efforts, Belascoarán is seriously wounded in a machine-gun attack that results in the loss of an eye. Even though he solves the mysteries, nothing changes. Unlike Philip Marlowe, who often suffered disillusionment at the end of his cases, Belascoarán is well beyond that for he knows, "In Mexico nothing ever happens, and even if something does, still nothing happened" (227).

No Happy Ending begins with what seems like a joke when Belascoarán's office mate announces, "There's a dead Roman in the bathroom" (3). The dead man, whose throat has been slashed, is dressed as a Roman centurion. But when Belascoarán later receives a photograph of a second victim with a slashed throat along with a warning to get out of town, he realizes there is nothing funny about the case. Soon he is narrowly escaping repeated attempts on his life. Finally getting to the bottom of things, he learns that his many pursuers are all members of the Halcones, a super-secret paramilitary group which was hired by the government to crush a student strike in 1970 that resulted in forty deaths. Now they all work as subway policemen. But what he learns does him no good. At the end of the novel, he kills two more of his pursuers before his luck runs out and he is finally gunned down. The novel ends with his dead body lying in a puddle on the pavement outside his office. Mexico's violent insanity finally catches up with him.

The novel has strong echoes of both Dashiell Hammett's *Red Harvest* and Franz Kafka's *The Trial*. Mexico City resembles Hammett's violent Poisonville, and like Hammett's detective, Belascoarán seems to find himself in the middle of a bloody shootout at every turn. But in many ways he's also like Kafka's Joseph K., who in the opening scene of *The Trial* is arrested for some unexplained reason and who then spends the rest of the novel trying unsuccessfully to find out why. Belascoarán is equally puzzled: "He'd learned to accept the chaos at face value," Taibo writes. "He had plenty of easy truths, empty platitudes. What he didn't have was the slightest idea of why they were after him, who they were or where they were from" (92). One year after Joseph K.'s arrest, two men mysteriously arrive to take him out and execute him. Belascoarán's death at the hands of his executioners is every bit as absurd as that of Kafka's protagonist.

But not even death can keep a good detective down in Taibo's surreal world, and Belascoarán is resurrected in *Return to the Same City*. In an author's note Taibo explains that restoring Belascoarán to life wasn't entirely his fault. Like Arthur Conan Doyle's decision to bring Sherlock Holmes back to life after his supposed death at the Reichenbach Falls, his was also largely prompted by his readers' insistence that he return. But elsewhere he confesses, "I can't keep a character like Belascoarán alive in this kind of reality, because reality kills him. Reality kills him, and I bring him back to life, and the readers accept this absurd, crazy game" (Martin 21).

Return to the Same City can also be called an absurd crazy crime novel. Belascoarán is hired by a woman to hunt down a Cuban named Luke Estrella who she says drove her sister to commit suicide. He locates Estrella and with the help of a *Rolling Stone* reporter who is also on his trail learns that under several identities, Estrella (who may or may not by a C.I.A. operative) has been involved in political activities ranging from the assassination of Swedish prime minister Olaf Palme to the murder of Che Guevara. Now he is the major figure behind a drug-trafficking scheme that uses its profits to buy arms for the Nicaraguan Contras. It will take a superhuman effort to take down such a giant of international crime. But in comic-book fashion, Taibo manages the task with the assistance only of his mysterious girlfriend, known simply as "the woman with a pony tail," and four marching mariachi bands.

Taibo intensifies the unreal in *Some Clouds* by giving the novel a metafictional twist. At the prodding of his sister Elisa, Belascoarán agrees to look into a case involving a childhood friend of hers whose husband and brother were both murdered following the death of their father, the owner of some furniture stores. He uncovers a secret scheme devised by a powerful police official that used the furniture owner as a banker through whom millions of pesos in illegal profits were funneled. During his investigation he overhears a mobster known as "The Rat" order an associate to physically assault a "dumbshit novelist" and make it look like an accident. Belascoarán tracks down the writer whose name just happens to be Paco Ignacio Taibo. Like Paul Auster in his *New York Trilogy*, by introducing himself into the novel Taibo subverts the line between the real and the fictional. And in a bizarre twist, this time Taibo doesn't kill off his detective but himself, or at least the fictional writer named Paco Ignacio Taibo, who dies in the company of the police official behind the money scheme in what is made to appear as a traffic accident.

The Uncomfortable Dead is the most unconventional of all the Belas-coarán books. In 2004, Subcomandante Marcos, the mysterious masked, pipe-smoking leader of the Mexican indigenous insurgency movement known as the Zapatista National Liberation Army, contacted Taibo with a proposal that the two of them collaborate on a mystery novel. Even though Marcos, a former philosophy professor, had previously written only political tracts and a children's book, Taibo, who hadn't published a Belascoarán novel since *Adiós Madrid* in 1993, readily agreed. Without consulting each other the two began writing alternative chapters that appeared in serial form in a leftist Mexico City newspaper. The final result is aptly described by Marc Cooper as a "dizzying, purposefully incoherent plunge into the multiple ironies, absurdities and injustices of present-day Mexico."

The odd-numbered chapters written by Marcos feature a Zapatista peasant named Elias Contreras (who confesses at the beginning of his narrative that he is already dead) who has been assigned the task of finding a man implicated in a plot to privatize part of the jungle where the Zapatistas live and sell it. His search eventually takes him to the "Monster," his name for Mexico City, where he meets up with Belascoarán. In the even-numbered chapters written by Taibo, Belascoarán is searching for a leftist activist who was reportedly killed by government agents in 1971 but who is now leaving messages on answering machines throughout the city.

The dual searches exist largely to give both authors an opportunity to offer their own commentaries on Mexican politics and its leaders, past and present. But the fractured nature of the narrative and the absurdities of both searches serve to highlight what has become Taibo's favorite theme of the absurdity of life in Mexico. Contreras discovers that the man he is tracking is either a "shape-shifting mutant" or that there are several of them with the same name, including one who kidnapped a taco vendor from Juárez the CIA was using as a double for Osama bin Laden. For his part, Belascoarán learns that the calls from the murdered activist are actually being made by his son, who dubs the voices of Scooby-Doo and Barney the purple dinosaur for Mexican TV. None of this surprises Belascoarán for to a Mexican like himself, "absurdity was his daily bread" (81).

A writer who lives in a beautiful city of manageable size that is designed for the pleasures of life like Paris is likely to celebrate its beauty and vitality, as Georges Simenon does. But for a writer who lives in a much different kind of city, one which calls into question even the very notion of a city, celebration is out of the question. Taibo devotes little effort to an actual representation of the city. Instead, he engages in the challenging effort of trying to give a sense of the bewildering mystery the city has come to embody.

In 1519, Spanish conquistador Hernán Cortés said of Mexico City: "I cannot describe one hundredth part of all the things that could be mentioned, but, as best I can, I will describe some of those I have seen which, although badly described, will, I well know, be so remarkable as not to be believed, for we who saw them with our own eyes could not grasp them with our understanding" (Caistor 4). Taibo confesses his own frustration at trying to capture the essence of his chosen city: "There is in this city a perverse condensation of madness and horror, mingled with a stack of myths. It's a frankly unstable city, full of malignant vibes and attempts at solidarity. Catastrophe pervades it and everyday protests nourish it. Lately it fucks me up, because it gets away from me, I can't get hold of it like I used to" (Braham 105).

Like his creator, Belascoarán enjoys a love-hate relationship with Mexico City. In *An Easy Thing*, he boldly proclaims his love: "Man, I love this city. It's magical, you know? I mean, where else? You never know what crazy ass-son-of-a-bitching kind of thing is going to happen next" (49). Flying over the city at night, seeing "the great spectacle of the unending sketch of colorful lights.... The erratic, geometric drawings, the great carpet of light" (*Return* 117), moves him to tears. In *The Uncomfortable Dead,* he reaffirms his "immense, infinite sensation of love for this ever-changing city that he lives in and that lives in him" (43). Then he goes on to list some of the reasons for that love: "It must be the demonstrations, the golden hue of the light at the Zócalo, the book stands, the meat tacos, the currents of deep solidarity, the friends at the gas station across the way who always say hello when he passes. It might be that marvelous winter moon. It might be" (43).

On the other hand, the city can also be a monster. Taibo seeks to convey this reality by strewing colorful epithets throughout his novels: Mexico City is variously described as being a "twelve-million-headed monster," "like the fetid entrails of a whale," a "national garbage dump," an "old whore," a "fucking mess," a "lousy sewer," "the cave of lies," "the cavern of cannibals," the "collapsed city," "the biggest cemetery of dreams," and "the city of his worst nightmares." Tossing out so many different descriptions like this can be seen as a strategy of trying to describe the indescribable. What emerges from the list of these terms is less a real place and more a symbol of a larger issue, i.e., the corrosive nature of political power wielded against its own people.

"Hallucinatory" is a word Taibo often uses to describe Mexico City, and he reinforces the notion of the phantasmagorical in interesting ways. Smog is one of the defining features of the city, but in Belascoarán's picture the pollution is designed to "provide cover for the ghost of James Dean who rode around on his motorcycle in those parts" (*Return* 39). The fluorescent streetlights that envelop everything in a "phantasmagoric atmosphere" create an unreal glow even though the city was already "unreal enough without special effects courtesy of city hall" (*Some* 78). The swans swimming on Chapultepec Lake also contribute their share to the overall effect by resembling "the faces of Treasury Department functionaries on the verge of retiring" (*Return* 58). Even the crowd in the Parque España is transformed into a surrealistic picture populated by "repressed rapists disguised as ice cream vendors," "a street cop from León, Guanajuato, who'd beaten his mother to death with a stone mortar," and "Sitting Bull's mother, condemned by poverty to sell squash seeds in the park, but who prepared love potions and strange poisoned brews at night" (*Some* 128–29).

Taibo suggests that the picture he paints of Mexico City is not an exaggeration, that he is not distorting for, say, satirical purposes. Rather, he would like the reader to accept his warped picture as an accurate representation of life in Mexico. In an author's note to *No Happy Ending*, he asserts, "Obviously, the plot and the characters in this novel belong to the realm of fiction. The country, however, although it may be hard to believe, is absolutely real."

Novelist James Sallis observed that Taibo's literary works "restore the balance between fabulation and objective social realism. Refusing to dispense with the representational, he refuses also to lash its materials to the mast of likelihood and verisimilitude." Taibo gets at the truth by reflecting it in a broken mirror. This is especially true of the way he portrays Mexico City, which as he often reminds us possesses its own surprising reality that makes life there "a mystery worthy of its own rosary" (*Some* 48).

14

Leonardo Sciascia

Sicily

For most writers, setting is largely a matter of geography and topography. For them, physical description of landscape is an integral component of their use of setting. But there are some writers for whom setting is more a matter of culture or mindset than geography. No author explores the implications of place as a state of mind more than esteemed Sicilian author Leonardo Sciascia.

Sciascia (1921–1989) wrote novels, short stories, essays, and journalism. Among his most popular works are several mystery novels. While many of these are set in Sicily, physical description of the landscape is virtually non-existent. Rather than describing the bright sunshine for which Sicily is noted, Sciascia instead focused on the shadowy world of the Sicilian mafia and on the mentality that allowed it to flourish.

The Sicilian mafia is different from that portrayed (and often romanticized) in American films like *The Godfather* and television series like *The Sopranos.* Unlike in the U.S., where the mafia operates at the fringes of society, in Sicily it is (or until recently was) the culture which dominates society. More than simply a criminal organization, it is, as Stefano Tani observes, "a 'moral code,' a way of acting and thinking that, as such, permeates Sicilian society and influences even people who think themselves beyond it" (59). It is the very milieu in which everyone lives, what Sciascia calls an "alternative state which the Mafia have themselves created" which is "infinitely more efficient than the one controlled by the central government" (Thomson 49).

Though Sciascia denied being an expert on the mafia, Gore Vidal for one felt otherwise: "What is the mafia mentality? What is the mafia? What is Sicily? When it comes to the exploration of this particular hell, Leonardo Sciascia is the perfect Virgil," he proclaimed in a cover blurb to a *New York Review of Books* reprint edition of *To Each His Own* in 2000. Sciascia's penetrating insights into the mafia and its pernicious influence are simply the result of spending a lifetime in the small town of Racalmuto, near Palermo:

> I am simply someone who was born, has lived and continues to live in a village in western Sicily and who has always striven to understand the people, the reality and the events which surround him. I am an expert on the mafia just as I am an expert on agriculture, on emigration, on popular traditions or on sulphur; at the level of things seen and heard, of lived, or endured, experience [Farrell 11].

Sciascia's crime fiction is as infused with the environment of the mafia as the novels of Tony Hillerman and James Lee Burke are informed by the Desert Southwest and the Louisiana bayous.

The Day of the Owl opens with the murder of Salvatore Colasberna, a small-time building contractor gunned down while running to catch a bus early one morning in a small Sicilian village. Though a busload of passengers witnessed the killing, no one offers the police any help. Assessing the difficulty of prying information out of witnesses, one policeman complains, "It's like squeezing tripe: nothing comes out" (22). To the locals, such killings are always more wisely (and safely) explained away as crimes of passion rather than, as in this case, retaliation for refusing the offer of mafia protection. Given the all-pervasive influence of the mafia in every aspect of local life, *omerta* (the code of silence) is always the wisest choice in Sicily.

Captain Bellodi, head of the local Carabinieri, is a northerner from Parma who is confident he can penetrate the web of secrecy and get to the truth. But he soon learns that his status as an outsider won't help him in his efforts. (As the locals insist, "Mainlanders are decent enough but just don't understand things" [16]). In the usual mystery novel, the focus would be on the efforts of the police to uncover the truth behind the crime. But Sciascia is far more interested in how the truth is kept hidden; for him the far more compelling mystery is Sicilian culture and society itself, especially as it relates to the mafia.

Bellodi soon rounds up a pair of suspects and cleverly pits one against the other to force them to reveal the truth. His hope is to use these two links in the chain to expose a third link, Don Mariano Arena, a prominent citizen suspected of being head of the local mafia. But what Bellodi soon discovers is that there are other, more powerful links in the chain, which are revealed to extend into the upper ranks of the Italian government. When an air-tight alibi is conveniently fabricated for the killer, the whole case melts into thin air.

What Bellodi eventually comes to understand is the power and influence of what virtually everyone refers to as the so-called mafia. The typical public response to questions about the very existence of the mafia is denial. As one local man asserts, "Is it really possible to conceive of the existence of a criminal association so vast, so well-organized, so secret and so powerful that it can dominate not only half Sicily, but the entire United States of America?" (62). Even the undersecretary of the interior in Parliament voices skepticism, arguing that "the so-called mafia ... in the opinion of the Government, only existed in the imagination of socialists and communists" (112). Against such a solid wall of denial, what chance does Bellodi have of bringing the truth to light?

At one point in the investigation, Bellodi discovers the body of a missing man, reportedly a witness to the murder, at a local *chiarchiaro*, or place of caves. Sciascia describes the site as looking like "a huge, black-holed sponge soaking up the light flooding the landscape" (85). The dark and mysterious *chiarchiaro* comes to symbolize the complex web of power, influence and secrecy that confounds Bellodi's search to bring the truth to light. It isn't that he isn't smart enough to solve the crime. But solving the crime and achieving justice are two entirely different matters.

At the end of the novel, Bellodi is back home in Parma on leave. When friends ask him about Sicily, he can only reply, "It's very complicated to explain ... it's just incredible" (118). His final thoughts about the place are mixed: at first he decides, "To hell with Sicily! To hell with it all!" Upon further reflection, however, he comes to realize "with utter lucidity, that he loved Sicily and was going back. 'Even if it's the end of me'" (120). That final line offers an ominous hint at the situation Sciascia will describe in his next mystery novel.

At the beginning of *To Each His Own*, Manno, a respected pharmacist in a small Sicilian town, receives an anonymous letter in the mail bearing an ominous message: "This letter is your death sentence. To avenge what you have done, you will die" (3). Manno can think of no reason why anyone would send him such a letter and so refuses to take it seriously. A few days later, while out hunting with longtime friend Dr. Roscio, the town doctor, both men are gunned down.

What the local police make of the incident and how they proceed in their investigation is never disclosed; the novel instead follows the efforts of Paolo Laurana, a teacher of Italian and history at the nearby classical *liceo,* as he works to solve the puzzle. Laurana is no intellectual genius along the lines of an Auguste Dupin or a Sherlock Holmes. Described as "an honest, meticulous, melancholy man; not very intelligent, and indeed at times positively obtuse" (40), Laurana is motivated purely by curiosity to get to the bottom of things. He has no desire, as Holmes and Dupin did, to demonstrate his intellectual superiority to the police. Indeed, "any sense that he was taking over the police's job, or that he was competing with them in their work, would have filled him with such repugnance that he would have let the matter drop" (43).

He undertakes a plodding investigation that, thanks to a few lucky clues and the chance encounter with an old friend who provides some key information, leads him to suspect a powerful local citizen named Rosello. He hypothesizes that the intended target of the murders was not the pharmacist but his friend Dr. Roscio. He speculates that Rosello was having an affair with Roscio's wife and Roscio was killed when he threatened to expose Rosello as someone "who holds the whole province in the palm of his hand, who made men and unmade them, stole, bribed, swindled" (55). Laurana naively thinks of the whole affair as "detached and distant, in style, form, and also somewhat in content delineated rather in the manner of a Graham Greene novel" (117).

It is obvious, however, that he poses a threat to someone powerful. Dr. Roscio's young widow (and the presumed lover of Rosello) arranges to meet him at a cafe to discuss her suspicions about her husband's murder. When she fails to show up, he heads for the station to catch a train back home. A car, driven by somebody he thinks he recognizes from his town, drives by and offers him a lift. He is never seen again. His body, the omniscient narrator tells us, ends up buried under a pile of lime in an abandoned sulphur mine. His death confirms what his suspicions had earlier warned him about ("his instinct, which in Laurana as in every Sicilian was sharpened by long experience and fear, warned him of danger" [87]) but which he had unwisely chosen to ignore.

In Sciascia's anti-detective novel, the truth is beside the point. What matters, and what Laurana's death demonstrates, is the presence of powerful hidden forces which, as in *The Day of the Owl*, can exercise that power at will in keeping the truth hidden. At the scene of the murders of Mammo and Dr. Roscio, eleven hunting dogs were present, but as the narrator remarks, even if they had the power of speech and could identify the killers, they would have wisely chosen silence: "Even had they had the gift of speech, the dogs would, in the given circumstances, have become so many mutes both with regard to the identity of the murderers and in testifying before the marshal of the carabinieri" (12). They are, after all, Sicilian dogs.

The novel concludes with a conversation among some local citizens a year after the murders of the pharmacist and the doctor. In the manner of a Greek chorus, they offer a commentary on the action of the novel. When one suggests they ought to discuss the murders, his friend retorts, "What good does it do to talk? ... What I know, you know and everyone else knows. Why talk about it?" (142). When the subject switches to the baffling disappearance of poor Professor Laurana, one man passes the final judgment: "He was an ass" (142).

In "A Straightforward Tale," a posthumously published novella, the mafia is never even mentioned, though its power and influence are fully exposed. The shooting death of Giorgio Roccella in his villa on the very day he returned to his Sicilian hometown after an absence of fifteen years presents a real puzzle, especially since just before his death he had called the police station to announce that he had just found something (which he did not identify) in his house. A case of suicide, concludes the inspector; murder, says his junior colleague, the brigadier. (To reinforce the fable-like qualities of the tale, neither is given a name.) In a surprising twist at the end, the inspector is shot and killed by the brigadier in the police station when he realizes the inspector is about to shoot him.

It is revealed that Roccella's killer was the inspector himself, a member of a local gang of drug dealers, who had been promoting the suicide story to cover up his crime. His police superiors conspire to cover up his actions and explain away his death as an unfortunate accident. In a final twist, the local priest summoned to perform the last rites on the inspector's body is recognized by a witness as one of the gang members he had earlier seen at the train station, where two other men were killed. Like any well-conditioned Sicilian, the man decides to tell no one. *Omerta* will insure that details about the complex network of corruption involving the police and the church will never be revealed.

Sciascia was an admirer of the works of Nobel Prize author (and fellow Sicilian) Luigi Pirandello. The two shared a common interest in exploring the disjunction between appearance and reality, in probing beneath deceptive surfaces for the complex reality lying underneath. "Scratch the surface, just lightly" in a typical Sicilian town, novelist Francine Prose notes in her travel book *Sicilian Odyssey,* "and what you uncover is the human equivalent of an ant colony, with its own occult laws, its limits, its prescribed patterns of behavior, and all of it ruled — ultimately, and beneath layers of subterfuge and obfuscation — by the Mafia" (85). Sciascia's genius is his skill in using the detective novel to expose the labyrinthine connections lying hidden beneath the beautiful surface of his homeland. A reader wishing to understand Sicily might do well to heed the advice of Frederika Randall: "Sciascia is the writer you need in your pocket when you travel around Italy. He demands that you look behind appearances and is the ideal antidote to sunny, mindless Tuscanophilia" (32).

15

Lindsey Davis

Ancient Rome

Not all mystery novels are set in the present. "Many readers are in love with the past," Robin W. Winks noted, but then added, "provided it does not make too many demands upon them and is not too difficult to understand" (1089). Historical mystery fiction has proven to be a very popular genre that satisfies a thirst for the past in an entertaining and informative way and also offers an imaginative escape from the anxieties of the present.

Choosing to set a series in the past presents a special challenge to the writer. *How* a writer decides to use setting is a matter of creative choice; the decision about *where* to set a novel, however, usually isn't. Most writers typically set their novels in places where they live or know well. (There are exceptions, of course: American mystery writer Elizabeth George sets her popular Inspector Lynley series in Britain, although she says if she had known how many times she would be asked why she did this, she would have chosen another setting.) In such cases, getting the details of setting exactly right doesn't normally present a serious problem. And because many readers are also likely to have some familiarity with the place, either through personal experience or from photographic images, writers can use them in a collaborative effort to create a sense of place.

However, when the setting is the remote past and the physical location no longer even exists, the task for the writer is to create a believable sense of place for readers who, like the author, have no personal experience of that location. The setting has to be created from the ground up, so to speak. The task facing the writer of historical mysteries is thus complicated: (1) The setting must be fully rendered so readers unfamiliar with the time and place will have an adequate understanding of the absent world being re-created; (2) Details of setting must be accurate to satisfy readers, especially those who already have some knowledge of the period; and then, most importantly, (3) the plot, characters, suspense, etc. must be fully developed for the benefit of mystery fans. All the elements must be kept in balance to prevent the details of setting from overwhelming the mystery.

Some popular examples that successfully combine rich historical setting with mystery include Umberto Eco's *The Name of the Rose* (set in 1327) as well as series by Robert van Gulik (seventh-century China), Ellis Peters (twelfth-century England), Anne Perry (Victorian England), and Elizabeth Peters (nineteenth-century Egypt). One contemporary writer who manages to combine mystery, history, and entertainment in an engaging way is British author Lindsey Davis, author of a series of novels set in ancient Rome.

Ancient Rome is at once both exotic and familiar. People dressed in togas, worshipped strange pagan gods, owned slaves, and threw Christians to the lions. On the other hand, today one can still visit the Colosseum and stroll along the Via Sacra through the ruins of the Roman Forum. We have own own Senate and enjoy modern versions of chariot races and gladiatorial contests. Latin is still taught in schools. One can even get a sense of Roman domestic life by actually walking though private homes exactly as they existed on that August day in A.D. 79 when Mt. Vesuvius erupted and buried Pompeii.

Ancient Rome has been an appealing subject for writers as far back as Shakespeare, whose *Julius Caesar* and *Antony and Cleopatra* still engage contemporary audiences. In the eighteenth century, British writers like John Dryden, Alexander Pope, and Samuel Johnson were so influenced by ancient Roman writers that the period is named the Augustan Age after the Emperor Augustus, during whose reign many of the greatest literary works of the classical Roman period were written. The groundbreaking 1976 BBC television series *I, Claudius* brought ancient Rome into countless homes. Popular films with a Roman setting ranging from the infamous X-rated *Caligula* (1980) to *Ben-Hur* (1959) and *Gladiator* (2000), both Academy Award winners as Best Picture of the Year, have entertained millions.

So it's not surprising that there are currently three mystery series set in Roman times being written. John Maddox Roberts's SPQR series featuring Decius Caecilius Metellus and Steven Saylor's Roma Sub Rosa series featuring Gordianus the Finder are both set in the declining years of the Roman Republic, roughly 70–50 B.C. Both are heavily influenced by the writings of one of the key figures of the era, Cicero, and draw heavily upon the famous political conspiracies and intrigues of the period, many of which are documented in Cicero's speeches. There are also overlapping real-life characters (Cicero, Crassus, Pompey, Marc Antony) and events (the Catiline conspiracy in 63 B.C.) in the two series which give both an emphasis more on history than mystery.

Lindsey Davis's Marcus Didius Falco series is set some 140 years later during the reign of Vespasian, who came to power in A.D. 70 after a brief period of civil war following the death of Nero. During The Year of the Four Emperors in A.D. 69, three ineffective leaders rose and fell in quick succession before Vespasian seized power and brought some measure of stability. While Vespasian and his sons Titus and Domitian, both future emperors, make brief appearances in the novels, the focus is neither on their accomplishments nor on the politics of the period. Davis is more interested in using the Roman setting to paint a vivid picture of life in the empire during the late first century A.D. She also exploits the comic possibilities of transporting the familiar twentieth-century figure of the private investigator to a period almost two thousand years ago.

Lindsey Davis was born in Birmingham, England, on 21 August 1949. After earning a degree in English at Oxford, she joined the British Civil Service, where she worked for fourteen years for the Property Services Agency, arranging contracts in connection with Ancient Monuments and the London Museums. When a novel she wrote was runner-up for the Georgette Heyer Historical Novel prize, she quit her job and with the help of the British government's Enterprise Allowance Scheme and a part-time job cooking lunches for a firm of tax consultants, she embarked on a new career as a writer.

Her first stories were romantic serials set in the period of the seventeenth-century English Civil War that were published in a women's magazine. However, a lifelong interest in historical fiction and a fascination with ancient Rome inspired her to write a novel set in classical times. Her first effort was *The Course of Honor,* based on the true story of the longtime love affair between the Emperor Vespasian and his mistress, an ex-slave named Antonia Caenis. Unable to find a publisher for the novel (it was eventually published in 1988), she used the research she had already begun in first-century A.D. Rome to write about the period again. This time she chose to write a mystery, a bit of a spoof featuring a kind of Roman private eye, a Philip Marlowe in a toga. The result was *The Silver Pigs*, published in 1989.

The Silver Pigs introduces Marcus Didius Falco and the exotic city of ancient Rome where he lives. A thirty-year-old veteran of the Second Augustan Legion in Britain, Falco is now back in Rome trying to estab-lish himself as a private informer. (Informers were familiar figures in Rome, especially during the time of Nero, when their activities earned for the pro-fession a well-deserved reputation for sleazy behavior.) When a sixteen-year-old girl he has rescued from her pursuers is later murdered, he feels obligated to find her killer. But the case turns into a much larger one when he uncovers evidence that silver pigs or ingots are being stolen from the imperial government and may be used to fund a conspiracy to topple the new emperor, Vespasian.

The case allows Davis to establish Falco's credentials as a classical equivalent of the familiar private detective. Part of the fun is watching a 1940s–type gumshoe walk the muddy streets of the ancient world. Davis gives him the requisite qualities of toughness and smart-alecky language, but he's far from the isolated figure Philip Marlowe and his successors were. Like them, he lives in a shabby apartment in a run-down tenement (his is on the sixth floor over a laundry that perpetually smells of the urine Romans used to bleach togas) and is always worried about coming up with enough money to pay the rent. Unlike them, however, his life is compli-cated by a growing family (which eventually includes two daughters and a dog), a large and demanding pack of fractious relatives, including five sisters and their obnoxious husbands, assorted nephews and nieces, and the girlfriend and child of his late brother who, under Roman custom, have become his financial responsibility.

Especially in the early books in the series, Falco is as antiestablish-ment as his modern private-eye counterparts. Republican to the core, he hates to see Rome "degenerate into a madhouse controlled by a handful of aristocrats manipulated by their cynical ex-slaves, while the mass of its citizens cannot earn a decent living" (*Silver* 23). Nor does he like the idea of handing control of the empire over "to one mortal, who may turn out insane or corrupt or immoral — and probably will" (23). And yet he finds himself working behind the scenes on behalf of the new emperor, Vespasian. His reason is simple: following the political unrest after Nero's death in A.D. 68, Vespasian's emergence as a strong leader promises to bring stability and order to the empire. So despite his anti-imperial views, Falco can't help but admire Vespasian and the qualities he brings to the position.

Davis incorporates material that sheds light on the extremes of the Roman world. To determine how the ingots are being stolen, Falco spends three months disguised as a Roman slave working the silver mines in Britain. His experience there exposes the brutal existence of a typical slave forced into doing hard labor in imperial times. At the other end of the social spectrum, Davis offers a vivid re-enactment of the ceremonial procession in Rome honoring Titus's defeat of Jerusalem in A.D. 70 that included legions of triumphant soldiers, seven hundred captured slaves, and so much gold and jewelry taken from Jerusalem that "the streets flickered with the glow of it as the molten tide flowed on towards the Capitol in one slow, swollen meander of heroic extravagance" (275).

Though proud of his plebeian background, Falco finds it complicates his life when he falls in love with Helena Justina, the independent-minded divorced daughter of a senator. Since the difference in rank prevents them from marrying, their future happiness depends upon his coming up with 400,000 sesterces, the amount needed to qualify for the rank necessary before they can marry, which will continue to be a thorny issue for the next several books.

Deciding to write a historical series always raises the question, why choose this particular time and place? For Davis, there are several reasons: although she lacks any formal training as a historian or a classicist, she first became interested in the Romans when she began studying Latin as a twelve-year-old schoolgirl; a teacher with a strong interest in archaeology further fueled her interest in the ancient world; living in Britain, where many traces of Roman presence still exist, also contributed; finally, an as ex-civil servant herself, she confesses to having a special fascination with how the vast Roman Empire was managed.

Historical fiction resembles science fiction in that it is capable of transporting the reader to an exotic place. And also like much science fiction, portrayal of an alien setting can be used as a commentary on the present by depicting attitudes and behavior that reflect on those of our own time. However, unlike the science fiction writer, the historical novelist is bound by actual fact. If one wishes to be taken seriously in re-creating a past world, then one has an obligation to be as accurate in terms of dates and events, as well as what the historical record shows as far as habits, attitudes, lifestyles, behavior, etc. are concerned.

The only real drawback with historical novels, Davis insists, is that if they are any good people sometimes start believing they are a substitute for real study of the period. She vehemently maintains her novels should not be read as textbooks. One way she ensures this won't happen is to make her books far more entertaining than a textbook, which she does by including plenty of humor. The comedy arises both from situations like the chaotic scene in *Venus in Copper* where Falco attempts to cook a giant turbot in his tiny apartment for a crowd that includes the emperor's son Titus as well as from Falco's characteristically witty comments and sarcastic put-downs.

The picture Davis paints of Rome in the first century A.D. is a mixture of research and imagination. Unlike writers who can actually visit the place they are describing, one cannot physically visit ancient Rome. However, because enough of the old city remains, and because many faithful reconstructions of the city are available, Davis is able to imagine what Rome likely looked like. By adding details gleaned from what we know about the nature of life in the teeming metropolis, Davis brings the city to life, as this description by Falco illustrates:

> As we walked along peacefully, Helena and I counted off the Seven Hills together. While we came west along the Esquiline ridge, we had an evening wind in our faces. It bore tantalizing traces of rich meat dumplings gurgling in dark gravies in five hundred dubious cook-shops.... Up to our high spot rose a distant murmur of the permanent hubbub below: touts and orators, crashing loads, donkeys and door-bells, the crunch of a marching Guards detachment, the swarming cries of humanity more densely packed than anywhere in the Empire or the known world beyond [*Silver* 178].

In order to ensure historical accuracy in her re-creation of Rome and the depiction of everyday life, Davis read the works of classical Latin authors like Juvenal, Martial, Horace, Ovid, Virgil, and Tacitus. (It is a tribute to these writers, Davis acknowledges, that she was able to write her first Falco novel before she had ever visited Rome.) When she departs

from the historical record, as she does when she has Vespasian's son Domitian murder a young girl by stabbing her in the heart with a pen in *Silver Pigs*, the action is at least plausible. As Ellen O'Gorman notes in her essay, "Detective Fiction and Historical Narrative," the action fits because "it is *congruent* with the narratives that we constitute as repositories of 'historical' knowledge — the ancient sources. We *know*, because Suetonius has told us, that stabbing living creatures with his pen was a favourite pastime of the emperor Domitian" (25). The reason why there is no record of this specific act is clear: Falco suppresses the evidence as a favor to Domitian's father, Vespasian.

The richest source of material about the reality of urban life in first-century A.D. Rome are the satires of Juvenal, especially his Third, entitled "Against the City of Rome." Juvenal takes a decidedly negative view of the city and colorfully catalogs a lengthy list of complaints. He gripes about crowded streets, the raucous noise at night when the city is open to the wheeled traffic that is banned during the daytime, the omnipresent danger of fires, and the constant threat of roofs caving in ("Rome is supported on pipestems, matchsticks," he grumbles [40]). He is especially outspoken in his warnings about the nighttime dangers of the city: "You are a thoughtless fool, unmindful of sudden disaster,/ If you don't make your will before you go out to have dinner," (43) he warns. If pieces falling from buildings don't get you, then drunks or holdup men with knives will.

Falco loves Rome more than the cranky Juvenal does, but his experience confirms much of what Juvenal says about the city. Until he gradually moves up the economic ladder, he knows firsthand what living in a tiny apartment in a rundown tenement building on the poor side of town is like. He knows too the exact kind of dangers Juvenal notes when he walks the streets after dark. Some of the most vivid scenes in the Falco books are those set at night.

> I had plenty of company on the streets that night. A couple of times I noticed groups of dubious characters huddled around the folding doors of lockup shops. Once there were scuffles above me as climbers scaled balconies on their way to upstairs burglaries. A woman called out, offering her services in a voice that reeked of dishonesty; having passed by in silence, I spotted her male accomplice in the next lane, hanging about waiting for her to bring a client for him to beat up and rob. A shadowy figure slipped from the back of a moving delivery cart, carrying a bundle. Slaves escorting a rich man's litter were sporting

ripped tunics and black eyes, having been mugged despite their sticks
and lanterns [*Time* 150–51].

Davis brings the ancient world to life by populating it with ordinary
characters whose problems are no different than our own. She isn't writing a political history of Rome nor does she adopt a "Lives-of-the-Emper-
ors" textbook approach. Her desire is to provide the reader a tasty slice of
Roman daily life as seen through the eyes of a somewhat cynical observer.
Just as 1940s L.A. still lives through Philip Marlowe's cynical eyes, Rome
pulses with life again thanks to Didius Marcus Falco.

Chandler's Marlowe was a key influence on the creation of Falco who,
Davis confesses, began as something of a joke: would it be possible to
place a forties-style private eye two thousand years ago? Some parallels with
Chandler are direct. For example, in *Shadows in Bronze* Falco becomes
acutely uneasy about his plebeian background when he is invited to speak
with Vespasian in his imperial office with its vaulted ceilings and ornate
gilt decorations: "I lay on the couch as if I was nervous my body would
leave an unpleasant mark on its silk" (38). His comment is an exact echo
of Philip Marlowe's similar concern while visiting a man in his elegantly
appointed living room in *Farewell, My Lovely*: "I sat down on a pink chair
and hoped I wouldn't leave a mark on it" (30).

At other times, Falco's moody ruminations sound like Marlowe at his
world-weariest:

> It was a night when professional burglars would glance quickly out-
> side, then decide to stay in and annoy their wives. Heartbroken
> women would be hanging around the Aemilian Bridge waiting for a
> quiet moment to edge over the parapet and jump into oblivion.
> Tramps would cough to death in the gateways at the Circus. Lost chil-
> dren and runaway slaves would huddle against the huge black walls
> under the Citadel, slipping into Hades by accident when they forgot to
> breathe ... it was a bitter, baleful, dolorous night, and I hated to be
> out in it" [*Poseidon's* 178–79].

Whether Falco is commenting cynically on the rise of Vespasian — "He had
no money and no famous ancestors. You cannot let people who own nothing but talent rise into the highest positions. What chance is there then
for the upper-crust bunglers and fools?" (*Shadows* 82) — or simply describing his methods — "All you can do is stir the mire, then keep prodding so
pieces of flotsam float to the top, while you stand there and watch for some
putrid relic to emerge and at last make sense" (*Silver* 284) — much of the

enjoyment in reading Davis's books comes from listening to a first-century character mimic the language and attitudes of his twentieth-century counterpart.

Davis achieves much of her effect through what she calls an "interlayering of perspectives" that mixes past and present. There are at least three layers of time in the novels. Patterning Falco on Marlowe invites a comparison between the near past (the 1940s) and the distant past. But while Falco steadfastly remains a first-century Roman who uses similes appropriate to his time ("This went down like a gladiators' strike at a five-day festival" [*Time* 218]), much of his language has a contemporary sound ("flimflammery," "zilch," "canoodling," "did the dirty"). Many of his remarks are also designed to sound ironic to the twenty-first century reader, who can't help but filter the past through a contemporary perspective. For example, when Falco derides the talent of a Gallic chef—"I am prepared to concede that one day the three cold Gallic provinces will come up with a contribution to the civilised arts — but nobody is going to convince me that it will be mastery of cuisine" (*Venus* 135) — modern readers can smile at how surprised he would be at the renowned excellence of today's French cuisine. Likewise, British readers may (or may not) chuckle at Falco's advice to anyone considering a visit to Britain, where he spent several unhappy years, mainly in the rain: "If you ever want to go there, I advise you not to bother" (*Silver* 87).

Over the course of the series, Falco's fortunes improve: he rises in rank, marries Helena Justina, becomes a homeowner, fathers two daughters, gets appointed by Vespasian to the position of procurator of poultry for the Senate and People of Rome, and expands his agency into Falco and Associates by taking on his wife's two brothers as assistants. He also becomes increasingly establishment himself, even to the extent of helping to track down tax cheats for the emperor. With respectability comes a price, however, as he comes to resemble Philip Marlowe less and less. The one thing that doesn't change, however, is the city he lives in.

Not all the Falco books are set in Rome. Some of his adventures are set in far-flung corners of the empire: Britain (*The Jupiter Myth*), Syria (*Last Act in Palmyra*), Germany (*The Iron Hand of Mars*), Spain (*A Dying Light in Corduba*) and Greece (*See Delphi and Die*). The descriptions of the various locations throughout the empire are more general than those of Rome as they are almost totally the product of the novelist's imagination. Thanks to the survival of ancient works like Juvenal's "Against the City of Rome," a richly detailed picture of the city and its people has come down to us. Being able to draw upon authoritative material like this enables Davis to paint a picture of Rome that is utterly convincing because it is based on the work of writers who actually lived there and described the place in such detail.

The first step in creating a strong sense of setting is establishing geography. Fortunately for Davis, many ancient sites in Rome are still standing: the Forum, the outline of the Circus Maximus, the Theater of Marcellus, the Pantheon, and most famous of all, the Colosseum (which did not exist when Vespasian became emperor, though one of his first tasks involved draining Nero's private lake and beginning construction of a huge new amphitheater on the site.) As Falco makes his way through the city, he always orients his reader to his location and the direction he is traveling. (Davis's books also include a detailed map of the city, so the reader can always visualize where the action takes place.) Davis also does an effective job of imagining scenes set in popular Roman locations, ranging from the games at the Circus Maximus to the more intimate activities at Plato's Academy, one of the city's many popular brothels.

In the best of her books, crime and setting are artfully woven together. In *Three Hands in the Fountain*, for example, a severed hand is discovered plugging up a fountain in Rome. Soon, more hands and other body parts are found, evidence that someone is killing and dismembering his victims and then dumping them into Rome's aqueduct system. The problem isn't just a serial killer on the loose. Rome's entire water system could soon become contaminated, undermining public confidence, so the local authorities are trying to keep the news under wraps.

In order to locate the likeliest place where the body parts are being dumped, Falco learns all he can about the aqueduct system, which allows Davis to incorporate plenty of useful information about the engineering marvel. Falco gets much of his information from S. Julius Frontinus, an actual historical figure who would in A.D. 95 become superintendent of the aqueduct system and later write an invaluable book on the history and workings of the entire system. From Frontinus we learn about the complex system of nine aqueducts that delivers water from rivers outside the city to sustain life in the teeming metropolis. We learn how water is distributed first to public fountains, then to the baths, and then if the supply permits to private homes of the wealthy. We also get to take an underground journey with Falco through the Cloaca Maxima, Rome's sewer system.

Falco concludes that the killer selects his victims from the Circus Maximus area during festivals. The Circus Maximus, with a seating capacity of 250,000 people, was the immense oval-shaped arena where chariot races and other games were held. Having Falco linger in the area hoping to spot the killer choosing his next victim gives Davis an opportunity to re-create the lively activities outside the arena, especially at night. When what Falco calls the "Circus vomitaria" disgorge the crowds after the games, the streets become filled with drunks, beggars, hustlers and "night moths," the prostitutes who swarm over the area, all of whom turn the area into a dangerous and sordid place.

Other books in the series shed light on different aspects of Roman life. In *The Accusers,* a prominent Roman senator named Rubirius Metellus commits suicide after being convicted of corruption. Falco is called in to investigate when it appears that Metellus may actually have been murdered. This case gives Davis an ideal opportunity to explore such matters as the Roman court system, wills, inheritance policies, funeral rites, even the role played by funeral comedians. In *Two for the Lions,* the killing of a man-eating lion who served as the empire's official executioner followed by the murder of a popular gladiator puts Falco on a case that allows Davis to explore the colorful world of the gladiatorial games. Woven into the plot are interesting bits of information about the different types of gladiators, the history of the games, and the ritualistic role they played in Roman society.

In *One Virgin Too Many,* a member of the Arval Brethren, one of Rome's oldest religious groups, is murdered. Shortly afterwards, another member of the family, a six-year-old girl who is the leading candidate to be chosen as one of Rome's six Vestal Virgins, goes missing. This gives Davis an opportunity to explore the Roman state religion. We learn about several of the many Roman festivals as well as the important ritualistic role played by such religious groups as the Vestals who tend the sacred flame that represents the life, welfare, and unity of the Roman state. Despite his own small role in the state religion as tender of the Sacred Geese, Falco is as cynical about the officials of Rome's religion as he is about virtually every other aspect of public life in the city. To him, all these "non elected, jobs-for-life patricians" do little more than dress up "in silly clothes for reasons no better than witchcraft" and carry out "dubious, secretive manipulation of the state" (*One* 72).

Davis is not interested in using the crime novel to reexamine the past, as James Ellroy does in much of his fiction, especially his L.A. Quartet. She is not interested in mixing real and historical figures to problematize the distinction between fiction and history as E.L. Doctorow does in *Ragtime*. Nor does she attempt to immerse the reader totally in the ancient world; we are never so trapped in the past that we forget we are not reading a narrative actually written by a person living in that distant time period. For her, history is never an end in itself, only a way of adding depth and texture to the action and characters. She uses ancient Rome to remind her readers of both the similarities and differences between modern life and life lived two millennia ago.

Davis's novels clearly demonstrate the power of setting. Her mystery plots aren't always suspenseful, Falco's fractious family's domestic complications aren't always compelling and often clutter up the narrative, and Falco's not the most original detective ever invented. But add the exotic Roman setting and Davis's detailed re-creation of life there and the books take on a fresh perspective that makes them lively and informative entertainment, a truly winning combination.

Works Consulted

Primary Sources

Burke, James Lee

Black Cherry Blues. New York: Avon, 1990.
Burning Angel. New York: Hyperion, 1995.
Cadillac Jukebox. New York: Hyperion, 1996.
Crusader's Cross. New York: Simon & Schuster, 2005.
Dixie City Jam. New York: Hyperion, 1994.
Heaven's Prisoners. New York: Pocket Books, 1989.
In the Electric Mist with Confederate Dead. New York: Avon, 1994.
Jolie Blon's Bounce. New York: Pocket Books, 2003.
Last Car to Elysian Fields. New York: Simon & Schuster, 2003.
A Morning for Flamingoes. New York: Avon, 1991.
The Neon Rain. New York: Pocket Books, 1988.
Pegasus Descending. New York: Simon & Schuster, 2006.
Purple Cane Road. New York: Dell, 2001.
A Stained White Radiance. New York: Avon, 1993.
Sunset Limited. New York: Island Books, 1999.

Davis, Lindsey

The Accusers. New York: Mysterious Press, 2003.
A Body in the Bath House. New York: Mysterious Press, 2003.
The Course of Honor. New York: Mysterious Press, 1998.
A Dying Light in Corduba. New York: Warner Books, 1999.
The Iron Hand of Mars. New York: Fawcett, 1994.
The Jupiter Myth. New York: Mysterious Press, 2004.
Last Act in Palmyra. New York: Mysterious Press, 1997.
Ode to a Banker. New York: Mysterious Press, 2001.
One Virgin Too Many. New York: Mysterious Press, 1999.
Poseidon's Gold. New York: Crown, 1994.
Scandal Takes a Holiday. New York: St. Martin's Press, 2006.

See Delphi and Die. New York: St. Martin's Press, 2006.
Shadows in Bronze. New York: Ballantine, 1990.
The Silver Pigs. New York: St. Martin's Press, 2006.
Three Hands in the Fountain. New York: Warner Books, 2000.
Time to Depart. New York: Warner Books, 1998.
Two for the Lions. New York: Warner Books, 2000.
Venus in Copper. New York: Ballantine, 1993.

Hiaasen, Carl

Basket Case. New York: Knopf, 2002.
Double Whammy. New York: Warner Books, 1989.
Flush. New York: Knopf, 2005.
Hoot. New York: Knopf, 2002.
Introduction. *The Deep Blue Good-By.* By John D. MacDonald. New York: Fawcett, 1995.
Kick Ass: Selected Columns of Carl Hiaasen. Edited by Diane Stevenson. Gainesville: University Press of Florida, 1999.
Lucky You. New York: Knopf, 1997.
Native Tongue. New York: Knopf, 1991.
Nature Girl. New York: Knopf, 2006.
Paradise Screwed: Selected Columns of Carl Hiaasen. Edited by Diane Stevenson. New York: Putnam, 2001.
Sick Puppy. New York: Knopf, 2002.
Skin Tight. New York: Fawcett Crest, 1990.
Skinny Dip. New York: Knopf, 2004.
Stormy Weather. New York: Knopf, 1995.
Strip Tease. New York: Knopf, 1993.
Team Rodent: How Disney Devours the World. New York: Ballantine, 1998.
Tourist Season. New York: Warner Books, 1987.

Hillerman, Tony

The Blessing Way. New York: Avon, 1970.
Coyote Waits. New York: Harper Paperbacks, 1992.
Dance Hall of the Dead. New York: Avon, 1973.
The Dark Wind. New York: Harper & Row, 1982.
The Fallen Man. New York: Harper Paperbacks, 1997.
The First Eagle. New York: HarperCollins, 1998.
The Ghostway. New York: Harper Paperbacks, 1992.
Hillerman Country. Photographed by Barney Hillerman. New York: Harper Perrenial, 1991.
Hunting Badger. New York: HarperCollins, 1999.
Listening Woman. New York: Avon, 1978.

New Mexico, Rio Grande, and Other Essays. Photographed by David Muench and Robert Reynolds. Portland, OR: Graphic Arts Center, 1972.
People of Darkness. New York: Avon, 1980.
Sacred Clowns. New York: HarperCollins, 1993.
The Shape Shifter. New York: HarperCollins, 2006.
The Sinister Pig. New York: HarperCollins, 2003.
Skeleton Man. New York: HarperCollins, 2004.
Skinwalkers. New York: Perennial, 1987.
Talking God. New York: Harper & Row, 1989.
A Thief of Time. New York: Harper Paperbacks, 1990.
The Wailing Wind. New York: HarperTorch, 2003.
_____, and Ernie Bulow. *Talking Mysteries: A Conversation with Tony Hillerman.* Albuquerque: University of New Mexico Press, 1991.

Leon, Donna

Acqua Alta. New York: HarperCollins, 1996. (Also known as *Death in High Water.*)
Blood from a Stone. New York: Atlantic Monthly Press, 2005.
Death and Judgment. New York: HarperCollins, 1995. (Also known as *A Venetian Reckoning.*)
Death at La Fenice. New York: HarperCollins, 1992.
Death in a Strange Country. New York: Harper Paperbacks, 1995.
The Death of Faith. London: Pan, 1998. (Also known as *Quietly in Their Sleep.*)
Doctored Evidence. New York: Atlantic Monthly Press, 2004.
Dressed for Death. New York: Harper Paperbacks, 1995. (Also known as *The Anonymous Venetian.*)
Fatal Remedies. London: Arrow Books, 2000.
Friends in High Places. London: Arrow Books, 2001.
A Noble Radiance. London: Arrow Books, 1999.
A Sea of Troubles. London: Arrow Books, 2002.
Through a Glass, Darkly. New York: Atlantic Monthly Press, 2006.
Uniform Justice. New York: Atlantic Monthly Press, 2003.
Wilful Behaviour. London: Arrow Books, 2003.

McCall Smith, Alexander

Blue Shoes and Happiness. New York: Pantheon Books, 2006.
The Full Cupboard of Life. New York: Pantheon Books, 2003.
In the Company of Cheerful Ladies. New York: Anchor Books, 2006.
The Kalahari Typing School for Men. New York: Anchor Books, 2004.
Morality for Beautiful Girls. New York: Anchor Books, 2002.
The No. 1 Ladies' Detective Agency. New York: Anchor Books, 2002.
Tears of the Girraffe. New York: Anchor Books, 2002.

Works Consulted

McClure, James

The Artful Egg. New York: Pantheon Books, 1985.
The Blood of an Englishman. New York: Pantheon Books, 1982.
The Caterpillar Cop. New York: Pantheon Books, 1973.
The Gooseberry Fool. London: Faber and Faber, 1974.
Snake. New York: Harper and Row, 1976.
The Song Dog. New York: Mysterious Press, 1992.
The Steam Pig. New York: Harper and Row, 1971.
The Sunday Hangman. New York: Avon, 1979.

Mosley, Walter

Bad Boy Brawly Brown. New York: Little, Brown, 2002.
Black Betty. New York: W.W. Norton, 1994.
"The Black Man: Hero." *Speak My Name: Black Men on Masculinity and the American Dream.* Edited by Don Belton. Boston: Beacon Press, 1995: 234–240.
Cinnamon Kiss. New York: Little, Brown, 2005.
Devil in a Blue Dress. New York: Pocket Books, 1990.
Fear Itself. New York: Little, Brown, 2003.
Fearless Jones. New York: Little, Brown, 2001.
Gone Fishin.' New York: Pocket Books, 1998.
Little Scarlet. New York: Little, Brown, 2004.
A Little Yellow Dog. New York: W. W. Norton, 1996.
A Red Death. New York: Pocket Books, 1992
Six Easy Pieces: Easy Rawlins Stories. New York: Atria Books, 2003.
What Next: A Memoir Toward World Peace. Baltimore: Black Classics Press, 2003.

Paretsky, Sara

Bitter Medicine. New York: Dell, 1999.
Blacklist. New York: Signet, 2004.
Blood Shot. New York: Dell, 1989.
Burn Marks. New York: Dell, 1991.
Deadlock. New York: Ballantine, 1985.
Fire Sale. New York: Putnam, 2005.
Guardian Angel. New York: Dell, 1993.
Hard Time. New York: Delacorte, 1999.
Indemnity Only. New York: Ballantine, 1983
Killing Orders. New York: William Morrow, 1985.
Total Recall. New York: Delacorte, 2001.
Tunnel Vision. New York: Dell, 1995.
Windy City Blues. New York: Delacorte, 1995.
"Writing a Series Character." *Writing Mysteries.* Edited by Sue Grafton. Cincinnati: Writer's Digest Books, 1992. 55–60.

Pelecanos, George P.

"Action Films." *GQ* 71.3 (March 2001): 318–19.
"Between Origins and Art." *The Writing Life: Writers on How They Think and Work.* Edited by Marie Arana. New York: Public Affairs, 2003. 85–89.
The Big Blowdown. New York: St. Martin's Press, 1999.
Down by the River Where the Dead Men Go. London: Serpent's Tail, 1999.
Drama City. New York: Little, Brown, 2005.
A Firing Offense. London: Serpent's Tail, 1999.
Hard Revolution. New York: Warner Books, 2005.
Hell to Pay. Boston: Little, Brown, 2002.
King Suckerman. New York: Dell, 1998.
Nick's Trip. London: Serpent's Tail, 1999.
The Night Gardener. New York: Little, Brown, 2006.
Right as Rain. New York: Warner Books, 2002.
Shame the Devil. London: Orion, 2000.
Shoedog. New York: Warner Books, 2004.
Soul Circus. Boston: Little, Brown, 2003.
The Sweet Forever. New York: Dell, 1999.

Rankin, Ian

Beggar's Banquet. London: Orion, 2002.
Black and Blue. New York: St. Martin's Press, 1999.
The Black Book. New York: St. Martin's Press, 2000.
Dead Souls. New York: St. Martin's Press, 2000.
Death Is Not the End: A Novella. New York: St. Martin's Press, 2000.
"Exile on Princes Street: Inspector Rebus & I." Accessed March 21, 2006. <http://www. twbooks.co.uk/authors/rebus.html>.
The Falls. New York: St. Martin's Press, 2003.
Fleshmarket Alley. New York: Little, Brown, 2006.
A Good Hanging: Short Stories. New York: St. Martin's Press, 2002.
The Hanging Garden. New York: St. Martin's Press, 1999.
Hide and Seek. New York: St. Martin's Press, 1997.
Knots and Crosses. New York: St. Martin's Press, 1995.
Let It Bleed. New York: St. Martin's Press, 1998.
Mortal Causes. New York: St. Martin's Press, 1997.
A Question of Blood. New York: Little, Brown, 2005.
Rebus's Scotland: A Personal Journey. Photographed by Tricia Malley and Ross Gillespie. Orion Books: London, 2005.
Resurrection Men. New York: Little, Brown, 2004.
Set in Darkness. New York: St. Martin's Press, 2001.
Strip Jack. New York: St. Martin's Press, 1998.
Tooth and Nail. St. Martin's Press, 1996.

Sciascia, Leonardo

The Day of the Owl/Equal Danger. Translated from *Il giorno della civetta* (1961) by Archibold Colquhoun and Arthur Oliver. Boston: David R. Godine, 1984.

To Each His Own. Translated from *A ciascuno il suo* (1966) by Adrienne Foulke. Manchester: Carcanet, 1989.

"A Straightforward Tale" ["Una storia semplice"]. *Open Doors and Three Novellas.* Translated by Joseph Farrell. New York: Alfred A, Knopf, 1992.

Simenon, Georges

Maigret and the Black Sheep. Translated from *Maigret et les braves gens* (1962) by Helen Thomson. New York: Harcourt Brace Jovanovich, 1976.

Maigret and the Bum. Translated from *Maigret et le clochard* (1963) by Jean Stewart. New York: Harcourt Brace Jovanovich, 1973.

Maigret and the Burglar's Wife. Translated from *Maigret et la grande perche* (1951) by J. Maclaren-Ross. New York: Harcourt Brace Jovanovich, 1989.

Maigret and the Headless Corpse. Translated from *Maigret et le cors sans tête* (1955) by Eileen Ellenbogen. London: Hamish Hamilton, 1967.

Maigret and the Hotel Majestic. Translated from *Les Caves du Majestic* (1942) by Caroline Miller. New York: Harcourt Brace Jovanovich, 1977.

Maigret and the Loner. Translated from *Maigret et l'homme tout seul* (1971) by Eileen Ellenbogen. New York: Harcourt Brace Jovanovich, 1975.

Maigret and the Madwoman. Translated from *La Folle de Maigret* (1970) by Eileen Ellenbogen. New York: Harcourt Brace Jovanovich, 1979.

Maigret and the Man on the Bench. Translated from *Maigret et l'homme du banc* (1953) by Eileen Ellenborgen. New York: Harcourt Brace Jovanovich, 1979.

Maigret and the Pickpocket. Translated from *Le Voleur de Maigret* (1967) by Nigel Ryan. New York: Harcourt Brace Jovanovich, 1985.

Maigret and the Spinster. Translated from *Cécile est morte* (1942) by Eileen Ellenbogen. New York: Harcourt Brace Jovanovich, 1977.

Maigret and the Young Girl. Translated from *Maigret et la jeune morte* (1954) by Daphne Woodward. London: Hamish Hamilton, 1955.

Maigret Bides His Time. Translated from *La Patience de Maigret* (1965) by Alastair Hamilton. New York: Harcourt Brace Jovanovich, 1986.

Maigret in Montmartre. Translated from *Maigret au "Picratt's"* (1951) by Daphne Woodward. New York: Harcourt Brace Jovanovich, 1989.

Maigret's Christmas: Nine Stories. Translated from *Un Noël de Maigret* (1951) by Jean Stewart. New York: Harcourt Brace Jovanovich, 1977.

Maigret's Failure. Translated from *Un Echec de Maigret* (1956) by Daphne Woodward. In *A Maigret Trio.* New York: Harcourt Brace Jovanovich, 1983.

Maigret's Pipe: Seventeen Stories. Translated from *La Pipe de Maigret* (1947) by Jean Stewart. New York: Harcourt Brace Jovanovich, 1978.

Maigret Stonewalled. Translated from *Monsieur Gallet décédé* (1931) by Margaret Marshall. In *Maigret at the Crossroads.* New York: Penguin, 1983.

When I Was Old. Translated from *Quand j'étais vieux* (1970) by Helen Eustis. New York: Harcourt Brace Jovanovich, 1971.

Sjöwall, Maj, and Per Wahlöö

The Abominable Man. Translated from *Den vedervärdige mannen fran Säffle* (1971) by Thomas Teal. New York: Random House, 1972.

Cop Killer. Translated from *Polismördaren* (1974) by Thomas Teal. New York: Vintage, 1978.

The Fire Engine That Disappeared. Translated from *Brandbilen som försvann* (1969) by Joan Tate. New York: Vintage, 1977.

The Laughing Policeman. Translated from *Den skrattande polisen* (1968) by Alan Blair. New York: Vintage, 1977.

The Locked Room. Translated from *Det slutna rummet* (1972) by Paul Britten Austin. New York: Random House, 1973.

The Man on the Balcony. Translated from *Mannen pa balkongen* (1967) by Alan Blair. New York: Vintage, 1976.

The Man Who Went Up in Smoke. Translated from *Mannen som gick upp i rök* (1966) by Joan Tate. New York: Vintage, 1976.

Murder at the Savoy. Translated from *Polis, polis, potatismos!* (1970) by Amy and Ken Knoespel. New York: Vintage, 1977.

Roseanna. Translated from *Roseanna* (1965) by Lois Roth. New York: Vintage, 1976.

The Terrorists. Translated from *Terroristerna* (1975) by Joan Tate. New York: Vintage, 1978.

Taibo, Paco Ignacio, II

An Easy Thing. Translated from *Cosa fácil* (1977) by William I. Neuman. New York: Penguin Books, 1990.

"Help! I'm Living in a Telenovela. (Assassinations in Mexico)." *The Nation* 24 (April 1995): 55–59.

Frontera Dreams. Translated from *Sueños de frontera* (1990) by Bill Verner. El Paso: Cinco Puntas Press, 2002.

No Happy Ending. Translated from *No habrá final feliz* (1981) by William I. Neuman. New York: Mysterious Press, 1993.

Return to the Same City. Translated from *Regresso a la misma ciudad y bajo la lluvia* (1989) by Laura Dial. New York: Mysterious Press, 1996.

Some Clouds. Translated from *Algunas nubes* (1985) by William I. Neuman. New York: 1993.

"So When Was it That This Guy Medardo Rivera Killed This Guy Lupe Barcenas." Translated by William I. Neuman. *The Armchair Detective* 26, no. 3 (Summer 1993): 44–46.

and Subcomandante Marcos. *The Uncomfortable Dead (What's Missing is Missing): A Novel by Four Hands.* Translated from *Muertos Incomodos (Falta lo que Falta), Novela a Cuatra Manos* (2005) by Carlos Lopez. New York: Akashic Books, 2006.

Secondary Sources

"Author Talk: Interview with Alexander McCall Smith." Accessed June 13, 2006. <http://www.bookreporter.com/authors/au-smith-alexander-mccall.asp>.

Baker, John F. "No Happy Endings." *Boston Review.* February–March 2001. Accessed October 11, 2006. <http://bostonreview.net/BR26.1/taibo.html>.

Becker, Alida. "Miss Marple of Botswana." *New York Times,* January 27, 2002.

Bell, Millicent. "On Venice." *Raritan* 13, no. 4 (Spring 1994): 124–45.

Berlins, Marcel. "Precious Ramotswe and Me." *The Guardian,* January 21, 2003. Accessed June 22, 2006. <http://books.guardian.co.uk/departments/crime/story/0,,879235,00.html>.

Bernell, Sue, and Michaela Karni. "Tony Hillerman." *This Is About Vision.* Edited by William Balassi, John F. Crawford and Annie O. Eysturoy. Albuquerque: University of New Mexico Press, 1990, 41–51.

Bertens, Hans, and Theo d'Haen. *Contemporary American Crime Fiction.* New York: Palgrave, 2001.

Birnbaum, Robert. "Robert Birnbaum Talks with the Author of *Soul Circus.*" *Identity Theory,* April 21, 2003. Accessed April 4, 2005. <http://www.identitytheory.com/interviews/birnbaum100.html>.

Breen, Jon L. "Interview with Tony Hillerman." *The Tony Hillerman Companion: A Comprehensive Guide to His Life and Work.* Edited by Martin Greenberg. New York: HarperCollins, 1994, 51–70.

Bremer, Sidney H. "Willa Cather's Lost Chicago Sisters." *Women Writers and the City: Essays in Feminist Literary Criticism.* Edited by Susan Merrill Squier. Knoxville: University of Tennessee Press, 1984, 210–29.

Bresler, Fenton. *The Mystery of Georges Simenon.* New York: Beaufort Books, 1983.

Breslin, Catherine. "Tony Hillerman." *Publishers Weekly,* June 10, 1988: 57–58.

Byrne, Jennifer. "Interview with Carl Hiaasen." *Foreign Correspondent,* May 16, 2001. Accessed December 30, 2006. <http://www.abc.net.au/foreign/stories/s297079.htm>.

Caistor, Nick. *Mexico City: A Cultural and Literary Companion.* Northampton, MA: Interlink Books, 2000.

Carr, John C. *The Craft of Crime: Conversations with Crime Writers.* Boston: Houghton Mifflin, 1983.

Carter, Dale. "Trouble in the Big Easy." *The Armchair Detective* 25, no. 1 (Winter 1992): 40–50.

Chandler, Raymond. *Farewell, My Lovely.* New York: Vintage, 1988.

_____. *The Simple Art of Murder.* New York: Vintage, 1988.

_____. *Trouble Is My Business.* New York: Ballantine, 1977.

Christgau, Robert. "A Darker Shade of Noir." *The Nation,* May 8, 2006: 31–36.

Churchill, Ward. *Fantasies of the Master Race: Literature, Cinema, and the Colonization of American Indians.* Monroe, ME: Courage Press, 1992.

Close, Glen S. "The Detective Is Dead: Long Live the *Novela Negra!*" *Hispanic and Luso-Brazilian Detective Fiction: Essays on the Género Negro Tradition.* Edited by Renée W. Craig-

Odders, Jacky Collins and Glen S. Close. Jefferson, NC: McFarland, 2006, 143–161.

Coale, Samuel. *The Mystery of Mysteries: Cultural Differences and Designs.* Bowling Green, OH: Popular Press, 1999.

Cochran, Stacey. "George Pelecanos." *Plots with Guns* 2004. Accessed April 18, 2005. <http://www.plotswithguns. com/PelecanosIntv.htm>.

Collins, Carvel. "Georges Simenon." *Writers at Work: The Paris Review Interviews.* Edited by Malcolm Cowley. New York: Viking Press, 1959, 143–160.

Connolly, John. "George Pelecanos." Accessed April 5, 2005. <http://www. johnconnollybooks.com/int_pele canos.html>.

Cooper, Brenda. *Weary Sons of Conrad: White Fiction Against the Grain of Africa's Dark Heart.* New York: Peter Lang, 2002.

Cooper, Marc. "Macho Libre." *LA Weekly*, October 25, 2006. Accessed March 7, 2007. <http://www.laweekly. com/art+books/books/macho- libre/14823/>.

Davis, Mike. *City of Quartz: Excavating the Future in Los Angeles.* New York: Vintage, 1992.

Dibdin, Michael. *Dead Lagoon.* New York: Vintage, 1994.

_____. Introduction. *The Bar on the Seine.* By Georges Simenon. London: Penguin, 2003.

Dinesen, Isak. *Out of Africa.* New York: Vintage, 1989.

Dunant, Sarah. *Fatlands.* New York: Scribner's, 2004.

Ellroy, James. "Magnetic L.A." *Publishers Weekly*, April 5, 1999: 49.

Farrell, Joseph. *Leonardo Sciascia.* Edin-

burgh: Edinburgh University Press, 1995.

Faulkner, William. *Requiem for a Nun.* New York: Vintage, 1975.

Freeling, Nicholas. *Criminal Convictions: Errant Essays on Perpetrators of Literary License.* Boston: David R. Godine, 1994.

Garis, Leslie. "Simenon's Last Case." *New York Times Magazine*, April 22, 1984: 20–33, 60–66.

Ghose, Indira. "Venice Confidential." *Venetian Views, Venetian Blinds: English Fantasies of Venice.* Edited by Manfred Pfister and Barbara Schaff. Amsterdam: Rodopi, 1999, 213–225.

Gill, Brendan. *A New York Life: Of Friends and Others.* New York: Poseidon Press, 1990.

Gross, Terri. "Interview with George Pelecanos." *Fresh Air.* August 25, 1998. <http://www.npr.org/templates/ story/story.php?storyId=1793525>.

Guttman, Robert J., and Marie-Laure Poire. "Interview with Alexander McCall Smith. *Transatlantic Magazine*, June 13, 2006 <http://www. transatlanticmagazine.org/inter- views/mccall-smith.html>.

Hardy, Thomas. *The Return of the Native.* New York: Modern Library, 1927.

Hemingway, Ernest. *The Short Stories of Ernest Hemingway.* New York: Scribner's, 1966.

Herbert, Rosemary. *The Fatal Art of Entertainment: Interviews with Mystery Writers.* New York: G.K. Hall, 1994.

"An Interview with George Pelecanos." *Time Warner Bookmark* 2000. April 18, 2005. <http://www.twbookmark. com/features/georgepelecanos/off thepage_interview.html>.

Works Consulted

James, Henry. *Italian Hours.* New York: The Ecco Press, 1987.

Jeffrey, David K. "James Lee Burke." *St. James Guide to Crime and Mystery Writers.* 4th ed. Edited by Jay P. Pedersen. Detroit: St. James Press, 1996: 126–28.

Jones, Malcolm. "Cool Eye, Cool Tales." *Newsweek,* March 17, 2003: 63.

Jordan, Jon. "George Pelecanos Interview." *Mystery One,* January 2002. Accessed April 6, 2005. <http://www.mysteryone.com/GeorgePelecanos Interview.htm>.

Juvenal. *The Satires of Juvenal.* Translated by Rolfe Humphries. Bloomington: Indiana University Press, 1958.

Kean, Danuta. "Ian Rankin Tells Danuta Kean Why Rebus Wouldn't Like Him." Accessed June 27, 2006. <http://www.orionbooks.co.uk/interview.aspx?ID=5814>.

Keates, Jonathan. *Italian Journeys.* London: Picador, 1992.

Kennedy, J. Gerald. *Imagining Paris: Exile, Writing, and American Identity.* New Haven: Yale University Press, 1993.

King, Peter B. "Antihero Detectives." *Pittsburgh Post-Gazette,* June 23, 2006. <http://post–gazette.com/pg/05058/462988.stm>.

Kinsman, Margaret. "A Question of Visibility: Paretsky and Chicago." *Women Times Three: Writers, Detectives, Readers.* Edited by Kathleen Gregory Klein. Bowling Green, OH: Popular Press, 1995, 15–27.

Kravitz, Peter, ed. *The Vintage Book of Contemporary Scottish Fiction.* New York: Vintage, 1999.

Lawrence, D.H. *Phoenix: The Posthumous Papers of D.H. Lawrence.* Edited by Edward D. McDonald. London: Heinemann, 1961.

Lee, Jennifer, ed. *Paris in Mind: Three Centuries of Americans Writing About Paris.* New York: Vintage, 2003.

Lehman, David. *The Perfect Murder: A Study in Detection.* New York: The Free Press, 1989.

Leonard, John. "Escape." *New York Times,* May 5, 1970, 43.

Locke, J.A. Kaszuba. "Interview: Sara Paretsky." August 2005. Accessed March 23, 2006. <http://www.book-loons.com/cgi-bin/Columns.asp?name=Sara%20Paretsky&type=Interview>.

Lodge, David. *The Art of Fiction.* New York: Viking Penguin, 1993.

Lomax, Sara M. "Double Agent Easy Rawlins." *American Visions,* April–May 1992: 32–34.

Lownie, Andrew. *The Edinburgh Literary Companion.* Edinburgh: Polygon, 2005.

Lundin, Bo. "Wahlöö, Per, and Maj Sjöwall." *The St. James Guide to Crime and Mystery Writers.* 4th ed. Edited by Jay P. Pederson. Detroit: St. James Press, 1996, 1014–15.

Lutwack, Leonard. *The Role of Place in Literature.* Syracuse, N.Y.: Syracuse University Press, 1984.

MacDonald. John D. *The Turquoise Lament.* New York: Lippincott, 1973.

Macdonald, Stuart. "Arresting Technology." Accessed March 21, 2006. <http://www.hackwriters.com/rebus.htm>.

Maidment, R.A. *American Conversations.* London: Hodder and Stoughton, 1995.

Mann, Thomas. *Death in Venice.* Edited and translated by Clayton Koelb. New York: W.W. Norton, 1994.

Martin, Jorge Hernández. "On the Case." *Américas*, March-April 1995: 16–21.

Mason, Anthony. "Capital Crimes." *CBS News.com*, March 24, 2002. Accessed April 8, 2005. <http://www.cbsnews.com/stories/2002/03/22/sunday/printable50443>.

Matzke, Christine. "'A good woman in a good country' or The Essence is in the Pumpkin: Alexander McCall Smith's Mma Ramotswe Novels as a Case of Postcolonial Nostalgia" *European Journal of Cognitive Psychology* 21, no. 1 (2006): 64–71.

McCrum, Robert. "Gothic Scot." *Guardian Unlimited*, March 18, 2001. <http://books.guardian.co.uk/departments/crime /story/0,6000,458332,00.html>.

Miller, Henry. *Tropic of Cancer.* New York: Grove Press, 1961.

Miller, Lynn I. "Sara Paretsky: Collaring White Collar Crime." Accessed February 21, 2006. <http:www.crescentblues.com/2_6issue/paretsky.shtml>.

Mok, Michael. "In Maigret's Paris with the Man Who Invented It." *Life*, May 9, 1969: 43–49.

Moore, Clayton. "An Interview with Ian Rankin." *Bookslut*, March 21, 2006. <http://www.bookslut.com/features/2005_04_005009.php>.

"The Mystery Man." *Réalités* No. 137 (April 1962): 22–29. Accessed August 24, 2006. <http://www.trussel.com/maig/realite.htm>.

Nayar, Parvathi. "Life and Times of a Serial Novelist." *The Hindu Literary Review,* June 4, 2006. Accessed June 27, 2006. <http://www.thehindu.com/lr/2006/06/04/stories/2006060400030100.htm.>.

O'Connor, Flannery. *Conversations with Flannery O'Connor.* Edited by Rosemary M. Magee. Jackson: University Press of Mississippi, 1987.

O'Gorman, Ellen. "Detective Fiction and Historical Narration." *Greece & Rome,* April 1999: 19–26.

Paul, Marcie. "The Search for Identity: The Return to Analytic Detective Fiction in Mexico." *Hispanic and Luso-Brazilian Detective Fiction: Essays on the Género Negro Tradition.* Edited by Renée W. Craig-Odders, Jacky Collins and Glen S. Close. Jefferson, NC: McFarland, 2006, 180–203.

Peck, Richard. *A Morbid Fascination: White Prose and Politics in Apartheid South Africa.* Westport, CT: Greenwood Press, 1997.

Pepper, Andrew. *The Contemporary American Crime Novel: Race, Ethnicity, Gender, Class.* Chicago: Fitzroy Dearborn, 2000.

Pierce, J. Kingston. "Ian Rankin: The Accidental Crime Writer." *January Magazine*, March 21, 2006. <http:www.januarymagazine.com/profiles/ianrankin.html>.

Plain, Gill. *Ian Rankin's Black and Blue: A Reader's Guide.* New York: Continuum, 2002.

Porter, Dennis. *The Pursuit of Crime: Art and Ideology in Detective Fiction.* New Haven: Yale University Press, 1981.

Prose, Francine. *Sicilian Odyssey.* Washington: Nation Geographic Society, 2003.

Randall, Frederika. "Fear and Loathing in Italy." *The Nation*, March 28, 2005: 32–35.

Raymond, John. *Simenon in Court.* London: Hamish Hamilton, 1968.

Reddy, Maureen T. "The Feminist Counter-Tradition in Crime: Cross, Grafton, Paretsky, and Wilson." In *The Cunning Craft: Original Essays on Detective Fiction and Contemporary Literary Theory*. Edited by Ronald G. Walker and June M. Frazer. Macomb: Western Illinois University, 1990, 174–187.

Ringle, Ken. "The Engagin' Cajun: In Tobasco Country, Novelist James Lee Burke Cooks Up Spicy Detective Tales." *Washington Post*, May 31, 1993: D1, 10–11.

Rosenbaum, Ron. "Hurricane Hiaasen." *Vanity Fair*, September 1993: 124–36.

Roth, Philip. *Reading Myself and Others*. New York: Farrar, Straus and Giroux, 1975.

Sallis, James. "Fantastic Metropolis: Incomparable Paco." January 2002. Accessed March 7, 2007. <http://www.fantasticmetropolis.com/print.html?ey,taibo>.

Schmid, David. "Imagining Safe Urban Space: The Contribution of Detective Fiction to Radical Geography." *Antipode* 27, no. 3 (1995): 242–69.

Schuessler, Jennifer. "Hard-boiled Family Values." *Publishers Weekly* 247 (January 3, 2000): 52–53.

Scott, Larry Emil. "Sweden and Detective Fiction." *The Mystery and Detection Annual, 1973*. Edited by Donald Adams. Pasadena, CA: Castle Press, 1974: 292–300.

Shea, Roz. "Interview with Carl Hiaasen." *Bookreporter*, May 19, 1999. Accessed December 30, 2006. <http://www.bookreporter.com/authors/au-hiaasen-carl.asp>.

Sherman, Charlotte Watson. "Walter Mosley on the Black Male Hero." *American Visions*, August-September 1995: 34–37.

Shields, Paula. "This Curmudgeonly, Old, Chain-smoking Bugger Will Die Some Day." *Fortnight*. Accessed May 29, 2006. <http://www.fortnight.org/rankin.html>.

Shoup, Barbara, and Margaret Love Denman. *Novel Ideas: Contemporary Authors Share the Creative Process*. Indianapolis: Alpha Books, 2001, 159.

Silet, Charles L.P. "The Other Side of Those Mean Streets: An Interview with Walter Mosley." *The Armchair Detective* 26 (Fall 1993): 9–16.

_____. "Sun, Sand, and Tirades: An Interview with Carl Hiaasen." *The Armchair Detective* 29 (Winter 1996): 9–18.

Soitos, Stephen F. *The Blues Detective: A Study of African American Detective Fiction*. Amherst: University of Massachusetts Press, 1996.

Stasio, Marilyn. "Lady Gumshoes: Boiled Less Hard." *New York Times Book Review*, April 28, 1985: 1.

_____. "A Wonderful Place for Murder." *New York Times*, January 12, 1997: Sec 5: 33.

Stavans, Ilan. *Conversations with Ilan Stavens*. Tucson: University of Arizona Press, 2005.

Stein, Jesse. "The Art of Fiction XII: William Faulkner." *Paris Review*, Spring 1956. Reprinted in *William Faulkner Critical Collection*. Edited by Leland H. Cox. Detroit: Gale Research, 1982, 5–25.

Swilley, Stephanie. "Big-City Setting Is 'Right as Rain' for Author George Pelecanos." *BookPage*, 2001. Accessed April 1, 2005. <http://www.bookpage.

com/0102bp/george_pelecanos. html>.

Symons, Julian. *Mortal Consequences: A History from the Detective Story to the Crime Novel.* New York: Schocken Books, 1973.

Szuberla, Guy. "The Ties That Bind: V.I. Warshawski and the Burdens of Family." *The Armchair Detective* 27, no. 2 (Spring 1994): 146–53.

Tani, Stefano. *The Doomed Detective: The Contribution of the Detective Novel to Postmodern American and Italian Fiction.* Carbondale: Southern Illinois University Press, 1984.

"Tartan Noir." Accessed March 21, 2006. <http://www.literaturefestival. co.uk/2004/ rankin.html>.

Thomson, Ian. "Sicilian Writers and the Mafia: A Conversation in Palermo with Leonardo Sciascia." *London Magazine*, April-May 1987: 39–70.

Tindall, Gillian. *Countries of the Mind: The Meaning of Place to Writers.* London: Hogarth, 1991.

Ulin, David L., ed. *Another City: Writing from Los Angeles.* San Francisco: City Lights, 2001.

Wall, Don. "Interview with James McClure." *Mysteries of South Africa.* Edited by Eugene Schleh. Bowling Green, OH: Popular Press, 1991, 113–24.

Welty, Eudora. *On Writing.* New York: Modern Library, 2002.

Westlake, Donald E. "Mess over Miami." *New York Times Book Review*, August 29, 1993: 6.

Wharton, Edith. *The Writing of Fiction.* New York: Scribner's, 1925.

Whetstone, Muriel L. "The Mystery of Walter Mosley." *Ebony*, December 1995: 106–10, 112.

White, Michael. "A Patron of the Arts of Opera and Murder." *New York Times*, August 10, 2003: 24.

Willett, Ralph. *The Naked City: Urban Crime Fiction in the USA.* Manchester: Manchester University Press, 1996.

Williams, John. *Into the Badlands.* London: Paladin, 1991.

Winks, Robin W. "The Historical Mystery." *Mystery and Suspense Writers: The Literature of Crime, Detection, and Espionage.* Vol. 2. Edited by Robin W. Winks and Maureen Corrigan. New York: Scribner's, 1998, 1089–1101.

Winston, Robert P., and Nancy C. Mellerski. *The Public Eye: Ideology and the Police Procedural.* New York: St. Martin's Press, 1992.

Index

Index